PRAISE FOR

HOME FIELDS

"From beginning to end, Coach Bill George crafts a beautifully written, compelling story of compassion and courage that will leave readers yearning for more. This deeply sensitive, inspiring novel artfully maneuvers between the past and the present, providing a poignant view into the personal lives of Syrian immigrants—real people who struggled to fulfill their hopes and dreams in a world that wasn't always fair. *Home Fields* is more than a story; it's a highly relatable, personal testimony to strength of character that takes the reader on an emotional journey of self-discovery."

—Sandra Stosz, Vice Admiral, US Coast Guard (Ret.), Author of *Breaking Ice & Breaking Glass: Leading in Uncharted Waters*

"Bill George's *Home Fields* provides all readers with an emotionally compelling story whose core reflects selfless commitment to family, faith, and country. He brilliantly shares his broad personal experience in roles as leader, coach, teacher, proud patriot, husband, father, and caregiver; Bill reverently and respectfully illustrates to us timeless life values of love, humility, and sacrifice; this multigenerational narrative also shows us genuine empathy for community, courage, perseverance, tragedy, illness, and loss. *Home Fields* is inspiring and deeply heartfelt!"

—Jeffrey Colt, Major General (Ret.), US Army

"As a former Coast Guard Academy football co-captain and former commandant, I have had many occasions to speak with Bill George and talk to his football teams. Bill has always understood that sports at the Coast Guard Academy become a metaphor for service as a Coast Guard officer. The discipline and teamwork required to compete on athletic fields becomes operative when a boarding officer leads a team boarding a drug-laden boat or positions a helicopter for a hoist to save a life. In *Home Fields*, Bill has created a very personal, intergenerational link that is framed by selfless service to the nation. He also effectively captures the human dynamic within families who shoulder the burden of taking care of each other while meeting the day-to-day challenges of their profession. These are timeless lessons in life, and Bill teaches us all."

—Thad W. Allen, Admiral, US Coast Guard (Ret.)

"*Home Fields* is a must-read story about how family history shapes the life of a father, son, and college football coach and the enduring love of family in the most challenging situations. Coach Bill George served as a positive mentor that influenced and shaped hundreds of leaders in the United States Coast Guard."

—John Loose, Assistant Head Football Coach, Army West Point, Co-Founder of Lauren's First and Goal Foundation

"I've had the honor of being a hospice RN for twenty-eight years. This memoir illuminates with stark honesty the tenderness, poignancy, and struggles of caring for a loved one at the end of life. As you read, timeless gifts are seared into your heart as childhood memories of love and loss are shared."

—Sandra Kim, RN, BN, BS, CHPN

"As the last words of *Home Fields* jumped off the page, I closed the book and sat in a dark room by myself with tears in my eyes. I have admired Bill, or 'Monker' as I have called him, for over fifty years; now my admiration turned to great love and immense respect. *Home Fields* is a must-read for anyone who has been or will become a caregiver, a fan of college football, a veteran, a student of history, or anyone who is faced with challenges they may not understand. COVID robbed me of attending my own father's funeral, a man just like Casper, gentle, humble, loving and close to God. *Home Fields* allowed me to finally and properly mourn my dad's passing, and for that I will be forever grateful to this extraordinary work. Bravo, Monker!!"

—Paul D. Kim, MD, Executive Director, Veterans Health Administration Office of Emergency Management

"A memoir that is at once a dying father's and a son's, a wife's and a daughter's. Filled with moments that break your heart and others that send your soul skyward, in *Home Fields*, Bill George paints a delicate tribute to his family, to the game of football, to the boys he inspired and that inspired him, and to a generation that sacrificed everything."

—Rona Simmons, Author of *A Gathering of Men*

"Honor, respect, and devotion to duty are the core values of the Coast Guard Academy. Coach George gives you a glimpse of what it's like to be a coach, father, husband, and son. Great book and outstanding read."

—C. C. Grant, Head Football Coach, US Coast Guard Academy

"I left Myers, and after two and a half years on the front lines, I came home and lived with the scars of war alive inside of me. So many others never came home."

—George "Gus" Isaac, Army Company L, 30th Infantry 3rd Division, Bronze Star, Purple Heart

"I was immediately pulled into the heartfelt story of a Division III football coach's family in New London, CT, that was inextricably tied to a group of children growing up in Upstate New York. Having worked at the Coast Guard Academy for the past eighteen years, many of the names and personalities were familiar yet seen anew through the eyes of Coach Bill George. Coach reveals himself as a vulnerable, loving, and uncertain son, husband, and father to his family as he struggles through the challenges that his father, wife, and daughter present, while revealing the strength, compassion, and determination of a coach.

"His narrative on his own relationship with religion, God, and heaven was so relatable as told through the conversations he had late at night with his father. But with every turn of human struggle in caring for his dying father are bright spots of youthful conversations on life seen fresh and new by his daughter, Lila. Equally compelling is the counternarrative of Puppy Moses and his friends growing up in a Syrian village in Upstate New York as the group experiences life and death as children and eventually on the shores of Normandy during World War II. While some certainty of life and death of the characters is inevitable, it unfolds with anticipation of a more hopeful future."

—Andrea Marcille, Captain, USCG (Ret.)

"I read this book through the lens of a son, a father, a grandfather, an athlete, and a coach. Bill hits on all aspects with his amazing storytelling ability, starting with the Greatest Generation and through his journey as the head coach of the United States Coast Guard Academy."

—David Palmer, Major League Baseball Pitcher for Twelve Seasons, New York State Baseball Hall of Fame

Home Fields:
Coast Guard Academy Football Coach Recounts
the Unfulfilled Lives of World War II

by Bill George

© Copyright 2023 Bill George

ISBN 979-8-88824-159-2

All rights reserved. No part of this publication may be reproduced, stored in a retrieval system, or transmitted in any form or by any means—electronic, mechanical, photocopy, recording, or any other—except for brief quotations in printed reviews, without the prior written permission of the author.

Published by

3705 Shore Drive
Virginia Beach, VA 23455
800-435-4811
www.koehlerbooks.com

HOME FIELDS

Coast Guard Academy Football Coach Recounts
the Unfulfilled Lives of World War II

BILL GEORGE

VIRGINIA BEACH
CAPE CHARLES

DEDICATION

To Lila, who came from heaven; to Anna and Casper, who left for heaven; and to my wife, Nancy, who lovingly took care of us all.

AUTHOR'S NOTE

The people, places, and historic events referenced in Home Fields are real. Character dialogue, and much of the intricacies portrayed throughout this novel, are what I imagined was said or occurred at the time based upon interviews and research. Myers, New York was, in fact, the home to my father and many of the characters of the World War II generation. Also real and much admired are the players, coaches, and military leaders who I encountered during my years as head football coach of the US Coast Guard Academy.

CHAPTER 1

A thin, white cloud lies motionless above the distant tree line, pressing against the endless, blue horizon as if it were an angel waiting for the perfect moment to travel between this life and the next. The tree line slopes down to the deep, still waters of the Thames River, which seems stagnant like a New England lake in the heat of a fading August afternoon. The Thames, however, rushes past in a silent, eerie way as it flows to the Atlantic.

The sun behind me pulls the life of the day westward, leaving my aging shadow stranded on the fifty-yard line of Cadet Memorial Field, in the middle of the United States Coast Guard Academy in New London, Connecticut. By the time the sun of an August summer day in 2014 fully sets, and my fifty-six-year-old shadow has blended into the darkness, I will have begun my sixteenth season as head football coach at the Coast Guard Academy. I study my silhouette and wonder if shadows stay here forever, following around our loved ones long after we are gone. My shadow stays frozen as if it is waiting for my next move. Maybe it's impatient for me to do something good for the world and will move on to wait for someone else. I gaze up to the vast, blue sky again, and far to the left I notice two small clouds painted pink by the departing sun. My eyes shift back to the thin, white cloud, which slowly disappears. There must be a spot, somewhere in the distance beyond the cloud, where the trees blend into the horizon and the heavens touch the earth, a spot we cannot see, where all the past souls travel back and forth between this life and another to live within our hearts. Or maybe it is us, I wonder, the living, who have traveled back to serve as angels and heal the world, here and now and only once.

"Hello, Daddy!" Four-and-a-half-year-old toothpick legs, as white as the cloud, race across my shadow from left to right. Her curly, orange hair follows her like a trailing flame. She curves her running path into the shade of the oak trees, which cover half of the south end zone. "Hello, Gido," she says, using the Arabic word for grandfather, as she comes to a halt and lays her head in the lap of a withered, dying man who sits sleeping in a wheelchair provided by hospice care.

My eighty-seven-year-old father's heavy eyelids rise and the whites of his eyes peer down from his vacant skull. His bony fingers, wrapped with deep blue veins, rest on her sweaty forehead. His tan arms, covered with pale blotches, are in deep contrast to hers. The two of them stay frozen in an exhausted embrace, one exhausted from youth, the other from life. His bald head still holds a few strands of his once thick, white hair, which now covers my head, as well. With great effort, he raises his eyes to me as I approach and then quickly lets them droop to Lila.

"I love you, Gido," Lila says, raising her blue eyes to my father. His touch on her head is gentle; he could not even leave a fingerprint.

"Lila Marguerite." Casper whispers her first and middle name into the evening. "You were sent from heaven." He smiles softly as he continues to whisper. "I love you more than anybody ever loved anybody."

Lila looks up and smiles back at Casper. She climbs onto his lap and takes his glasses out of his pocket and puts them on his long nose and around his big ears. She delicately studies the features of his head with slow, soft touches from her tiny fingers. She does not realize the muscles of his skull have recessed. All she sees is his loving face.

"Lila," calls my wife Nancy, seated a few feet behind the wheelchair on the end zone padding. "Stay with Gido in the shade." At fifty-five, her petite frame and cropped blonde hair disguise her age. Her life was spent dreaming of being a mother and when she was fifty-one and I was fifty-two, we adopted the first and only child for either of us, Lila, who was placed in our arms at one-minute old. Lila was a result of Nancy's never-dying quest.

"She thinks he is her brother." Nancy says to me as I sit next to her.

"Those boys," Casper says. "Why do I think of those boys so much lately and those two girls?" His whispering voice carries an echo of sadness.

"I don't know what he thinks," I say to Nancy. "I do know that Lila has brought him back to life. The hospice nurses and caregivers love Casper, and once they cut out all of his meds his mind became clearer, but Lila is keeping him alive."

"Those boys," Casper tearfully whispers again.

Nancy pauses. "I know at least she brought his memory back to life."

I start to think that Lila's youth has somehow ignited Casper's. "I don't know," I wonder aloud to Nancy. "Maybe those boys and the other children he grew up with never left him. Maybe they were with him all along. Maybe they are more than a memory. He told me all of those stories years ago and now they are coming alive again."

Nancy gives me a quizzical glance. "You sound as confused as Casper."

"You always say Lila was a miracle and you say miracles can multiply," I answer as I move beside Casper and Lila.

Casper's eyes open wider, and I can tell his mind is suddenly clearer for a moment. "Why do I think of Myers and those boys and those girls?" Casper asks, referring to his childhood in the tiny village of Myers, New York. "Does Lila make me think of them?" Then his eyelids droop again, nearly shut, and I cannot not tell if he is looking at me through the cracks.

"I am here, Gido," Lila says to Casper as she gently pats his face. "I am here," she repeats as if she believes her love will cure all his ills.

My attention abruptly shifts to the upcoming Coast Guard football season and my eyes search the area around the stadium for a player, any player, but I see none.

The bleachers of the stadium run up into a twenty-foot stone wall that surrounds half of the stands and gives it a touch of Roman architecture. The players will soon all be beyond the wall, seated for lectures in the large McAllister Hall, the engineering building at the back of the stadium, waiting for me to walk in and start the football season. The team has arrived at the Academy after a summer of military training, and before the return of the rest of the Corps of Cadets, giving up a precious week of summer leave to begin the football season.

I look away from the bleachers and out to the Thames River again. *It's like Myers and Cayuga Lake*, I think. *A train runs through a national service academy and along the water.* The scene reminds me of Cayuga Lake and the train that runs along its eastern shore and through the hamlet of Myers. My mind drifts back to Casper and his childhood in Myers. I remember stories told of the town years ago, and now they are coming back to Casper, and me.

I close my eyes to football for a moment and let Casper open my memory to Myers.

In May of 1935, Takla (pronounced *Tutla*) Moses watched the morning sunshine creep into the bedroom of her youngest child. The sunshine moved like a soothing wave that did not recede, but instead stayed ashore and covered her twelve-year-old son like a warm blanket.

The sun was cresting above the hills and into the tiny valley of Myers, which lay almost directly on Cayuga Lake. Route 34 ran from the city of Ithaca and up the east side of the lake to Auburn. Seven miles north of Ithaca, at a crossroads, was the Ludlowville school. Ludlowville Road led, of course, to the village of Ludlowville. The left turn, Myers Lane, sloped down toward Cayuga Lake and into the valley of Myers, where the International Salt Company had created a community for its Syrian and immigrant workers. The only stop for the immigrants between Syria and their new paradise had been Ellis Island.

All along sloping Myers Lane were small, two-story houses built by International Salt—all two-stories with two bedrooms, coal furnaces and no indoor toilets. They were mansions to the immigrants. At the bottom of the hill, where Myers Lane turned right, was the only grocery store, Myers Grocery, which was smaller than the houses. Alongside the store was a short dirt road, which led away from Myers Lane and back to the Moses house.

Myers Lane continued toward a bridge about twenty yards long that crossed Salmon Creek. The road forked thirty yards after the bridge. The left turn led to the salt plant, which was on the lake. There, salt mined from the ground was processed. The road split to the right, curving upward and connected back to Route 34, led to Syrian Hill, which overlooked Cayuga Lake and the salt plant. The road that sloped down into Myers was called American Hill because most of the people were not first-generation immigrants. In the valley, where the Moses house stood, there were a few Syrian families, a family from Poland and another from Czechoslovakia. At the center of the village was the Eastern Orthodox Church, perched on the end of Syrian Hill, overlooking the valley of Myers, Cayuga Lake and the salt plant.

Takla Moses stretched her thick calves and leaned her stocky frame over the youngest of her seven children. "My baby," she sighed as she thought, *My twelve-year-old little baby. You will always be my little baby.*

She wondered if the demands of survival had made her too mechanical with her first six children, or if it was the gentle, shy kindness she saw in her youngest boy that made her feel a deeper affection for him. Or perhaps it was the fact that he did not talk until he was five and then suddenly spoke in full sentences. *He was silent for so long. I thought he was deaf,* she thought. *But no, he was studying the world, letting all the good in the world enter his heart, and stopping all the evil.*

"Michael, I will kiss you while you sleep. You will feel it, but you will not know I kissed you. I love you," she whispered, barely mouthing the words. "If you felt my kiss in your dreams, maybe it is trapped within your heart or dreams. I wonder if long after I am in heaven you will feel that kiss in your dreams and it will awaken you then. And you know I will love you forever, even from heaven."

Takla Moses looked at Michael's feet and gently touched each of his toes on one foot. "One, two, three, four, five," she whispered to herself. *You were born right in this room and it seems like only moments ago. I counted your toes on the day you were born and I have counted your toes every day I have seen you sleeping since that day.*

She ran her fingers through his bushy, black hair. *He looks like my husband when he was young and my other two sons,* she thought. *And he has hair like his four sisters.*

When Michael Moses opened his eyes, his mother bent down, cupped his face and kissed him as if he were only a minute old.

The room he shared with his brothers was empty, as was his sisters' room. He followed his mother downstairs to the kitchen next to a small living room, which turned into his mother and father's bedroom every night.

Michael Moses ate his breakfast quietly. He slowly broke off pieces of flat, round loaves of Syrian bread and dipped it into a bowl filled with *shanklish*, a Syrian cheese that tasted like feta made from aged cottage cheese. It was the size of a baseball, covered with oregano and swimming in olive oil. He felt the house shake lightly from a train, which traveled only a hundred feet behind his house as it traveled through Myers on its journey up and down the east side of the lake. He ignored it in the daytime but at night, when he lay awake, he would listen to the tracks rattle as the cargo cars rolled by. When he finished breakfast, he walked with his mother from his house to Myers Grocery, which was only a hundred feet in the opposite direction of the tracks.

On the store's cement porch, his mother met with two other Syrian ladies, Helanie, the wife of Abraham George, who ran the grocery store, and Helanie's sister, Atina Saleem. They were about her age, but thinner and taller than Takla. The sister's maiden name was also Moses, but their families weren't related. They all wore dull-colored flowered dresses, simply made and fit for housework. Their true faces were hidden behind the tired mask of hard immigration woes. Takla bent to kiss her son and went into the store.

Michael peeked inside to see if he could see two of Atina's five children, Michael and Martha, but he did not. He saw Abraham, the grocer, standing near the small butcher's block in front of a wall lined by cans and behind a glass counter with penny candy. He looked for Abraham's son Casper, who was four years younger. Casper had two younger brothers, Alfred, called Otsie, and Nicholas. Abraham caught his eye through the glass and smiled. He was shorter than his wife, Helanie, and he spoke gently. Abraham had traveled to America on the *Lusitania* and left a daughter and his son Abraham Jr., who everyone called George, behind in Syria along with Abraham's wife. When the RMS *Lusitania* sank on its return voyage, World War I had begun, and Abraham's family was stranded. His daughter died in Syria before he ever saw her again. Helanie and George had to wait until the end of the war to rejoin Abraham in America. Abraham had spent years working in the salt plant and then opened Myers Grocery.

Michael turned away from the window and stepped his stocky frame out into the street. He looked around and paused; he had felt confused lately. He could feel himself maturing emotionally but he did not understand the changes. He looked to where the road sloped toward American Hill, a hovel where non-Syrian workers lived.

Myers, he thought. *It is like the rest of the world but I also think it is not. I think someone like the President of the United States could stop the sad stories of the world, but I also wonder if I could, too.*

Michael started down Myers Road past a row house that looked just like his. Two houses before the bridge he stopped at the small cement pillars marking the entrance to the Georges' house. He waited a few minutes, but no one appeared. He then walked to the bridge, stopped and leaned over and watched the clear, thin water of the creek run beneath the bridge. He watched the water run over the gravel and create white bubbles that faded as they floated downstream and entered a wider, quiet pool where he swam in the summers. The pool stretched beneath the railroad trestle and then moved on to Cayuga Lake. Michael lifted his head up and looked out to where the mouth of the creek flowed into the shallows of the deep lake.

He looked to where the creek ran against the steep shale bank for a hundred yards downstream until it reached the bridge. The small bridge was a truss type with a large metal lattice skeleton extending up from both sides and spanning overhead its entire length. The deck of the bridge was supported on each end by two concrete and metal girders. From where he stood, he could see a part of the big bridge, which ran along Route 34B and over the creek. *The bridges,* he thought, *run over the same creek, but one is so high and big and the other is so small and short. Yet they both take people to the same place.*

Michael leaned his head back and felt the cool breeze of the May morning blend with sunshine that covered his face. When he opened his eyes, he immediately noticed the beauty of the cumulus clouds racing across the sky. Almost instantly, he felt a tap on his arm.

"What do you see?" Casper George asked.

Michael looked at Casper and thought back to when he was five and did not speak out loud. He thought back at how his mother, Takla, would visit with Helanie in the store or at their house, worried about him, thinking he was deaf. When he was alone with baby Casper, he started to talk to him, sometimes in baby talk and sometimes with his own words. Michael remembered a simple story he would repeat over and over to Casper.

"Do you remember when I would tell you the story of the good cat and the bad cat?" Michael asked Casper.

"Yes, but tell me again," Casper smiled.

"The bad cat went from house to house on the Syrian Hill and asked everyone, 'Do you have any candy for me?' Everyone would say, 'No, we have no candy for the bad cat.' Then the bad cat would walk from the Syrian Hill down to your house and ask you, 'Do you have candy for me?' And you said to him, 'I do not have any candy for the bad cat.' Then he would stop at your father's store and ask everyone at the store for candy and everyone would say, 'No candy for the bad cat.' Then the good cat would go to everyone's house on the Syrian Hill and ask, 'Do you have any candy for me?' and everyone would say yes and give him candy. Then the good cat would walk down the hill to your house and ask you for candy and you would say, 'Yes, I have candy for you.'"

Michael finished the story, saying, "The good cat would go to the store and then ask for candy, and everyone would give the good cat candy."

"Why did one cat get candy and one cat did not get any?" Casper asked.

"The good cat helped people who needed help. He shared things. The bad cat, he was not really a bad cat, he just did not share, he did not help other people," Michael explained.

"Oh," was all Casper said back, although smiling.

"Yes, you know it well. Now you can tell it someday to another little child," Michael said to Casper.

Michael suddenly realized that repeating the story to Casper is what drew his own voice outward. *I still keep most of my thoughts to myself.*

"You stand on the bridge a lot. I can see you from my house," Casper said.

Michael wanted to say something, but he did not answer. *Maybe,* he thought, *maybe if I practice on Casper like I did with the cat story, I can practice expressing my thoughts. Maybe someday I will be able to tell others what I really think.*

Michael began to speak softly. "The clouds are big and white like giant bubbles, sometimes they have a shade of gray underneath the white, or sometimes a shade of orange or pink around them. The bubbles of the clouds change every moment, like a painting that is not finished. Every day we forget what they looked like yesterday. We might remember that they were beautiful, but we forget what they looked like. They are always more beautiful than the day before. Almost always we walk by them day after day without looking up."

"A lot of times I see you looking down," said Casper.

"Yes, I watch the water as it flows down the creek to the lake."

"And at night? When I see you standing out here in the dark?"

"At night I sometimes see the stars and stare at how they make the night alive. And sometimes I just wonder what is out there and where it all goes to."

"You mean like outer space?" Casper asked, confused.

Michael did not answer. He turned his head back to the morning sky. "Casper, you can stand on the bridge in Myers, and you can feel like you are at the center of this world, or maybe the universe."

A few minutes later, Casper's mother, Helanie, and Aunt Atina Saleem led Casper across the bridge, up to Syrian Hill and out of sight. Michael looked at the creek and then the sky and then the creek again. When he crossed the bridge and came to the fork in the road at the bottom of Syrian Hill, his eyes followed the empty lane leading to the International Salt Plant. When it was quitting time, he would stop at the split in the road and watch the men walk from the salt plant and down through Myers or up to Syrian Hill. He started up Myers Road as it headed back to the main highway, but before he reached the turnoff to Syrian Hill, he stepped off the road and onto a path cutting up the side of Syrian Hill through the brush. The ground of the shortcut was hard dirt beaten down by those who traveled to the salt plant for work or to Myers Grocery. The trail cut through the underbrush covering the slope of Syrian Hill. The smaller trees and bushes on the side of the hill were not yet thick with their summer growth. He followed the path as it angled upward. When he neared the top, he kneeled and looked out onto Syrian Hill. In front of him was a small patch of grass leading to the green-shingled sides of the Syrian Orthodox Church. The church had been built for the Syrian workers eleven years before, in 1924, by International Salt. The house on the left belonged to the Isaacs and the next to the Solomons, then the Caliels and across from them was Abraham's brother John's house, then the Saleems, where he was headed, and the Abrahams. Michael Moses turned away from the houses on the hill and looked out onto Myers. *When I stand on the bridge in the daytime, I can see the whole world but the whole world can't see me. On the path I can see the whole world but sometimes I can hide from the world.*

He looked down at the bridge where he had just stood and could see the trail of the water heading out onto the vast blue lake. Only the tall, white concrete of the salt plant off to the right detracted from its beauty. His eyes found the train tracks as they crossed by the salt plant and moved across the creek and out of Myers. He looked down on his house and Abraham's grocery store. *Yes, I can see the whole world better from up here,* he thought. He studied Myers as if it was a painting. *I think that the railroad tracks must lead to the rest of the world. The world outside of Myers.*

He emerged from the brush-covered path and walked across the small lawn of the Isaacs' house and stopped at the front of the church. In the middle of Syrian Hill, on the dusty dirt road walking toward him, were three children his age, and Casper. Martha Saleem tiptoed over the scattered pebbles with her bare feet. Her wavy black hair fell to her shoulders. When she stood in front of him, she kept her lips sealed to hide her slightly buck teeth, but she had been born with an instinctive smile when she approached people. Martha was thirteen, one year older than Michael Moses, and her younger brother, Michael Saleem, was his classmate and friend. The Saleems had a family of five children: Michael and Martha, Sam, Scandera, and Mary. Michael and

Martha who were inseparable and Michael Moses paired with them both in the tiny confines of Myers. Michael Saleem was longer than him, skinny in terms of immigrant children and pale compared to the other Syrians. His eyes were always alive, peering at the world through his thin-rimmed glasses, which he rarely took off.

They look like cousins, he thought as he compared Michael Saleem to Casper George. *They have a soft, slim handsome look about them.* He glanced at Martha and the butterflies in his stomach stirred. *Not like me.* His comparisons stilled the butterflies.

Next to him was Dawn Worsell. She lived on Ludlowville Road across from the Ludlowville school on the other side of Route 34B. Dawn was ten years old, one year younger than Michael Saleem and two years younger than Martha. Dawn was shy and blond, with skin as white as milk that bruised easily. When she was cold, the blue veins and arteries bulged against her white skin. Dawn was also in the same classroom as both boys.

They walked from where they had met at the front of St. George's Syrian Orthodox Church, the only building on the hill that was not a home inhabited by immigrant workers from the salt plant. They stood next to the small, one-story oval building covered with green shingles.

"I can see all of the world from here," said Michael Moses, looking down on the valley and taking it all in. "The creek looks silver from up here. I can see all the older children on the bridge. And all the people going to Abraham's store to get their mail or maybe ice cream. I can see my house but not my mother."

"Here comes the train," pointed Michael Saleem. The engine chugged in unison with the iron wheel rattling against the steel rails as it moved north across the creek and to the salt plant. It echoed throughout the valley and through the hills.

"It came from Ithaca."

"My father went to Ithaca once, told me I could go someday," Dawn said shyly.

They gazed across the deep blue darkness of the last seven miles of Cayuga Lake to the city nestled on its southern hills.

"I think the train must stop at Cornell," said Michael Moses. He remembered a teacher, Mr. Smith, at the Ludlowville school was from England and was studying for his doctorate at Cornell.

"He told us all we had wonderful parents but they had to take care of us. He said that we should think about life beyond Ludlowville school and the salt plant."

"Beyond Myers, what did he mean by that?" Michael Saleem asked.

"He means over there, where the rest of the people of the world are." Martha Saleem pointed across the width of the deep blue lake to the rising hills on the western bank. She traced the tree line until it blended into the horizon, as if the two were connected.

A small whimper rose from just beneath their feet at the edge of the brush as the hill sloped down.

They all looked at each other.

Again, a soft whimper repeated itself.

Michael Moses slowly parted the thin brush with his hands. The sad, watery eyes of a tiny, brown-and-white beagle puppy stared at all four of them.

"It's a puppy!" shouted Casper.

"How did that get here?" Michael Saleem wondered.

"There are no dogs on this hill or all of Myers," said his sister.

Michael Moses cupped the tiny dog underneath its front legs and picked it up with the gentleness of a newborn baby. He held it close to his neck and the puppy settled against him. The dog whimpered again.

"What do we do with it?" asked Michael Saleem.

"Let's take it down to Myers Grocery. Someone there will know where it came from and what to do," Martha answered as she leaned her face into the puppy.

Michael Moses felt the dog turn slightly in his arms, reach its neck out and gently rub its face against Martha's cheek. Martha looked into Michael Moses's eyes and smiled.

CHAPTER 2

"I do not know how we are going to make it through the season," I say to Nancy before I start to help her, Lila, and Casper off the field and head to the team meeting.

"We'll make it," Nancy answers with such ease, as if somehow she believes she can predict the future. "We moved Casper in with us after your mother died four years ago when he was fine and healthy. Lila was a few months old, and she grew up with him. We can't kick him out now. We must take care of him as well."

I know the burden will fall on Nancy. The long hours and weekends will now be filled with Casper.

"The hospice nurses and caregivers will help. Hat will too," I add, referring to a local senior citizen, Harold Fengar, who is shaped like Humpty Dumpty and is on assisted living himself. Hat arrives every morning at eight and sits with Casper.

"You know you could quit your job." I do not mean what I just proposed, and Nancy knows why.

"And what if you lose yours? We went through this once, before your championship seasons," Nancy says, referring to a decade earlier when the Academy did not renew my three-year contract and instead gave me a six-month deal for not winning enough games. "Besides, what if you were to die or have a stroke or heart attack?" Her tone is nervous, as if she has lost her ability to predict the future. "We are fifty-five and fifty-six with a four-year old child and a dying old man. I'm not sure how it all came to this, but we will get through it."

Then I remember. A few months ago I found a letter Nancy had written to herself thirteen years earlier, nine years before Lila was even born.

5/19/01

Today is the day that I realize that I will never be a mother, biologically or adoptive. In my heart I think I have sensed that this day would come. Especially lately, I have had this feeling of impending doom or more specifically an overwhelming sadness that I cannot seem to shake. It is as if I'm afraid to admit to myself that my life has to go on, without a child. I think that since I moved away from my family, the one thing that has kept me going was the thought of a little one that needed me as much as I would need them. But the time has come for me to accept that God has chosen another path for me, and I need to move on because the sadness I feel constantly is slowly taking over. I am not at all the person I used to be. I can barely get through the day and then my energy is gone. I have no will to fix the house or to exercise or any of the things I used to want to do. And I know that even though Bill occasionally suggests he may adopt (when I'm having a sad day, he'll say, "We'll get what you want... or we'll look into it"), I know he has no real intentions of doing so. In fact, if I never brought up adoption again he would secretly be very pleased.

What I don't know is how to live with this finality. That is something I will have to get professional help for, you see, although I know that I do not have a choice in the matter. I am having a terrible time trying to accept it. It is almost as if I am giving in and losing faith, and being Catholic and losing faith makes me feel like God may say, "If only you had more faith in me, I would have granted your wish." When is it time to give up? Maybe it was Bill's decision, so although I have to live with it, God will know that I never fully gave up.

"It seems like it has been a long four years since Lila was born, and then a few months later your mother passed away and Casper moved in," Nancy says.

Casper's head perks up from the sound of Nancy's voice. "Was your mother stoned to death?" he asks me.

"No!" I answer abruptly to change the direction of the conversation.

"Lila, come here, I want to give you a drink of water," Nancy says, and she picks Lila up and puts her on her lap. Nancy is always ready to move Lila away from Casper's sudden thoughts.

"Mom fell and hit her head," I say.

"Was it my fault?" Casper asks with a quivering voice.

"No, she fell and hit her head," I repeat.

As if to soothe his pain, Nancy places Lila back in Casper's lap in the wheelchair. He looks down at her as she places her head on his chest as if she is ready to fall asleep.

I think back to my mother's death. I was lucky Anna and Lila had a short meeting and crossed paths. Four years ago, three months after Lila was born, my mother, at eighty-two, was visiting her eighty-eight-year-old sister on the porch of their childhood home and they bumped into each other. My mother's head hit the concrete of the one-hundred-year-old front porch. The blood flowed into her head and packed her brain tightly into her skull. Anna did awaken five days later; even though she had severe brain damage, she did seem to recognize people and smile. I was lucky again. How many people, after death has arrived, get a chance to say goodbye one last time? Anna never walked or talked again and lay bedridden for a few months, suffering minute by minute. A few months later the doctors gave her twelve hours to live. The next four days, she lay unconscious, breathing her last breaths. On the fifth day, Nancy brought six-month old Lila into the room and changed her diaper on the bed right next to Anna's chest. I kissed her cheek like I had done a thousand time before. This time I did not taste the perfume, or the soap, or the baby powder, and I did not feel softness of her face. Instead, my lips could taste the minerals of her body leaching through the skin of her cheek. A few moments later after we had taken Lila out of the room, as if Anna had been waiting to see Lila one last time in the flesh, she passed from this life to the next.

"Those boys," Casper says to me. "Those boys and those girls that come back to see me... will I see them soon?"

I look at his sad face, but I do not answer. I want to say to him that I do not know if they will creep into his memory again here on earth or if he will travel and visit them instead.

I gaze back to the empty field and think of my boys instead of his, the Coast Guard football players. Then I shut my eyes and travel back to the most surreal moment of my career. Through my closed eyelids I can see the brightness of the August sun. The hidden sunshine takes me back three years to an earlier homecoming on September 24, 2011.

I was walking off the field, the victory fresh. The officers had all patted me on the back, and I felt I was the hero to all who were shaking my hand. I had hugged and laughed with every current and former player I could find. I moved down the right hashmark, on the twenty-yard line on the south side of the stadium, ready to exit into Billard Hall.

"Coach," a gentle finger barely touched the hair on my right forearm.

I turned and vaguely recognized the solemn, worn face of a gray-haired lady in her mid-fifties. Her name eluded me. *I should know her*, I thought. Her face looked gray like her hair, as if she had been in prison or hidden from daylight for years. Her eyes were swollen and red, as if the volcanic pain inside her was erupting through her tears.

Behind her, a few yards away on the opposite hashmark, a tall man stood silently as if he were at funeral, not a football game. He looked like a grim statue with skin, a statue that did not breathe. His arms were folded loosely like a child holding an imaginary baby. I knew something was wrong. Their faces did not wear the same joy as the other Coast Guard people who milled about.

"Coach, I don't know if you remember me. But I am Matt Krueger's mother. I just wanted to say hello."

"Matt, where's Matt?" Now the face had come back to me. "Where is he?" I shouted. My mind was back to football, back to the joy of the heroic victory. "I have to give him a hug!" After years of tough, losing seasons, the 2006 and 2007 teams were league champions. *Street & Smiths Sports Annual* magazine had ranked us twenty-fifth in the nation. Matt was the starting center and an All-League and All-East player.

"No, Matt's not here," she paused as if not wanting to continue. "He is in Michigan flying helicopters for the Coast Guard."

There was a short silence and then her voice cracked. "Today is my other son's birthday, my son Sean's birthday."

Sean Krueger, whom I had never met, was Matt's older brother and his hero. The only reason Matt came to the Academy was he wanted to be like his older brother and fly helicopters for the Coast Guard. Sean Krueger had tragically lost his life with three other Coast Guard personnel off the coast of Washington State just months earlier when the MH-60 Jayhawk helicopter he was flying crashed. Sean had left behind a wife and three children under the age of ten.

"We sat up all night and could not sleep." Her words crept out of a throat fighting back cries of pain. "We stayed up all night and then drove hours just to get here, to sit in the stands and be around people, Coast Guard people, Coast Guard family. They got us through the day."

Almost as instantly as the Kruegers had appeared, they disappeared into the moving football crowd. No goodbyes. Not today, not ever for the Kruegers. Sean, like all Gold Star families, did not get to say one last goodbye to his wife or children or parents. Mrs. Krueger did not even get to kiss his cheek one last time like I kissed my mother Anna's cheek.

I search for the thin, white cloud above the tree line, but it has dissipated like my mother or even Sean Krueger. I wonder if they all can travel back from time to time, or do we all wait forever to see them again? Do Sean Krueger's children live in waiting, or maybe he is with them now.

CHAPTER 3

"I'll be done by the time you get them to a drive-through for ice cream and let them finish. It's a forty-five-minute administrative meeting," I tell Nancy.

"Ice cream!" Lila yells. "What do you want Gido, vanilla or chocolate?"

"What?" Casper hears his name but nothing else.

"Ice cream. Nancy is taking you for ice cream," I say.

"I scream, you scream, we all scream for Ludlowville," Casper smiles as he sings a childhood phrase from his school days in Myers. Then his face freezes in fear; his quick moment of happiness slides into depression.

I think about how he was always a kind man who was sad much of the time.

"It was a long time ago," I tell him.

"It does not seem like a long time ago," Casper says as if he is young again.

"Yes, Dad, a long time ago."

I wonder, *Maybe it is us who take time for granted and it is the dying who feel the pain of lost time.*

"Am I supposed to tell them about Lila?" he asks.

"I guess," I answer to end the conversation, but not really understanding his question or my answer.

Casper perks up and asks, "Did I tell you how we got our nicknames in Myers?"

"Yes." I answer. "You told me years ago and then talked about it the other day."

"Good," is all Casper says.

Nancy starts toward the silver SUV parked on the entrance ramp to the stadium and I follow pushing Casper and Lila in the wheelchair. I look down at his scalp; a few strands of gray remain across the top but not enough to cover the brown blotches that have appeared on the top of his head. I think back to how handsome he looked in his high school graduation picture standing in front of his house with his parents in Myers. With her forefinger, Lila touches a spot on his aging face as if she is searching for something, then she leans forward and replaces her finger with a kiss.

We all converge on the passenger side of the SUV. Lila hops off the wheelchair and, as if to instinctively mimic Nancy and me, she tries to help by holding Casper's hand while we hold him up by the armpits. He cannot stand on his own.

"Turn," Lila says to him as we shift his stance and prop his rear end on the seat. I swing his legs around and tuck his feet beneath the glove compartment. "Buckle up, Gido," she instructs, as she climbs into her car seat in the middle of the back seat. She does not know he cannot buckle up on his own.

Nancy buckles Casper's seat belt. She drapes a large cotton bib across his chest and loosely ties the strings behind his neck.

"Casper is not eight or seven on hospice, he is eighty-seven. His time is passing like it should," I add.

I know she is aware of Lila's attachment to Casper but is afraid to say it to me.

"We are lucky," I say. Casper is easy to take care of in hospice care. I have three diapers on him for when he urinates. He has a bowel movement every two days and can tell when he needs to be brought to the bathroom. And he can feed himself the soft foods we serve him. The hard part is we must change him and clean him. I continue. "Also, his biological system slows down if we have a chance to get him out."

"He is not going to get out again once you walk into that meeting room and start the season," Nancy states.

"I just want to get him to the second game, the Merchant Marine game on September 13," I say.

"Your mother died a week after the last time you beat them four years ago. And you do not think you will be able to beat them ever again. You're chasing your own ghost," Nancy scolds. "And you can't drag a dying man along with you."

I follow the car uphill away from the field and walk to the top of the stadium and lean onto the flat stone surface wall and stare over the field out onto the Thames River.

I think of the train tracks that run below the stadium, through the Academy, and separate it from the baseball, soccer, and softball fields that stretch to the Sailing Center and the crew house on the shores of the Thames River.

It is like Myers and Cayuga Lake, I think as my mind drifts back to Casper and his childhood in Myers.

Michael Moses carried the dog from behind the church toward the top of the path on Syrian Hill, as Michael and Martha Saleem, Dawn and Casper walked along with him. They all stopped at the top of the path and looked down into the valley of Myers.

"Who are all the kids on the bridge?" Martha pointed downward to the bridge which had a gathering of fifteen children.

"Myers kids, from the hill and the houses down below," her brother Michael answered.

"What do you think they will say about the puppy?" Michael Moses asked.

No one said anything. They stood silent for a few minutes, each trying to guess what might happen.

"Let's just walk past them to the store," Michael Saleem said.

"Hide the dog as best you can. They won't see it or even stop us."

They traveled single file down the path but stopped when they reached the road at the end of the path. Slowly, they moved out into the open and onto the bridge.

The first three children they tried to sneak past and avoid were the Isaac brothers who lived in the first house next to the church at the top of the path, George (Gus), Michael (Decker) and Jack (Jacko) Isaac.

"Stop," said Jacko, who was a few years older, with dark curls. It was Jacko who gave the nicknames to all of those in Myers.

The five of them froze in their tracks in the dead center of the bridge.

"Who are you boys?" Jacko asked knowing the answer.

The bridge was filled by a long line of older children with given nicknames. The Georges from the hill, John George's sons, John (Johnny Boy) and Casper (Coach); Abraham's other sons, Casper's brothers, Nicholas and Alfred (Otsie,) The Solomons from Syrian Hill and George and Nicholas Solomon from the valley of Myers. Abraham Caliel Jr. (Cal) and Cal Abraham from the hill along with the Marshalls who lived across from Casper and came to Myers by way of Czechoslovakia and had changed their name once they set foot in America. The Burin brothers and Eddie Kowalski from Poland, who lived next to Myers Grocery, were there also.

Michael Moses and Michael Saleem had no answers. Casper stood motionless with Martha and Dawn.

"It is time to name you both," said Jacko. "And since you are here," he pointed to Casper, "I will name you also."

"You will be called Monk," Jacko said to Casper. "You always follow the two Michaels around Myers and never say a word. Like a monk in a monastery."

Casper stood silent. He liked Jacko, if for no other reason than a month ago Jacko had given Casper his entire collection of marbles.

Casper and his mother had been walking by the Isaacs' house on Syrian Hill when Jacko called him over and handed him a dark green canvas bag filled with over one hundred marbles.

"I am too old to play with them," Jacko had said. "You can have them."

"All of them?" Casper shouted as he ran his hand through the bag filled with marbles of all shapes and colors.

"Yes, all of them," Jacko said. "Until you are done with them. Then you have to give them away to someone else."

Jacko turned to Michael Moses. "And you, step forward. What shall we call you?" he asked like a king would ask a follower as he stared at Michael Moses.

Michael Moses held the tiny puppy so tightly to him, no one had noticed.

"What is that, a squirrel or a kitten?" Jacko asked with amazement.

Everyone circled tightly around Michael Moses, who said nothing, but clutched the puppy lovingly between his neck and chin. He looked up at them with his soft, amber eyes surrounded by his round head of bushy hair. The puppy looked up at them also. Four eyes looked out at the group in perfect unison, as if they had been together forever on the same face.

"It's a little dog! It's a puppy!" came shouts of joy.

"Where did that come from?" Jacko asked.

"Behind the church!" Martha yelled.

"From where? There are no dogs in Myers," Jacko answered.

"Maybe it came off the train when it stopped at the salt plant," a voice yelled.

"And climbed from the tracks to the hill and then up the backside of the Syrian Hill, through all that brush? No that is impossible," Jacko stated. "It could have come from one of the barges that goes up and down the lake and stops at the salt plant."

"Maybe it fell out of the sky," Casper quipped.

The whole group looked at Casper but said nothing.

"What are you going to do with it?" Jacko asked.

"We're going to take it to the store and see who might know

about it or want it," Martha answered.

"No," Jacko said and pointed to the salt plant. "I will take it to the salt plant and ask the people there."

"No!" Michael Saleem yelled at him. "It's his dog! He found it!"

Jacko stood with his hand on his chin, thinking deeply. He moved his face close to Michael Saleem's face and stared through Michael's glasses and into his eyes.

"I was going to name you 'Doc' because I heard you say you might want to become a doctor someday. But I have changed my mind, you will be named Nemo for the rest of your life."

"Why Nemo?" rang out from the crowd and echoed across the bridge.

"It's from Captain Nemo in the book *Twenty Thousand Leagues Under the Sea*. He loved his crew and felt their pain. He stuck up for his crew and believed in them as people. You stuck up for Michael and his puppy."

Jacko turned to Michael Moses and said, "I was going name you Silent because you never talked until you were older, but now I have a better name for you. You shall be called *Puppy*, you will be *Puppy Moses* for the rest of your life."

"Proceed." Jacko said, waving as the crowd parted.

The five of them crossed the bridge to the store where Abraham placed a small bowl of milk on the porch of Myers Grocery. The dog sipped it as if he was barely alive.

"Who will love this dog?" Abraham said to the few people on the porch.

"Dawn, we have to go," her father said. "We cannot keep it until you feel better all the time." Her father pulled her away.

Michael Moses noticed how she had sometimes missed school.

"Can we keep it?" asked Martha.

"No," her mother Atina said.

Takla Moses bent down to the bowl, her thin, long skirt bundled on the dust of the porch. Her son Michael picked up the puppy and held it to his face.

The four empty, desperate eyes were attached again, and they looked up at Takla. She could feel her son's affection for the puppy.

Takla's heart reacted before her brain could, as if love could solve every problem. She took his hand without saying a word and they walked back down the dirt road to their house with the tiny animal tucked underneath his chin.

Puppy Moses did not understand what was happening to him, but he felt himself changing, as if he were experiencing his own birth. He was joyous and he could feel love flowing through his veins.

CHAPTER 4

The moment I step into the meeting room to start the football season, I search the faces of the Coast Guard Academy football team for the smile of the Mona Lisa. My eyes quickly circle the lecture hall in the engineering building. I hear the jovial laughter quickly subside as the faces turn toward me. In the front row are this year's seniors, or first-class cadets as they are called at the Academy. They have been on summer assignments serving the Coast Guard since their academic year ended in May. They were granted only three weeks leave, and they sacrificed one of those to return early and play football. Some of the *firsties* have shown up sloppy and unshaven as part of a rebellious tradition and without the normal fear of being reprimanded. Within hours, they will be neatly groomed and in the assigned military uniform of the day, or the mandated physical education apparel for every waking moment the rest of the year. The now quiet faces turn to me with respect, but none show that famously wry smile.

I have seen the smile of the Mona Lisa only once in my life, a decade ago, on the face of a Coast Guard football player in this very meeting.

A few rows behind the first-class football players sit the sophomores, or third-class cadets; they too have been on summer assignments since last May, but their young faces are clean, as they dare not violate the dress code even for a moment. I can see the mixed tension in the faces due to the start of the grueling football season. The juniors, or second-class cadets, all look like officers or enlisted, dressed in the Coast Guard working blue uniform as if they were actively working on a Coast Guard vessel. They have been at the Academy all summer in leadership roles over incoming freshmen, fourth-class cadets, who are still called swabs until the Swab Summer ends next week. The swabs sit in the back. They started their six weeks of summer on the last Monday in June. The freshmen have lost significant amounts of weight and muscle mass after spending each day from the morning calisthenics at six until lights out in either military training, academic preparation, or endless physical athletic activities such as the obstacle course, physical fitness development, swimming, and diving. Their hollow eyes glare at me and their faces are expressionless.

A decade ago, I was standing in the same spot I am now when I looked down at one of the senior football players in the front row. Adam Bryant watched me intently. I was ranting like a young, hungry football coach when the most peculiar of smiles caught my attention. It was simple, barely traceable on the gentle expression of Adam's face. His brown hair was neatly cropped.

Adam was a receiver; he looked like the average cadet and not the average college football player. He was fit and lean, but not skinny. He possessed no football skills that would separate him from an average receiver at the Academy. I had always thought of him as a quiet person who spoke little and let his work ethic and actions define his personality. I remember thinking that Adam Bryant was the symbol of every cadet at the Coast Guard Academy, a symbol of honor, respect, and compassion. If he were sitting in uniform in the middle of the entire Corps of Cadets, you would not be able to distinguish him from anyone else.

The next morning, after seeing Adam Bryant's smile in the meeting the previous night, I arrived at the Academy for the first day of football practice. The sky was dark and gray when I got out of my car and walked through the thick humidity to Billard Hall. I could feel the perspiration slide down my forehead and thought, *This is not good for the first day of football.* I climbed the steps of Billard Hall. Built more than fifty years ago, it once served as the main gymnasium of the Academy. My office was on the top floor, which had been the balcony of the old gym, and the rows of tarnished wooden seats still looked down on the gym floor. I was dressed in my coaching shorts and shirt and carrying my football playbook. When I reached the top step, I stopped for a moment and looked across the rows of seats. Adam Bryant was sitting in the first bleacher a few feet from me. He was the only other person in the building. Adam sat alone waiting for the first position meetings of the morning and the season. He looked up at me but unlike so many cadets who were quick to address you with a solid "Hello, Coach," or "Good morning, Coach," Adam said nothing but instead smiled. Then it hit me, I had seen him smile before, normal smiles, but this smile and the one he flashed the night before were faint. *His smile is just like the Mona Lisa*, I thought. *Here is a young man who is content with life. He is going to go through life enjoying every moment. He is here early, he is the kind of kid who can't wait for football to start and he can't wait for the rest of his life to continue.*

Adam never said a word as I walked past him toward my office.

Adam graduated from the United States Coast Guard Academy, then went to flight school in Pensacola, Florida, and became a pilot. On October 29, 2009, while conducting a search-and-rescue mission as a co-pilot on a HC-130 Hercules aircraft from Coast Guard Air Station Sacramento, his plane collided with a Marines Corps AH-1 Super Cobra Marine Aircraft Wing helicopter that was stationed out of Marine Corps Base Camp Pendleton. Adam was killed instantly, as were six other Coast Guard service members and two United States Marines.

The following year after his death, in late May when the Academy was quiet after graduation, and before Swab Summer training started, a memorial service was held for Adam on the main parade field in the front of the Academy at four in the afternoon. I stood off to the side of the ceremony, underneath the walkways surrounding Hamilton Hall (the historic Academy headquarters) and looked out onto the parade field. The ceremony finished at five, the summer sun still decorating the horizon. The plush green grass of the parade field had absorbed the golden sunshine and created a color I had never seen before. For a moment I drifted away, thinking, *I wonder if you travel far away from here, to another universe or galaxy, if you would see colors never seen before on earth?* As I watched the solemn ceremony I wondered, *Time goes on for us still here, but does time go on for Adam Bryant?*

I watched his classmates, his teammates, and Coast Guard people mingle about until the crowd had diminished to only a few. Adam Bryant's mother stood alone beneath the flagpole when I approached her. She was clutching a triangular flag, enclosed in glass and inside of a wooden frame, to her chest with one of the corners of the dark wood touching her chin. The new colors of the earth behind her did nothing to hide the pain in her face.

Maybe time cannot go on for her, I thought. I could not tell if she recognized me. Her lips were closed and jaw clenched, as if the emptiness she was feeling was alive and pulling her from within.

"I am Coach George," I said.

As Adam's mother looked at me, she forced a slight parting of her lips attempting to smile, but it was not the smile of the Mona Lisa. "He loved his teammates, he loved being on the team," was all she said.

Whenever I went recruiting across America, in the big cities and small towns, I would search thousands of nameless faces for that smile. Some faces ignored my eyes, some turned away quickly, some glanced back with no expression, a rare few even smiled, but never once has the smile of the Mona Lisa appeared on a face before me. Adam Bryant's face is forever painted in my memory, smiling at me like the Mona Lisa.

Back in the meeting, Derek Victory, our five-foot, nine-inch sophomore quarterback, sits in the middle of the group and cracks his friendly smile at me. In March of his senior year of high school,

Derek had been reviewed off the admissions wait list but did not get an appointment. He was reviewed again in May and received and accepted an appointment just one month before reporting for Swab Summer.

The United States Coast Guard Academy is one of the most selective schools in America, with academic entrance requirements equal to or more competitive than West Point, the Naval Academy, the Air Force Academy, or the Merchant Marine Academy.

The challenges to maintain the football program were becoming obvious to everyone. After the graduation ceremony last May, Admiral Robert Papp, the commandant of the Coast Guard, and I were talking with our athletic director, Tim Fitzpatrick.

"I don't know how you are going to do it with thirty-eight percent female out of around a thousand cadets," the commandant said.

"Character," he added sternly before Tim Fitzpatrick or I could say anything. "You're running the program on character."

I was thrilled that the Coast Guard commandant had said that in front of the athletic director, who was starting his fourth year. Fitzpatrick had been the associate athletic director at West Point and held the same position at Indiana University in the Big Ten, both Division I schools. Our team played in Division III. I was not certain he knew that I wanted to win more than him.

In January of 2012, Admiral Sandra Stosz addressed the faculty on the future of the Academy. "We will be decreasing in size, and we will be increasing our female enrollment," she stated. "We will be getting smaller and more diverse. The one person most affected will be Coach George."

I was not flattered to be the only faculty member she mentioned by name, considering the reason. I somehow sensed she understood my situation better than anybody. She had always impressed me as an insightful military leader.

I want to beat Merchant Marine, nicknamed Kings Point for its location in Kings Point, New York, worse than anyone. To us, the game against Merchant Marine is as big as the rivalry between Army and Navy. As an added incentive, it is played each season for the Secretaries' Cup, with Coast Guard representing the Secretary of Homeland Security and Kings Point playing for the Secretary of Transportation. It is always our most intense game of the season, but this year it involves Casper.

I set a meeting with the team to review the daily schedule, Academy rules, and a bevy of other topics. They listen but I can tell they are thinking about Kings Point.

Afterwards, I let the players mingle and rush out of Mac Hall. I jump in the parked car with Nancy, Lila and Casper. I take a quick second to look at the cement on the top of the stadium then drive off. We all exit one life and head into another.

CHAPTER 5

Our home in Salem, Connecticut, is almost a straight shot up Route 85 from the Academy. On this August evening, I drive with Lila and Nancy in the back, while Casper sits quietly in the front. His glasses hang over his stoic face. The drive always seems to put him in a peaceful trance.

"There is that same guy," Casper says, referring to a man walking along the side of the road. "We saw him right there in that same spot and same time last night."

Nancy and I say nothing about his statement. We are used to him often saying he saw someone walking, jogging, or riding a bike in the exact spot at the exact time the night before when he had not. Then I think, *Maybe he was here somehow or in some other time. Maybe he is not crazy.* Then I think, *Maybe I'm crazy for thinking, even for a moment, that he might not be crazy.*

We are home by nine and summer is over. We pull off the main road to our gray, old house, which sits on a corner. The day has been too long for Casper, but it was a day away from the monotony of farmhouses built in the 1930s.

"Stand up straight," I pull him up by the armpits. I hold him by the belt and shirt collar as he grips the walker I have placed in front of him.

"Where are we?" he asks. His sundown syndrome is in effect as his brain tires from a day too long. Unlike many seniors whose days end in confusion, he adds curious statements about a different world.

The manageable part of Casper is that he can still feed himself with small, soft, foods that are cut up. He can also tell us when he needs a bowel movement, although he cannot clean up after himself.

The red flash of hair races past me to get the door as I hold Casper up and push his shuffling steps along.

"You're moving him too fast," Lila warns me.

"One foot up!" I shout.

I struggle with the dead weight of a tired body up the one-step entrance and up a second step and through a five-foot kitchen to the bathroom. The entire summer for Nancy and I has consisted of coming home from work, sending the caregivers home, getting Casper in the bathroom, and getting everyone fed and to bed.

"I can't stand up," he worries as I shove the walker aside in the bathroom and place his hands on the sink. The toilet is directly across from the sink, and a dresser is next to the toilet. They are both perfect hand grips placed long before Casper's deteriorated state.

"Yes, you can," I answer sternly. My patience is gone. The burden of these duties at the end of the day has changed me again.

I pull the first three diapers down and tear off the fourth, which is only slightly wet with urine. Trying to avoid a disaster, I quickly lower him to the toilet.

"Ouch!" he screams as he hits the seat with a quick thud. "You broke my back," he whimpers.

"You hurt Gido," Lila sighs softly. "Gido, are you okay?" The concern of a little girl has once again made me realize I have lost a degree of compassion about my father and this life.

He puts his elbows on his knees and buries his face in his hands as if he has just realized his life will never be what it once was. Lila walks in and rubs the top his head. He lifts a sad, lonely face out of his hands when he feels the flesh of her palm.

"I'm okay," he whispers.

"Lila, give Gido his privacy. The rule is you're not be in the bathroom with Gido. There are too many germs," I tell her, knowing we go through disinfectant like it is water.

"Come on. We are going upstairs to take a quick bath and then you can read a book with Gido and Daddy," Nancy says as she pulls Lila away.

In the bathroom, with an eighty-seven-year-old man on hospice care, the nightly ritual is a blur of plastic gloves, wipes, and garbage bags that get filled with soiled diapers.

Once he is sitting on the toilet, I layer him with diapers to get him through the night. In the early days of his dementia, he would wake me up and I would have to either drag him into the bathroom at 3:00 a.m. or hold the urinal cup underneath him and then put us both back to bed.

"Up," I instruct as I pull him up by the armpits back to the original spot gripping the sink. I have become immune to the fact that I have been cleaning my father at least once a day for the last year. Sadly, I have become more immune to the fact that Nancy has also had her share of bodily cleaning, a share which dramatically increases tomorrow when the season starts and I'm at work.

I feed Casper a Trazodone. He will sleep through the night, which is what makes this survivable.

"Wait, I want to say goodnight to your mother." He makes the sign of the cross out through the kitchen window to a spot in between the two maple trees in our backyard. "Is she buried there?"

"No. She is buried in Glens Falls," I remind him. I know we have made the day too long for him and now his tired mind is entering another dimension.

"Is the Blue Sky still open?" Casper asks.

"No," I answer. Casper is referring to the Blue Sky Restaurant where his older brother, Abraham George Jr., was the proprietor, and Abraham's wife, Esther, was the cook. Casper spent his entire life as the bartender, and my mother spent her entire life there as a waitress.

"I spoke to your mother today," Casper says.

"Again?" I ask sarcastically. I try to ignore his words. Often, he says my mother called on the phone or he spoke to his long-lost childhood friends.

He looks out the kitchen window. The spot in the backyard seems to have significant meaning to Casper, a spot my mother thought looked beautiful.

"Come upstairs with me," he says. "The greatest words ever spoken. Never bet on a horse again after that." He is referring to the time twenty-five years ago when he asked me to lend him $2,500 to pay off a bookie. I was in our basement, and I took him upstairs and explained to my mother that he had to stop. Somehow, he stopped after that. Cold turkey. Shame or guilt, but it ended.

Our living room is a hospital ward. A clear plastic sheet covers most of floor, but it does not hide the ragged, stained carpet. One couch is draped as a bed where Casper spends his day. It is lined with plastic and sheets. Across the room and taking up the greatest space is the hospital bed where he spends the night. A commode is off to the side in front of our living room window, halfway between the hospital bed and the couch. All the extra spaces on the ground look like a hospital closet filled with buckets of gloves, diapers, towels, and baby wipes.

I start to read to Lila, and Gido, in his hospital bed, listens. Lila looks at the book, occasionally glancing back at Casper and smiling.

When Casper first moved in with us, he would read to Lila, but now he just sits. As she gazes at him, I think she knows that he is not listening, but she is still happy to be with him. Casper stares at Lila the entire time I read. Some nights he is on the couch when we read, but it's late tonight, and I do not want to make the second move from the couch to the bed later.

"Good night, Gido," Lila kisses him and crawls into his hospital bed. "I want to sleep with him."

"I'm in heaven, I'm in heaven," he starts to sing as they hold each other.

"Time for bed," I pull them apart.

"She's sent from heaven," he says as the lights go out and I carry Lila upstairs.

I rub Lila's back until she falls asleep between Nancy and me, and then head downstairs to sleep on the couch near Casper.

I lean over him to see if the Trazodone has kicked in.

"Why do I think of Nemo at night? And of Puppy, too? Why am I still here? Where is Anna?"

"She is in heaven," I answer mechanically.

"Oh no," he sobs, remembering my mother is gone forever.

He is caught in some world where confusion and reality mingle, where the next world and the past world invade this one.

"You are here for Lila. You are here to tell them all about Lila." I pause and look at his sad face. "You are the connection, I guess."

Casper's face widens. "Was Mary stoned to death?" he asks.

"What?" I ask. "Enough with these stoning questions."

"Mary was pregnant, and she was not married," he says.

"No, Joseph married her. Now go to sleep," I tell him.

Casper curls his lips into a small circle and then says, "Oh, that's right. Anna is in heaven with Jesus." He talks about Jesus now more than ever.

I have no more answers. I have drifted too far from a religion I never learned and went through the motions with anyway.

"What's Anna doing in heaven?" Casper asks.

"She is in heaven doing what she is supposed to do, and we are here and supposed to be doing the same. You know on earth as it is in heaven," I answer.

"Can I ask you something?" Casper asks with a wary sadness.

"Let's just get some sleep," I huff in frustration. Casper's nightly routine has gradually turned into a philosophical awakening.

"What is going on in Syria, where my mother and father came from?" He looks up at me with hollow eyes. I know Nancy or I or the caregiver must have had the news on and, although most of the time he cannot follow television shows, something has jogged his mind. Certain sights on the television trigger memories or deep thoughts.

"They are having a revolution," I say.

"A war?" he asks.

"Yes, a lot of people are dying."

"Children?" he asks.

"Yes, a lot of them. Some with bombs and some with poison gas."

"Oh," he whimpers with sorrow. "Do we have relatives there?"

"Your parents and Mom's parents came to this country when they were young. I guess we have relatives, but I do not know any of them."

"Are we doing anything to help the dying children in Syria?" he asks me.

"No. You are too old, and I am too busy trying to win football games," I answer roughly.

"I know you're a good boy. I know you're helping the people in Syria, especially the children," Casper says with kindness as he closes his eyes.

Guilt wracks me as I fall to sleep. I do not walk through life treating people as God would treat people, let alone how I wish to be treated back.

CHAPTER 6

One week after the puppy had been found in the spring of 1935, Michael Moses sat on his front porch steps in the dim light of the early morning and waited for the sun to create a new day. He looked down and smiled at the slim body of the tiny dog resting on his lap. He ran his hands across the brown chest fur. The puppy looked back up at him with its eyes wide, seeming to smile back at him. After seeing the face of the boy holding him, the puppy closed its eyes slowly as if it was now expressing how content and safe it felt.

"The sun is coming up," Michael said to the dog. He watched the sun creep over the tops of the trees of American Hill. The sun peeked into the valley of Myers for a moment as if to test where it should shine and, after finding Myers to its liking, the sun sprayed rays of sunshine over it.

"Here it comes," he said to the dog. The sun moved like a slow, gentle wave that had tiptoed out of a quiet body of water to gently massage the sand of a beach and then slide unnoticed back into the water. From his front porch step, he watched the rays of sunshine light up the side of Abraham's store, then flow down the gravel road to his feet.

Puppy Moses let his palm rest on the thin hairs of the tiny dog's chest, his hand moving with the animal's lungs as they inflated and deflated. After a short while, he fed and groomed the dog, ate his own breakfast, returned to the porch and waited. A few hours later, Michael Saleem, his sister Martha, and Dawn Worsell followed the same path that the sunshine had traveled and walked past Myers Grocery, down the gravel road and to the front porch. The resting dog yelped slightly and came alive with happiness when he saw the children. The dog started to squirm out of Puppy's lap, but he held it securely.

"You're protecting it like you're the father," Michael Saleem said.

"I did not think of it that way, Nemo," Puppy said to Michael Saleem. "But that is right."

Michael Saleem paused and looked at him for a moment. "Puppy, that's the first time you have ever called me Nemo," he said.

"And that is the first time you have ever called me Puppy," Michael Moses said, smiling back.

"You still have not given the puppy a name," Martha Saleem said, reaching her hand forward and letting the dog sniff the tips of her fingers.

"I do not know what to call him. I just keep saying 'Here, little puppy' whenever I talk to him," Puppy Moses said.

"That's a perfect name," Nemo said. "We'll call him Little Puppy. You can be his father and I will be his godfather."

"Yes," Martha added. "And I will be his godmother."

"Then I will be his fairy godmother!" Dawn Worsell added excitedly.

"If Little Puppy has all of these godparents, maybe we should get him baptized," Nemo joked.

"You are both altar boys," Martha Saleem interrupted. "The priest is not going to baptize a dog."

"No, but we can," Nemo answered. "We can sneak him in the church and do it ourselves."

"Yes, we could do that, but if anyone saw us, they might take the dog away from us," worried Puppy Moses.

"Do animals have to be baptized to get to heaven?" Dawn asked. "Do people have to get baptized to get to heaven?"

They all stood silent for a moment before Nemo said, "What do you think, Puppy? You are the one who thinks about all these things."

"I do not think so. Heaven must be full of animals and people who do not get baptized," Puppy answered. "God wants everyone in heaven. Although I suppose we could, just to be sure."

Puppy held the dog gently in his arms as if it was a baby, as they all walked together up the gravel road. They cautiously stopped at the cement porch of Abraham's grocery, but everything seemed quiet, so they walked to the bridge. They all stopped and watched the water beneath them fill with white bubbles as it raced across the larger gravel stones. The bubbles disappeared and turned flat as the water rolled into the long pool, which ran beneath the railroad trestle and then out to Cayuga Lake.

"I am going to hold you tight," Puppy said as the little dog tried to free himself from the boy's arms. "This creek can be dangerous for you. Maybe in the summer we will take you for a swim."

The children moved from the bridge, took the right at the fork in the road, which led up to Syrian Hill and away from the lake and the International Salt Plant. Thirty yards up the road, they cut into the path up the side of Syrian Hill. When they reached the top, they scurried undetected across the grass yard between the Isaacs' house and the small church, which was never locked. When they entered the empty church, they stood frozen in relief for a few moments, studying the silence. To the left of the entrance was a small, square metal table painted gold. The table had a rising crust around its sides and held pure white sand, which was three inches deep. Parishioners would enter the church, light a candle and say a prayer for someone ill or someone deceased. Next to the table was an open doorway leading to a cramped staircase, winding down into the basement of the church. From front to back, the church was only seventy-five feet long and twenty-five feet wide. The church, which had no pews, had ten rows of chairs, three on each side of an aisle wide enough for a priest to walk though.

"What do we do now?" Nemo whispered.

"You two boys are altar boys," Martha said, keeping her voice down as well. "You should know."

"We are not going to fill the baptismal tub up and dunk him under like the Syrian babies," Puppy said. "But maybe if we had some holy water, we could sprinkle it on him."

"Maybe up on the altar," Nemo said as he pointed to the front of the church, less than sixty feet in front of them.

In the front of the church, two steps in the middle led up to the altar, which was only fifteen feet deep. On the back wall was a large crucifix painted in detail with Christ nailed to it, his head hanging, and his eyes closed. On each side of the steps were curtains hung eight feet high, which led down to the floor and blocked the rest of the altar so the only thing that could be seen during Mass was Christ on the cross or the priest in front of him.

They all moved quietly toward the altar.

"No girls on the altar," Nemo warned.

"We know," Martha snapped back.

"You wait here. I will try to find some holy water," Nemo instructed.

"Wait, I hear voices," Puppy whispered.

"Oh, no," Nemo whispered back with the same fright in his voice.

"Quick, everybody behind a curtain," Martha ordered.

All four of them darted up the two steps and onto the altar, then crouched behind the curtain to the left. Puppy could feel his heartbeat in panic. *If they find this dog in the church they will take him away from me. Why did I not think that somebody might come in?*

The church door creaked open and all four of them froze in silence. Puppy held the dog tightly, but suddenly it wiggled away. Instantly, Martha scooped the dog up, lifted her red wool sweater up over her belly button and pressed the dog against her shirt and pulled her sweater over the dog.

The puppy nestled against her stomach and, feeling her body heat, lay still and content. They could hear several male voices speaking in deep Arabic accents. Then the door closed, and the voices stopped, but soft, slow footsteps approached the altar.

Puppy's breathing stopped. He shut his eyes tightly as if it all was a bad dream that would somehow go away.

"Hi!" The cheerful voice of Casper instantly turned all of their heads toward him.

"Who's outside?" Nemo whispered frantically.

Casper's face turned serious with fright the instant he realized Martha was on the altar and, worse, had the dog under her shirt. "Abe Caliel, my father, and my Umo John," Casper whispered back, using the Arabic word for uncle. "And your father," Casper added, referring to Martha and Michael's father, Abraham Saleem. "They are coming to clean the altar and replace the candles of the altar."

Then the door opened and the men started toward the altar.

"Smoke!" Casper screamed at the top of his lungs. "I smell something burning in the basement. The furnace is on fire." Casper knew the church had a coal furnace just like the one in his house and the grocery store.

All four of the men bounded down the basement steps. At the exact moment the last man disappeared Casper said, "They're gone."

"Let's get out of here right now," Martha said as they moved from the cover of the altar. She held the dog tightly against her stomach as they all quickly moved back through the church, out the door and to the safety of the path. They raced down the path and stopped halfway and sat on the ground. Martha lifted her sweater and looked down at the dog. The puppy looked back at her as if nothing had happened.

"That was close," Nemo said with his heart still racing. "Monk saved us," he said, referring to Casper.

"I thought we would get caught," Puppy huffed as his body still trembled. He looked over at Martha, still holding the dog, and noticed how much love she was giving the dog. "Thank you, Martha," he said to her. He paused and wanted to say more, but his tongue locked against the bottom of his mouth. *She is a quick thinker.*

Martha said nothing but looked up and smiled at him. Puppy swallowed the smile like a starving twelve-year-old boy.

CHAPTER 7

Christian George, the greatest athlete I have ever seen at the Coast Guard Academy, or anywhere else for that matter, drifts back and forth between my waking thoughts and the cracks of daylight in our living room the next morning. As the sunshine grows, it sends Christian to where he belongs, which is on a boat or a plane or somewhere all the former players are supposed to be, helping the world as officers in the US Coast Guard.

With the sunshine also brings the question, "Did the darkness of the night, as it snuck away with the stars, carry Casper along as well?" Just as I put my ear directly on top of his mouth, I look up as I feel Nancy brush by me.

"What?" she asks as she cups Lila's red head against her shoulder.

"I'll get him up and over to the couch before I leave," I say.

Nancy places Lila down on the opposite couch, now knowing that Casper is still alive.

"I was thinking of Christian," I say.

"Oh, what a wonderful young man," she says.

Although she is married to a football coach, we hardly talk football. Over the years, Nancy judges players by how kind and humble they are when she meets them. At the Coast Guard Academy, that could describe anyone.

"Even Christian is not fast enough to help you catch your own ghost," she adds.

"I find it the oddest of circumstances," I say to her. "You can't make it up."

"What, this?" she says, opening her arms for emphasis.

"No," I answer. "Christian George. He is no relation to us. But he could have been our child. His father is Lebanese and looks like every one of my uncles, and his mother is Irish like you. He even has the same last name. You couldn't make it up in a million years."

Nancy says nothing as she glances over at Lila.

Christian played quarterback three years before Lila came into our lives. I would stand behind him in practice and watch with amazement. His slim, five-foot-eight, 160-pound frame was entirely muscle. He was wind in the form of a human. Just like a wind gust, he could instantly come out of nowhere, rush past anyone, and then stop and start again.

"He was the best," Nancy adds, "but you surrounded him with all those other great players. He would step out onto the field, and you could see everyone light up."

"And the fear he put into the other teams and most of all the other coaches," I add gleefully.

Nancy looks at me as if I am wrong. "It was not fear, it was respect and admiration."

"We won a lot of football games over two years, and we beat Merchant Marine his senior year," I say. "There were a lot of NAPS guys." I'm referring to the Naval Academy Preparatory School in Newport, Rhode Island.

The Coast Guard Academy sometimes places prospective cadets there who do not get a direct appointment to the Academy. During Christian's time, we had a cadet who would go on to be a Navy Seal, and we had John McDonald, who as a football captain gave a no-drinking order, which coming from him was more powerful than any Academy regulation. I have had enough of memories for now and close my eyes quickly, as if I could make the players disappear from my mind. Those players are in the record books, and they now wear a different uniform for the Coast Guard.

I open my eyes, look around the room and let the past disappear into the past.

Casper is awake and so I slowly spin him out of the hospital bed and onto the seated side of the walker to take him to the bathroom.

Lila studies a cartoon on the television, ignoring the routine of the morning.

When Casper and I return from the bathroom, I lay him on the opposite couch from Lila, which is his daytime area. He opens his mouth like a helpless baby robin in a nest waiting for its parents to drop food down its gullet. I drop in a Lorazepam for Casper's nerves.

"Hi, Gido," Lila says as she eats her daily breakfast of peanut butter and pancakes.

"Hi, honey," Casper says as he makes the sign of the cross on her and then rests his head back on the pillow and keeps his eyes half open as he gazes at her. Tears drip slowly from the corners of his eyes and onto his ears.

"You can go," Nancy says as she watches Casper. "I'll take care of him."

It will be her day to be the caregiver as football starts. All Sundays will be like this. Today she will wake him at 11:00 and feed him his Cheerios. If he has to go to the bathroom during the day, she will push him along as he shuffles with the walker. Nancy will have to clean him up and change his diapers.

"Casper, close your eyes. Get some more sleep. It will make you feel better," she says with love.

"Thank you, Nancy," Casper weakly whispers as he follows her instructions. "I was thinking of those boys," he says with his teary eyes closed.

I start to worry I have become too mechanical in the process of caring for him. I worry more that it will only become worse with the start of the football season.

The hospice nurses and health aides will not be in until Monday. It will be a longer, harder day for Nancy than for any football coach on the planet, yet she will do it with more patience and care than any football coach could even fathom.

I think of Casper crying on my drive to the Academy, not of the first day of football. I always remember him being emotional when I was young. A lot of times he would just get quiet and stare out into space and I would see his eyes start to cloud.

After I park my car, I head toward the football stadium instead of my office. I watch a few Swab Summer companies march by in the heat and notice a few freshman football players, but they keep their eyes straight ahead and their ears focused on the cadre who are barking instructions. I will not see them until they are given a few hours of escape from Swab Summer for practice at 4:30 today. The amazing thing about the cadre is that every one of them just finished sophomore year of college and are now in charge of shaping the lives of eighteen-year-old cadets. I see a few upper-class football players walk in and out of Billard as they double-check their equipment in the locker room or visit the weight room before the position meetings start. The stadium is empty as I stroll to midfield.

Just one game five weeks from now is all I want. The thought wakes the butterflies in my stomach for a few moments, but the butterflies are smarter than me and know the game is not today so they go back to sleep.

The thought of one game reminds me of Jim Butterfield, the coach I played for and later coached with at Ithaca College. "Anybody," he would say with his deep Maine accent, "can beat anybody on a given day." Coach Butterfield preached family and said, "Always have class, have class in everything you do." He scattered three national championships between three decades of winning seasons. He always appeared strong, organized, and in charge. Often though, I would see his eyes water when he was talking to the team, when he was talking about something emotional after a practice or at a team meeting. You could see his feelings through his eyes.

I remembered when his twin brother, Jack Butterfield, who was vice president of the New York Yankees at the time, was killed in a tragic car accident the night before we left to compete in the first round of the NCAA playoffs my senior year. Coach Butterfield stood strong and tall when he told the team at five in the morning. You knew then why he said, "A football team has to be a family." Everyone had to stay strong for him.

I only saw him cry once. It was a few hours before his last home game in early November of 1993, just two years removed from his last national title. I was at Ithaca as an assistant coach. At times during his final season, I would walk by his office and see him sitting at his desk and staring at the vastness of Cayuga Lake. He would look up at me, smile softly, and without saying a word he would turn back to the blue waters of the lake. I would stop for a moment and look out to Myers and Syrian Hill, which was ten miles away on the eastern shore where the lake turned slightly to the northwest.

Ithaca College announced his retirement the Tuesday before his final game against rival Cortland State. Just moments before he would head out in front of fifteen thousand people for his last home game, I stood in the doorway of his office. He was looking out at the lake; he knew I was standing there but he did not look up. I could see the tears running down his face.

I look out to the Thames River and watch a submarine from the Naval Submarine Base in nearby Groton cut the water in half. Suddenly I realize that the two men I have admired most both show their emotions with their eyes. It is also ironic that I have watched the two men I admired most both die slowly. Jim Butterfield stayed physically strong as he aged, but his brain was eaten alive by Alzheimer's disease. Casper's brain is on a similar path as he wonders and searches for answers. His mind sometimes gets clearer as his body weakens and fades. Nancy's words pop into my head, "I have never seen you cry, not even when your mother died."

I have heard Casper's stories so many times that they wake me with nightmares that should be reserved only for Casper.

On the Fourth of July in 1935, it started raining in Myers and it did not stop for three days.

Just after midnight on July 7, Puppy Moses started to wake and, for a few moments, could not tell if he was dreaming. He could hear rain pelt against the side of the house. For an instant he wondered, *Has the lake come crashing up to Myers, ready to carry the houses away and eat them?* Then he heard movement around him in the darkness of the room.

"Is it still raining?" Puppy Moses said as he cracked open his sleepy eyes and looked into the eyes of his mother, who was staring at him as he slept. The background of the room was unfamiliar.

"Yes," Takla whispered, "for the third straight day and night. It is like Noah's Ark here on the Syrian Hill. Go back to sleep, my baby. We are safe here on the Syrian Hill."

In the morning, Puppy Moses started to wake, and the silence popped his eyes open. He listened and heard nothing. Then he opened his eyes and could see the light of the clear skies creep into the unfamiliar room.

Puppy Moses reached down and touched the nose of the dog he had named Little Puppy. It jumped nervously from its wicker basket and softly knitted afghan. The dog sniffed his hand and ran its nose and ear across his hand. The dog stepped out of the basket, lay on its stomach and stretched its body.

The door creaked open, and he could see Martha and Nemo peeking in. "Are you awake?" they said in unison.

The three days and nights of rain had flooded the creek to the top of the banks. The deceiving beauty of the creek had turned poisonous, its brown water threatening to spill over the bridge. Puppy's father had taken the two older brothers and sisters to the

Solomon house, which was two houses up from the church, while Puppy and his mother stayed with the Saleems.

Puppy swung his hips around, sat up on the side of the bed, and picked the dog up. The orphan and the boy had been inseparable for two months, like a mother and a child, since they found each other.

Martha and Nemo walked in followed by Casper, who had just turned eight. They all sat on the bed and watched the dog curl up on Puppy's lap as if it was going to drift back to sleep.

"Everyone is going down to watch the creek. It's like a tornado," Nemo said.

In the middle of the night, the hard floodgates of three days and nights of constant rain had stopped. The clearness of the day brought a small gathering in the yard between the church and the Isaac house. They could all see the creek move like an uncontrollable train charging downstream at the speed of light.

As the rain stopped, a small group moved down the muddy path off Syrian Hill and to the creek, listening to the thunder of the rushing water, which had already washed away the home of Nick and Helen George, Abraham the grocer's brother and his wife.

At the edge of the bridge, where it met the road, Puppy stood in awe with Martha and Nemo. Next to him stood Abraham's son, Casper, who was holding the bag of marbles Jacko Isaac had grown out of and given him.

Jacko and four other boys milled about while other adults and young people stood on the side of the bridge yelling for them to get off. The five boys faced upstream and watched the water as if it were a runaway train rushing beneath them. The water spit out at them in anger, trying to reach out and grab them.

"Get off the bridge! Get off the bridge!" John Solomon, the father of two of the boys, screamed as he raced down the path from Syrian Hill. The raging water had deafened the world.

Two of the boys, Johnny Boy and Eddie Kowalski from American Hill, stood on the bridge, but just a few feet out from the road. Puppy

Moses stood at the edge of the bridge and watched the brown water thunder by. It moved with such force and speed that it seemed alive, like a beast, not a force of nature. *I would not want to fall in,* he thought. Puppy Moses took two steps out onto the bridge to get a better look at the churning muddy mass below. *I wonder if it will ever turn back and become beautiful again?* he thought.

"Ouch!" he screamed as he felt the strong teeth of the small dog violently tear through his lower lip. Still standing on the bridge, he bent down and put the dog down, but held the dog's leather collar. "Yow!" he screamed again as the teeth of the animal sunk into his bare calf.

The dog gripped tightly and turned its tiny body to pull Puppy off the bridge. Puppy Moses shook his leg free of the small dog and, for a fraction of a second, he lost his grip on the collar as he stepped away from the bridge and back onto Myers Road.

BOOM!

From behind him, Puppy heard the loud collapse of the bridge over the rush of the flooding creek. He looked up and instantly saw the face of Casper frozen with shock. At the very same instant, a crazed John Solomon rushed past him and leaped into the flood water after his two sons, neither of whom the father could see. The father and boys vanished in the torrent.

Puppy Moses turned with a numbing fright that was running through his body like lightning and saw nothing but raging water. "MY PUPPY!" he screamed. "MY PUPPY!" he screamed again. The racing blood that had surged back and forth between his brain and his heart with adrenaline now thickened with horror. He turned frantically in every direction, praying the brown, angry water had not swallowed his baby dog. People raced in all directions alongside the road. He looked again at Casper, frozen in shock like a statue, not even breathing.

Puppy Moses watched as two of the boys who had been on the bridge, Johnny Boy and Eddie Kowalski, jumped to the edge of the road as the bridge teetered up. Eddie had managed to get to the bank and was pulled out by a bystander. Johnny Boy was holding on to the metal frame of the bridge only a few feet from the bank. Another Syrian boy had gathered a rope and tossed to Johnny Boy just as he was about to slip back into the raging waters. He grabbed it with both hands and was pulled ashore, vomiting quarts of muddy water.

"My puppy!" Puppy Moses continued to cry. A split second of fear had turned into a minute of horror and then the horror turned into a black emptiness that he somehow knew would always be part of him.

Puppy saw nothing else but the top of the upstream side of the bridge rolling up and down, nearly sideways. The brown, angry water had swallowed them all. People raced and screamed in all directions along the side of the road. He looked again at Casper, still frozen in shock. Then he took two steps closer and saw the whiteness of his eyes swell around his pupils. He could feel the pain of death for his puppy in his stomach, but he knew Casper was in danger.

"Let's get back to my house," Nemo said frantically as he moved next to them. "His eyes, what's wrong with him?"

"I don't know, he's having a seizure or a convulsion or something," Puppy answered.

Puppy and Nemo slowly turned Casper, lifted his arms and draped them around each of their shoulders. They each gripped one of Casper's hands as they stood at his side. Then, gently, they started dragging Casper's numbed body up the path. Casper's feet scraped across the ground and his head hung down low with his lips open and dripping until the fluids of his mouth were gone. When they reached the top of the path, dragging past Jacko Isaac's house, Nemo and Puppy could hear the screams of horror. They looked at each other, both with pity and fear. They said nothing as they continued across the hill until they reached Nemo's house. They dragged Casper up the steps. Women, screaming prayers in Arabic, followed them as they lay him on the gray couch in the small living room. Then all three mothers went silent. Casper's white eyes stared upward into the dull, tan paint of the ceiling. The lack of sunshine entering through the lace curtains transformed the room into a living wake.

Casper did not move for an hour. Puppy and Nemo sat in the room with him.

"Casper," Puppy whispered softly, "you are the good cat in the story I used to tell you. Do you remember, the good cat, bad cat story? You need to be the good cat as you get older so you can help people. You need to come back to Myers to be with me and Nemo. We need your help. Casper, Casper."

Nemo and Puppy both watched and waited but Casper did not move.

Puppy started whispering again, "Casper, do you remember when you were learning to talk, and I was keeping all my words inside of me? When I was alone with you, I would say words to you in the corner of the store or at your house. The first word we said together was *cat*."

Puppy Moses took a deep breath as he watched Casper lay motionless. Then he raised his voice from a whisper. "The puppy is lost Casper. You have to come back and help me find him. He is lost, here in Myers, he is not where you are. You have to come back to Myers and help me find him."

Casper's brown eyes slowly rolled forward, and he moved his head slightly to glance at Puppy and Nemo. When he saw their faces, he turned his head away and looked up at the ceiling.

Two days later when the water receded, Jacko Isaac's body emerged pinned between the railings of the submerged bridge. Jacko's head and arms could be seen be seen facing upstream for two days until his body could safely be retrieved. For two days, people would stand and stare at it in silence.

Anthony Isaac, Jacko's father, stood screaming when the bridge fell. He wanted to jump into the creek to end his grief. Now he kept a silent vigil, standing on the side of the road watching the water wash over the trapped body of his son. The Solomon boys and their father were found later washed well out into Cayuga Lake. The family went out and bought white shoes for Jacko, something Jacko had always wanted and talked about getting, and they buried him in his new, white shoes.

Almost every day for the next year, Puppy would stand at the edge of the creek and watch the water flow. Sometimes he would be joined by Martha and Nemo, and sometimes Casper. They would walk down the banks of the creek, then along the lake down to the salt plant looking for the dog. Sometimes, Puppy would stand at Abraham's grocery and if any of the workers from the salt plant stopped for lunch or to buy beer he would ask, "Did anybody see my dog anywhere?" His desperate eyes would look into the faces of the tired men and wait for them to deliver a faint sliver of hope.

The men would look back at him with expressionless faces, beaten and weathered by the hard decades of the salt plant. "No," they would always reply. "Nobody has seen the puppy."

One hot day the following summer, Puppy was walking across the newly built bridge toward Syrian Hill and he saw Jacko's brothers, Gus and Decker, leaning over the side rung of the new bridge and staring at the dry creek barely moving. The coverless bridge had three thick iron rungs on each side, which reached four feet high, and when he came near the Isaac brothers, Gus looked up at him with tears and swollen eyes. They were locked in silence, neither caring to say a word. Then Gus turned back to the creek and let the tears fall off the bridge. Puppy Moses kept walking to the path, and when he reached the brush, he sat and watched Jacko's brothers and cried. He did not know if he was crying for Jacko or Jacko's brothers, or for the dog. *Maybe I am crying for everyone,* he thought. He never again asked about the dog or ever looked for it again.

CHAPTER 8

At 4:30 in the afternoon on the first day of practice, the sun turns the artificial turf of the stadium into an inferno. Bruce Cobb, the Academy equipment manager, and I stand at the entrance to Billard Hall waiting for the freshman football players to be released from Swab Summer for their first college football practice. Bruce looks at me, and I can see the calm patience in his face. But I look back at him with the impatience of a football coach who is behind schedule.

"Where are they?" Ray LaForte, who coaches the quarterbacks and runs our offense, yells over from the end zone across the street from the Billard entrance. The rising temperature on the artificial turf draws beads of sweat off his head. "Good thing we built extra down time into the practice plan."

The coaches stand together under the south goal post, milling around with all upperclassmen who are dressed in helmets and jerseys. The coaches already held position meetings at one o'clock without the freshmen, so practice will already be at a slower pace, waiting for the fourth-class to catch up.

"Again, every year," says Ulysses "CC" Grant, who coaches the linebackers and is co-defensive coordinator. "Every year a fourth-class player has to come to his first practice all confused before he gets here. We're used to it," he says as he takes his hat off and wipes the sweat beaded on his scalp.

"Here they come, or some of them anyway," says Dana Fleischmann, who is the other co-defensive coordinator and coaches the defensive backs. "It is what it is," he adds without emotion.

Dana, CC, Ray and I are also members of the Academy faculty and teach, as well. I will also coach the offensive line.

"The freshman D-line looks like they lost thirty pounds apiece in the last six weeks," says Jay Driscoll. Jay will rush over to the Academy every day to coach after he finishes teaching English at one of the nearby high schools.

Among the other coaches are Pat Knowles, a retired Coast Guard officer, and Don Miller, who spent his career as the longtime head coach at Trinity College in Hartford.

The exhausted fourth-class stagger up in waves from the depths of Swab Summer and stand frozen in formation in the road in front of Bruce and me, waiting for orders. They have not moved a muscle without instruction in six weeks.

Their tired faces make me forget about our practice plan. "Relax, fellas," I say. I know I have to make football as enjoyable as possible. At every other college, football is the hardest part of the day. At any of the five national service academies, it is the easiest.

Ten minutes later, Coach Grant blows a whistle and the upperclassmen start to jog from the back of the end zone to the fifty-yard-line and back, and then repeat with slow stretching movements before they break into stretch lines to begin the day. The freshmen fall in behind them.

The first day of no shoulder pads moves along, to the coaches' surprise, with us looking like a football team instead of the typical Academy confusion on the start of day one.

Football players at Coast Guard move at full pace at all times; it is their nature, their persona, it is how their hearts beat. The drills, some of which have an underlying factor of preparation for Kings Point, move the day quickly along. I have instructed each position coach to have at least one drill that pertains to Kings Point, even though it is mainly basics for the first practice.

"Cut blocks! Get your hands down!" I hear Coach Driscoll

yelling all day at the defensive line in anticipation of the Merchant Marine offensive line crab blocking—offensive linemen attacking an opponent's knees by crawling on their hands and feet.

I walk off the field and stop on the concrete walkway that leads out of the stadium when Coach LaForte says, "They might not become the 2005 or the 2006 team. But who knows?"

"I just want them to be the 2006 team for a day," I answer.

"It could happen. It did for a day in 2010," Jay Driscoll says, referring to the last time we beat Kings Point.

"Anybody can beat anybody on a given day." I repeat what Jim Butterfield would say to his Ithaca teams.

I listen to the sound of the cleats scraping against the concrete as the players shuffle past me and out of the stadium. The sight of the sweating, healthy bodies of the young players strangely conjures thoughts of the picture of Casper standing with his parents in his high school graduation robe. Casper's young face may be frozen in memory, but time does not stop for memories. The picture I always thought of as so beautiful now defines itself as sorrowful, and suddenly the sorrow ignites a jolt of panic inside of me which erupts into an explosion of frayed nerves.

I race past the players, through Billard Hall and into the coaches' locker room in Roland Hall. I quickly strip my clothes off and jump into the shower room. I hide my face in the rushing hot water of the shower, hoping it will melt away the panic of fading time.

After practice, food is delivered to the Billard Hall balcony and the players eat and then race to meeting rooms. The freshmen sit and feast like starving animals and drag extra food, like animals with a carcass, off to their meetings. The summer meetings end before nine so the freshmen can get back to the military world. After this week, athletic time is four to six, dinner six to seven, and then study time starts at eight.

I tiptoe into my living room at nearly eleven. The glare of the TV illuminates Casper's motionless face.

"He's breathing. I just checked him," Nancy stands up from the opposite couch and hands me Lila.

"Dad, I am hungry," Lila whispers through sleepy eyes.

"She is still up," I say and smile softly to myself.

"It's the first night in a long time you have not put her to bed," Nancy says.

"Gido was all alone," Lila adds. "I think he was scared."

Nancy coughs deeply, brought on by her asthma at the end of a long day. Her eyes droop as the asthma drains her.

"What did he eat?" I ask.

"A half of a peanut butter and jelly sandwich and a spoonful of Lila's mac and cheese."

The love and sympathy Nancy has for Casper does not equate to her patience for me, and she wants to tell me to go to hell, but she does not because she is too tired to fight, and Lila is in the room.

"I am hungry," Lila repeats.

Her words draw me to Syria, the land where my grandparents came from and where now-starving children are running away from bombs. I am not sending a child to bed hungry in my house.

"You know the rule, Cheerios and milk and that is all," I say.

Lila sits on my lap and scoops a small spoonful from the bowl, studying the floating Cheerios on her spoon for a moment before eating them. After four more spoonfuls, she is done and nestles into my shoulder.

I carry her upstairs and put her next to Nancy.

Back downstairs, I debate whether to get Casper up and over to the hospital bed or leave him sleeping on the couch. If we are going to make it through the late nights of football and he ends up on the couch, it will be for the best, but tonight I decide to move him. Tomorrow is Monday, the first day in after the weekend for the caregivers, hospice nurses, and hospice aides. I better get it set up correctly. Casper has been surviving and they may reevaluate him in a month.

Nancy carries Lila back downstairs and into the room. "She

wants to say good night."

Lila lifts her head from Nancy's shoulder and stares down at Casper.

I help a sleeping, dying old man to stand then sit him back down on his walker. "Dad, I am going to move you over to your bed."

He says nothing as I slide the walker across the room and lift his dead weight up from underneath his arms.

Once I have his rear end on the bed, I swivel his feet around.

"Bill, is that you?" his brain finally stirs.

"Yeah, Dad. It's late. I'm going to get you in the bed."

His hollow, glassy eyes look up at me in the darkness. I bend down and kiss his scratchy face. His eyes are expressionless.

Nancy bends and lets Lila lean down to kiss him.

"Oh," he sighs softly with love.

"I was dreaming about the flood. Why am I the only one left on earth who saw what happened?"

"I don't know, Dad," I say. I've heard the story many times from him throughout my life.

"I am going to cry about those boys in the flood. All my life they make me sad." Casper's weak voice starts to crack.

"I know, Dad," I say sympathetically.

"Where is your mother?" The end of his life has left Casper alone and his mind moves from one lost soul of his past to another. "Where is Anna? Is she in the kitchen?" He has forgotten Anna is gone.

"She is in heaven," I answer, hoping that it will satisfy him.

"Oh, oh," he sighs deeply with sorrow as he begins to remember. "In heaven with Jesus."

"Yes."

"Will I get there with your mother and those boys in the flood?" he says as tears mix with his voice. "And those other boys?"

"Yes," I again answer.

"Why or how do you know?" he asks.

"You made the world better with kindness. You did what was

expected of you from what was given to you," I say, doubting my own words and questioning myself as I judge Casper and watch him start to fall back to sleep.

"Is Christmas coming soon?" Casper asks as his eyes close.

"Santa's coming?" Lila perks ups.

"No. Not for a while," I huff, knowing that now Lila will be up and thinking about Christmas.

"What was that Christmas song Anna loved?" Casper asks.

"It was Nat King Cole singing, 'Chestnuts Roasting on An Open Fire,'" I tell him.

"Yes, she used to sing along every time she heard it." He waits a moment, as if his mind stalls for a second, then he says, "I am trying to hear Anna. Can you still hear her voice?"

"I can hear it in my mind." I think back and I remember the softness of her words. "But I cannot remember her singing."

"Where did her voice go when she sang? Did her words go on forever?" he asks.

"I suppose they went on until they bounced off some planet in another universe." I play along with his confusing questions.

"You are being cruel," Nancy warns.

"Do you think that when she sang her words stopped in heaven?" Casper pauses for a moment, but he keeps talking when I do not answer. "I think that everyone in heaven would listen to her when she sang."

"I told you, now you have the poor man going," Nancy says.

"Do you think Anna is in heaven right now singing Christmas songs? Maybe we can hear her sing."

"I'm sorry, Dad," guilt softens my mind. "Rest now and sleep."

"Is it Christmas in heaven today?" Casper whispers. His eyes are still shut, and his mouth opens for air as his head tilts back on the pillow. "Are people born again when they go to heaven?"

Nancy and Lila look at me waiting for my reply.

I look up at both of them. "I don't know. Maybe they are born again and start new or maybe they move on from where they left off in this world." I try to remember my mother when we were all younger, but the only vison I have is of a thin, shrinking woman. It is as if the good thoughts have been swallowed by passing time. I search my memory for happy moments.

"Maybe it is like Christmas in heaven every day and we all get to live again."

Nancy looks at me with an odd expression as well as exhaustion.

"Today is Christmas," Lila says and smiles as Nancy carries her upstairs.

At 2:00 a.m. I am awakened by something, but I do not know what. I stare around the darkness of the room, listening to the silence.

"Billy," Casper whispers hoarsely but loud enough for me to hear.

"What?"

"Did I ever tell you about the baseball game with Freeville?"

"Yes, a million times. The game when you hit the massive home run in high school," I answer him.

"No," Casper says, "not that game. The game when I was batboy in the seventh grade."

"Once," I answer. "You only told me that story once."

On an unusually warm afternoon during the first days of April in 1939, Puppy Moses stood in right field for the Ludlowville Bobcats and ran his right hand across the back of his neck where his thick hair touched to the top of his wool collar. His maturing body was short and slightly stocky, and he had neither the speed or power to excel at sports. But, he had heart.

With two outs in the top of the ninth inning and Ludlowville leading by one run, the opponent, Freeville, had baserunners on first and second. There was a pause in the top of the ninth inning as a new pitcher, Gus Isaac, warmed up. The afternoon sun was dimming as it moved away from Cayuga Lake and Myers and on its way past the Finger Lakes. The warmer air of the day was cooling but it had no effect on Puppy, who could feel the nervous moisture on his fingers. He took a deep breath, trying to steady his nerves, hoping the break in the action would go on forever and he could run off the field and never return.

If it was not such a small team, and the regular right fielder had not broken his leg, Puppy would not even have to be out here.

How did I get into this nightmare? he had thought.

Puppy watched the white clouds swell and bubble across the richness of the blue sky. *The clouds move so fast sometimes that I think they are alive. They are in a hurry to get somewhere,* he thought. *Maybe they are chasing tomorrow before it is too late and they are left behind. Or maybe they are afraid they will be stuck here today like me, stranded in right field. Then again, maybe they are trying to get back to yesterday before it is gone forever.* Puppy closed his eyes. *I thought the baseball uniform would make me like Lou Gehrig, handsome and invincible. Gehrig never stops. He looks like a movie star and never comes out of a game. He plays baseball as if his life was a movie. But I am not Gehrig.*

Puppy bent forward, putting his gloved hand on his left knee and his bare hand on his right knee, and looked down into a bare patch of the outfield ground where the grass had not grown. He used the bill of his cap to shield his face from the world, but it could not shield the world from him. Puppy spit and watched the wad of fluid hit the dried outfield dirt and free a trapped puff of dust, which rose as if it were escaping earth and fleeing into the atmosphere.

Puppy shifted his gaze to the spot midway down the third-base line where there was a small section of bleachers beyond the Ludlowville bench. He had spent almost all the last two innings staring at the same spot, and, more specifically, at Martha Saleem, who sat next to Dawn. He could not keep from looking at Martha, with her black hair lying on the top of her shoulders and her bare knees peeking out from her skirt. He could see her soft smile as she talked and giggled. The thought of her added a heavy layer of fears to his usual baseball nerves.

I wish I could sit and be that close to Martha, Puppy thought. *I could talk with her and make her smile like that. I wish I could do that for just one conversation. I wonder if people feel like this their whole life about somebody.*

Puppy looked into the infield in front of him where Nemo was playing second base. *What an athlete,* Puppy thought. *He plays like Gehrig and he is handsome like Gehrig, too. Lou Gehrig of the New York Yankees and Nemo Saleem of Myers could be one and the same, but not me... I was made differently.*

Puppy glanced inside the dugout and saw Nemo's young cousin Casper George, who was the batboy. *Both of them have such handsome faces. If I had a face like Casper or Nemo or I looked like Lou Gehrig, I would not be so afraid to talk to Martha.*

Suddenly, sounds of baseball action stirred and Puppy readied himself. The pitcher's first offering raced toward the middle of the plate and the right-handed hitter took a powerful swing that was a fraction of a second late as he connected solidly with the ball, driving it into right field.

The explosion of the ball against the bat drew groans from the home crowd as the baserunner instantly jetted forward.

Puppy raced back as quickly but he was a moment behind the line drive as it raced over him. He lunged his arm upward and thrust his hips up to leap toward the ball, but his stubby thick legs stayed glued to the ground and only the tip of his brown leather glove touched the ball. The speed of the ball hardly slowed as it hit the ground five feet beyond him and skidded through the brown patches of grass in the outfield. Puppy's legs churned as he chased after the ball and when he scooped it up and turned to throw into Nemo at the edge of the infield, he could see both baserunners in the background easily score the tying and go-ahead runs.

When he returned to his spot on the dried grass of the outfield, his nerves had been replaced by the swelling sorrow of shame. *I am trapped in this outfield like it is a prison and this uniform is my straight jacket.* When the inning ended after the next batter, he hustled to the bench with his head down, avoiding eye contact with everyone, especially Martha.

In the bottom of the ninth, Puppy sat nervously alone.

"It was a shot," Nemo said as he plopped down on the bench next to him.

"I had a chance at it. I could have grabbed it with another inch," Puppy answered.

"Gus Isaac threw the pitch, not you. There are a million things that could have happened," Nemo said. "Besides, that kid from Freeville hits like Gehrig."

"A million things always happen, and in this case it was that line drive," Puppy said.

The first two Ludlowville hitters went down swinging and then Nemo stood and looked down at Puppy. "Maybe we will get our chance; you're after me," he said as he moved from the bench to the on-deck circle. Nemo hardly had time to practice a swing when the Ludlowville hitter in front of him stroked the first pitch up the middle for a single. Nemo stepped into the batter's box and Puppy moved to the on-deck circle.

Puppy took a few swings so that his body would turn enough to glance at Martha. His butterflies from the outfield returned.

Nemo bent forward in his right-handed stance and watched a fastball brush the inside corner. On the next pitch, he stood sturdy in his stance as the Freeville right-hander threw a big curveball that appeared to be coming right at him, but as the ball bent inward and down Nemo timed the breaking ball perfectly and shot it over the shortstop's head and out into the left-center field gap. The speedy Freeville center fielder cut it off and held Nemo to a double, with the tying run stranded on third base.

I have a chance to save myself, to save the team, Puppy thought as he rose from the on-deck circle. *If I get a hit, maybe Martha will say something to me.*

Puppy walked up to the plate and thought, *If he throws curveballs, he will make me look foolish.*

Puppy stood and waited, and the first pitch was a fastball down the middle just like he had thrown Nemo. Puppy swung and hit the ball solidly, but his swing was late, and the ball went foul inside first base.

The next pitch was a curveball and when it came toward him, his knees buckled.

"Strike two," the umpire yelled.

Now he knows I cannot hit a curveball, Puppy thought. *I must sit in there. I cannot move.*

The next pitch was a curve coming right at him. Puppy stood tight and held his ground but the curveball bent inward, causing him to swing off balance and late. His heart sank as he heard the ball hit the catcher's mitt. He blocked out the cheers as the Freeville team rushed onto the field.

He stood frozen at the plate for a moment then turned and jogged back to the bench with his head down and holding the bat in front of him, both hands on the wide barrel. *I wish it was a log I could throw off the bridge in Myers and watch it float away to the lake.* Suddenly, out of nowhere, a vision of the beagle puppy's happy face appeared, and his pain turned into grief for the dog. By the time he reached the bench, he was about to cry but fought back tears.

Puppy bit his lip and felt Nemo's arm on the back of his shoulder. "It is just a game, not life or death."

Puppy looked out toward where Martha had been sitting. Instantly, as their eyes locked, he felt a tear, so he looked away.

Puppy stalled his exit, slowly picking up balls and bats in silence with Casper, the batboy. Casper said nothing; every few minutes Puppy would glance at Casper and all Casper would do is glance back, his eyes filled with sorrow for Puppy. As the bench and bleachers cleared and he looked around again, Martha was gone. He grabbed his glove and bat and started out to Ludlowville Road and down American Hill to his house. He saw Nemo and Dawn across from the baseball field on the tennis court. He watched them from the road. Nemo, like Puppy, was still in his baseball uniform and he would hit the tennis ball with a powerful serve and Dawn would float around the court after it.

She looks like Cinderella with a magical wand. And he looks like Gehrig.

Back and forth the ball went. When one missed, the other would chuckle and tease. Then they stopped and both walked and met each other at the net; while they held their rackets, they leaned forward with arms at their sides until their faces were very close, but their lips never met. Puppy could not see if they were whispering to each other or just staring in each other's eyes. It was only ten seconds but to Puppy it seemed like an eternity. Puppy turned and started down American Hill to Myers and again the happy face of the beagle appeared in his thoughts.

Halfway down American Hill, he could see the deep beauty of Cayuga Lake as it basked in the last sunlight of the day, as the sun hung over the hills on the opposite side of the lake. The water was a deeper blue and its beauty strangely fed into his sadness. He thought of Martha and looked at the houses he was walking past as the road sloped down into the valley. *Maybe someday I will stare into her eyes and she will stare back into mine, and she will lean forward when our faces are close and kiss me.* He felt a twinge of self-created hope but again was quickly consumed by melancholy. He walked to Myers Grocery, but instead of turning into the cinder road next to Abraham's grocery store, which led to his house, he walked to the bridge. He leaned over and pressed his chest against the iron railing, and he could feel the solid metal press against the sadness in his stomach. He took the baseball bat with both hands and threw it into the water beneath him, which was swirling quickly from the spring runoff. He watched it splash and disappear as the fast water dragged it away. Moments later he saw the bat emerge in a slow pool as it floated away beneath the trestle. He looked up and across the lake to the far side, where the orange sunset was cresting on the hilltops, and he thought of the puppy, then put his face in his hands, leaned over the bridge and cried uncontrollably.

CHAPTER 9

Monday morning begins as an attempt at a routine that I hope can carry us through the season. I pluck Lila out of bed at 6:30 a.m., carrying her downstairs, and plop her on the couch. Her breakfast is the same every day—two frozen pancakes cooked in the oven and made into a peanut butter sandwich that is cut into quarters. She sips her milk from the plastic cup before she starts to eat.

Nancy walks in and kisses her goodbye. Lila looks up and smiles with a milk mustache.

"I'll pick her up at four at the CDC," Nancy says to me referring to the Child Developmental Center at the Coast Guard Academy.

The developmental center is our first stroke of good luck. It is run like an elementary school. It is provided for military families, but as an employee of the Coast Guard I am able to pay into the system.

Casper is next. I let him sleep if I can, but most days I wake him up quietly by lifting his shoulders off the bed as I stand in front of him. This lightens the load. Casper's eyes and mouth open wide at the same time as if he has been hit by a bolt of lightning. His breathing instantly increases, but I am not sure his brain is awake. I move him like cargo onto the walker, through the kitchen, and into the bathroom where the routine repeats itself day in and day out. I methodically go through the motions as I ready him for the day ahead. I feed him his meds and when we are done, I rush him back from the bathroom and I lay him on the couch.

"Hi, Gido," a now perky Lila says to him as she looks up from the children's morning show on television.

"Lila Marguerite, the most loving, beautiful girl in the world," Casper says.

After I dress, I return to the living room to get Lila ready, and she is sitting on the side of the couch with Casper and finishing her breakfast. Casper just stares at her.

Five-foot, four-inch Hat Fengar waddles through the kitchen door and limps his sixty-eight-year-old body. He's morbidly overweight and in need of new shoulders and knees. His small, rounded shoulders and bald head sit atop his round frame and give him the appearance of Humpty Dumpty. When Hat walks, he moves like a wobbling egg. He is far from a picture of health himself. When the head hospice nurses arrived on the first day to check Casper, they walked past Casper and over to Hat, thinking he was the patient.

But Hat is perfect for Casper, and not just because we can afford him. He loves to talk, watch television, and take naps. The television is their companion; they watch any Western and baseball game or any sports show. Hat always flips to the news, and although neither Hat nor Casper are Catholic, they never miss the noon Mass. The basis of caretaking, the talking, is what saves Casper. Hat gets him to talk about Myers, his childhood, and about all of his years at the Blue Sky Restaurant in Glens Falls, New York, where Casper and Anna spent their lives together. Hat's poison in life was the same as Casper's but much worse.

"The damn bookies owned me, all because of college basketball," he told us after he had been with us a few weeks. Then he added, "I live better now than I ever have. Except for Mom, of course. But I'll see her again."

Hat had lived with his mother his whole life and, like Casper, his heart beats for those gone. Hat was married once years ago but has no children. After his mother died, Hat was homeless.

"When you're homeless all you have is God to talk to, you're all alone," he said to me. "Nobody else but God knows you're alive." He ended up living in a press box above the Babe Ruth league field and then ended up in assisted living for the elderly. Bob Bono, an assistant basketball coach at the Academy, hooked him up with me a year ago, just before Casper was placed in hospice. I bought him a used car for five grand, and we pay him a small amount each week as well as feed him.

Lila and I race out and Hat sets the other couch up with sheets and pillows for himself as Casper returns to sleep.

Debbie, the hospice caretaker, arrives at ten each morning. She is a humble, sweet woman about fifty-five. Love and kindness are the two traits that best describe her. Hat swivels up to a sitting position and then, using one hand, he pushes off the couch, using the other to hold onto Casper's walker. Together, Debbie and Hat pull Casper's covers off and swing him to a sitting position. They put the green walker in front of him.

As with most mornings, Casper's face is confused, as if he is still asleep. His gray T-shirt hangs off his frame as he grips the handles of the walker. Debbie and Hat each hold an armpit and together they raise him to a standing position over a round, plastic mat covering the living room carpet in front of the couch. Hat pulls Casper's diapers and pajama bottoms down to his ankles. Debbie pulls a warm washcloth out from a bucket of sudsy water and scrubs his body. When she is done, Hat pulls up the diapers and pajamas. Debbie lifts off his shirt and washes his chest and arms. Each time, she uses a new rag, never dipping a soiled one into the clean water. Then Debbie brushes his teeth and rinses his mouth, keeping most of the water he spits out from falling on the plastic mat beneath him. Hat towels up any water from the mat while Debbie cleans his feet and toes and rubs them with lotion. In the years before Casper faded badly and he could still walk, I would take him down to the coaches' locker room at the Coast Guard Academy and shower him there. It has been over a year since I have been able to do that.

"We have to scrub him from top to bottom in a full shower," Nancy once told me. And with that, the two of us take him once a week to the downstairs bathroom. It has been our Saturday morning "wet-down" for the past year. No summer Saturdays at the beach, just a swim in the bathroom. I take my clothes off except for a pair of gym shorts. The two of us get his legs over the side of the tub and support him in the shower as we lean him against the front wall of the shower underneath the shower head.

"I'm falling, I'm falling," he screams.

"Don't be scared, Gido," Lila says softly.

Casper looks down at her until I move his face over into the spray of the shower and he shuts his eyes and lets the spray cover him.

I hold him up from behind with my arms wrapped around his chest and underneath his armpits. Nancy scrubs him from head to toe as the water sprays all over the bathroom.

"I'm all wet," laughs Lila, as she thinks she is helping by watching and talking. After we dry him off, Lila holds Casper's hand as we clip his toenails and fingernails. Her touch soothes his fear of the clipping. The shower ritual on Saturday will move to Sunday mornings now that football season has started.

After Debbie's daily sponge bath, Hat gets Casper's breakfast, the same every day—a bowl of Cheerios, the primary food which keeps him alive. Then come the hospice nurses. It is either Amy or Jessica who come to check him out. They all love Casper; he is a gentle man who was, and is, still kind and loving, unlike his son, the football coach. He sits patiently while they check his vitals. It is unusual that he is so calm, as Casper has had a fear of doctors and always worried about being sick. Casper has now associated the hospice nurses with only positive medical results. No matter what happens, he somehow understands they will not send him to a hospital. He does not know he is dying so he thinks every time they check his vitals he is fine.

Hospice nurses are different from any human being. They walk into families where there is no return. They face no family outcome but one, the death of a loved one. We see the end from afar and the hospice workers and nurses see it in their heart every day. They hold his hand and talk to him. They know him not as old and gaunt and dying, but as alive as a new rosebush.

My cell phone rings, "Coach, this is Jessica. I'm here with Casper."

"Is everything all right?" Panic strikes.

"Yes. In fact, he is doing well. Thriving is the term. His health has improved since being put in hospice. One of the administrators will set up an appointment to reevaluate him in a few weeks. They may have to take him off hospice."

My heart sinks and drags the panic away. "I was hoping to get him through the first two weeks of the season. You know with all the extra care it is saving us."

"I know," she says. "He is not a hundred percent there yet, but he is certainly stabilizing. By the way," she adds, "his stories of Myers are getting clearer."

"I know," is all I say to end the conversation.

"Wait," she says quickly to catch me before I hang up. "Hat wants to talk with you."

"Billy," Hat says. "Your father has been telling me that when Lou Gehrig was playing for the Yankees he came to Myers in his baseball uniform. He wore his uniform at the church and served as an altar boy in his baseball uniform."

"No. Gehrig never came to Myers," I tell Hat. "I know what he is talking about. I will tell you later," I say as I hang up the phone.

Monday goes well, but Tuesday is hectic. Members of the athletic department must attend a reception at Admiral Stosz's quarters later in the day, and our freshman players don't arrive until about forty-five minutes before practice ends. To top it off, our backup quarterback has a dead arm, and the two freshman quarterbacks don't make it on time. We end up practicing for one hour and fifteen minutes with one quarterback.

At three o'clock, I look down at the beauty of the lower athletic fields and track that border the Thames River. Swab Summer is still in full swing with some of the freshman companies running around the turf field and track, while others are at the obstacle course. The sun seems exceptionally bright, and my eyes trace the width of the Thames River to the tree line. Above, a few bulging cumulus clouds make the sky a masterpiece. I wonder how often I have ignored the beauty of the moment, the sky, the breathing people around me, and let the worries tied to football steal life away.

The lower field, where we practiced prior to the renovation of Cadet Memorial Field, reminds me of the 2003 season.

We went 4-5 that season, winning our last three games after an overtime loss against a team ranked in the top twenty. We were led by captains Johnny Oscar, an old-fashioned linebacker out of Moeller High in Cincinnati, and Brian Whisler, a six-foot, six-inch tight end from California. We ended the season with a win against Merchant Marine.

In 2004, we went 1-9. In a meeting with then-athletic director Ray Cieplik, I was told, "The admiral is only going to give you a six-month contract in June when your three-year contract is up. This is the admiral's last year, and he is not going to renew your three-year contract," Cieplik told me, adding, "He does not think you have won enough games." The following year we beat Norwich University in the second game of the season and Cieplik set up a meeting with the new superintendent, Admiral James Van Sice, on Monday after the game. Admiral Van Sice agreed that my three-year deal would be renewed.

As I stand at the entrance to the admiral's quarters, a beautiful home which overlooks the entrance to the Academy and the parade field, I am greeted by Admiral Stosz. "Coach, where's Nancy?" she asks politely.

"She had another commitment," I answer, wracked with guilt. She would have loved to have been there with the other spouses, but

I took it for granted that she would take care of Casper.

The house is quiet when I walk in at around eight-thirty. Casper is sitting up on the couch, staring into space, oblivious to Nancy and Lila who are sitting next to him and reading a book.

Nancy's words are quick, with a slight tone of anger. "Michelle LaForte called me and said we were the only wives not there. You and Ray, two big-shot football coaches."

Casper turns and looks up at me. "Oh, hi, Bill."

Before I can say anything, Lila says, "Mommy gave me a talk about strangers again."

"Yes, I know you are going to a new school in a couple of weeks," I say.

Lila has been lucky we have had her in day care with the Coast Guard Academy and she has been well cared for and protected. Now, she is not only going to new surroundings, but she is also getting more mobile and verbal.

"Did Jesus get kidnapped by a stranger when he was little?" Casper asks as I move him from the couch to the hospital bed.

"No, Dad," I answer.

"Yes, he did. Your mother told me. Today from heaven, she told me."

Nancy starts to pick Lila up, but Lila crawls off the couch to the hospital bed and sits on Casper's lap.

"Casper, Jesus was separated from his parents in Jerusalem when he was twelve."

"He was kidnapped," Casper says. He wraps his arms tightly around Lila. His eyelids droop, his face worn near to death, each day taking its toll.

Lila reaches her hand up and with the tiny, soft palm of her right hand she gently rubs Casper's forehead as he lowers his head and closes his eyes. Lila keeps rubbing gently, as if she were touching a newborn baby.

"No. Mary and Joseph could not find him and when they asked

a Roman soldier, he told them that children were often kidnapped," clarifies Nancy.

"Anna told me he was kidnapped," Casper says with his eyes shut as Lila leans up and kisses him. His eyes flicker.

"No, they found him in the temple teaching," Nancy says.

"Oh, Jesus was found. That's good that he was found," Casper says. He opens his eyes and looks at Lila. His eyes are watery. Then he turns his face to me and with his hand resting on his chest he motions me to come closer to him.

I move closer and listen to his cracked voice say, "I told Hat about the time Lou Gehrig came to church in Myers in his baseball uniform."

"I remember the story, but it was not Lou Gehrig."

"Yes. It was Lou Gehrig in his baseball uniform," he convinces himself.

"I remember now, Dad, you're right," I say, and watch Casper close his eyes now that he is content and believes he is correct.

On Friday evening, April 7, 1939, just a few days after his last baseball game, Puppy Moses stood motionless in his baseball uniform on the bridge in Myers. Puppy had struggled through practice, still rattled by his poor performance. Today there was a game scheduled against Dryden, but their bus broke down and the game was canceled. Relieved that the game was canceled, Puppy walked past his house and stopped on the bridge. Suddenly, he thought of the puppy and walked toward Cayuga Lake. He thought of what Nemo and he had talked about earlier that day.

"Please, give baseball one last chance," Nemo had begged him.

"I can't. It is not my game. It is a game for people like you and for people like Gehrig. Let Casper play. He is four years younger and four times better than me."

"Try for me," Nemo pleaded one last time.

"Okay, okay," Puppy answered, knowing deep down he could not quit. "I just wish the season would end today."

"I know you do, but thanks," Nemo said.

Puppy listened to the water slowly brush against the cinders along the shore as the tiny waves rolled in and out. The soothing sound and his tearful memory of the puppy let the pain of baseball pass.

Eventually, he ended up back on the bridge, standing for nearly an hour, leaning forward and staring down into the flow below him. Occasionally he would hear a few footsteps passing on the bridge, but he ignored them. He leaned farther forward, folded his arms and felt the cool metal of the bridge that had been built after the flood three years ago.

"Puppy."

Puppy Moses cringed as the sound of his name broke the silence. He turned to see Casper George standing next to him and dressed in his Sunday suit.

"What are you doing?" Casper asked. "You are still in your uniform."

"I started to go home but took a walk instead," Puppy said.

"You are a good baseball player. I am not."

"I am too young to play on the high school team," Casper answered.

"Life is not about age or time," Puppy said. "It is about facing whatever and whenever the future crosses your path. And the future can be swift and uncertain."

At first, Casper was befuddled but then thought of the flood, the boys, and the puppy. "I have to get the altar ready for Good Friday Mass. You better change out of that baseball uniform and help me."

"I am getting too old to serve on the altar," Puppy answered.

"No!" Casper raised his voice. "You can leave me alone in right field, but not alone on the altar. Not in front of all of Myers."

Puppy Moses thought of Martha Saleem. He knew he would see

her in church. "I will be there," he said as he watched Casper walk away and toward the path.

Puppy looked up and saw Nemo and Dawn on the tracks. He watched as they slowly tiptoed across, balancing on one railroad tie at a time. They would hold hands for a few steps and break their grip if one lost their balance, then as if they were lost in the world without each other, their hands would reach out to regain their hold. When they reached the end, they walked down a short dirt path on the embankment and started walking upstream toward him. Puppy watched Dawn reach her hand out and touch Nemo's face gently. She traced her hand along his cheek to his neck and tickled him underneath his chin. He smiled and looked down at her, and she ran her hand back up across his face and through his hair. Then Nemo turned his face to hers and stared straight into her eyes as if they could speak directly into hers. She stared at him for a moment and then, as if his eyes had told her she was the most beautiful, wonderful person on the face of the earth, she stretched up on her toes, closed her eyes and kissed him on the lips.

Nemo Saleem felt his heart race and when she lowered her face away from his lips, he stared into her eyes again as if he would never notice another female on the face of the earth for the rest of his life. Dawn blushed, looked away and took his hand and led him toward the bridge.

He is so handsome and strong, like Gehrig, Puppy thought. *And he plays baseball like him, too.* Puppy looked down at the black hair on his forearms and brushed his bushy, curly hair, comparing himself physically to his friend on the tracks below, wishing he was walking hand in hand with Nemo's sister, wishing he could hit a curve ball. *I cannot strike out again.*

Puppy watched as the two of them walked up the bank and on the bridge to his right and toward him. Also approaching was his mother with Abraham's wife Helanie, Nemo's aunt. They wore long, flowered dresses made of cotton. They walked in thick, black shoes that clicked against the pavement. As they approached, Helanie was carrying a baby, two-year old Marion George, her grandson. Her oldest son Abraham, Casper's brother, had married Mary Caliel from Syrian Hill, but a year later she died moments after giving birth. Helanie was raising Marion as if he was her child.

Puppy looked down at Marion George as he was being carried across the bridge in Helanie's arms. Marion opened his eyes and looked directly into Puppy's.

I wonder, Puppy thought, *what he sees, if his eyes can see inside of me, if he knows I feel sorry for him. It is odd, you can be the unluckiest person on the face of the earth if all you get is a few moments with your mother before she leaves for heaven. Then your tragedy turns into a miracle if Helanie George becomes your mother. What if you have no Helanie George to save you? Then your tragedy stays a tragedy. The world must be full of never-ending tragedies.*

"Michael," Takla Moses said, "I will see you in church. It is Good Friday." She leaned in and kissed him on the cheek. It was a soft kiss, and her lips touched his cheek and before she moved her lips away, she slid her face up to his ear and whispered, "I love you, my baby."

The ladies turned and started walking across the bridge toward Syrian Hill. When their backs were turned, Dawn kissed Nemo on the cheekbone just below his wire-rimmed glasses and ran away giggling in the other direction and toward American Hill.

Puppy watched Nemo's face, which was much lighter than the other Syrian boys in Myers, turn red.

"I wish she would not do that. She is such a goofy kid," Nemo said, trying to hide his true thoughts.

"There you are, chaps," a thick British accent cut the air and approached them from the direction of Abrahams's store and American Hill. A tall young man in his early twenties approached them.

"Mr. Smith," Nemo said. "How did you find us?"

"This is Myers. There are not many places to hide," Mr. Smith answered. "And I know Puppy loves to stand on this bridge."

Puppy said nothing but thought it odd that Mr. Smith, an English teacher, was looking for him. Mr. Smith, who was from England, was getting his doctorate from Cornell and teaching English and coaching track at the Ludlowville school as part of his studies. Puppy realized for some time that Nemo had wanted them all to connect.

"Puppy," Mr. Smith started, "I want you to come and see me about trying some of the track events."

"I am not that good at sports," Puppy answered.

"We're all good at something," Nemo added.

"Yes," Mr. Smith cut in. "We are all good at what we are good at. We all have strengths, and we all have weaknesses."

Puppy looked at him, confused. Then he looked over at Nemo. "I am not good at baseball, and I am very average with schoolwork. I am not good at math and science like Nemo. He will end up at Cornell like you."

"Ah, yes," Mr. Smith cut in, "but you are a thinker, and you are quiet, and you analyze people and the world. There are people at Cornell who are not good at math and science, but they are good at deep thinking. And that is what you are good at. Your mind works like a runner. The body moves and the mind thinks. It is not like ball sports where you react. Or a mathematical formula."

"I am slow and thick. How could I be a runner?" Puppy asked.

"I'm not saying you will be a great runner. All I'm saying is let me help you try. I think it will fit your personality. You can run against yourself as you think," Mr. Smith said. "I have a few months left before the school year ends and I return to England. That will be enough time to get you started."

"What will you do back in England?" Puppy asked.

"I'm going to learn to fly. I want to be a pilot," Mr. Smith answered. "It is something I have always dreamed about doing. Just like you two have dreams beyond Myers, I have dreams as well."

"Will you ever come back to Myers?" Puppy asked.

"Someday. I may come back someday just to watch you run like a champion," Mr. Smith smiled at the two boys before he turned and walked off the bridge and toward Abraham's store.

Puppy looked over at Nemo. He knew his friend had put Mr. Smith up to this. He watched Nemo's gentle eyes look back at him. Puppy felt his warmth and love. A short while later they walked arm and arm up the path on Syrian Hill to be altar boys at the Syrian Orthodox Good Friday Mass.

Puppy and Nemo raced around to the far side of the church near where they had found the puppy and down the cellar steps into the basement. Puppy and Nemo donned their altar boy robes over their baseball uniforms and tiptoed up the steps and into the back of the church. Once they reached the altar, they started the incense burning. Then they moved quickly around the tiny church lighting candles. The only other person inside the church besides Casper, Puppy and Nemo was the priest.

Abouna (priest in Arabic) Khalouf looked at the three boys as they moved around and went about his quiet chanting in Arabic.

When they finished lighting the candles, they stood on the altar and watched the priest move from icon to icon and quietly pray.

"This is my last time as an altar boy. I'm getting too old," Nemo leaned to Puppy and whispered so the priest would not hear. "After Easter tomorrow night, I'm done. What about you?"

Puppy hardly shook his head in response as he stared at the priest across the empty church. He knew the people would come in at any minute. *I will stay here for a while longer,* he thought.

A crowd started filtering in, a few at first, and then the church filled.

When the Mass started, Puppy could not help himself. He kept glancing out to the left side of the church where the women sat. All the men sat on the right.

He saw Martha in the middle of the women's section. Martha sat with her sisters Mary and Scandera, and her mother Atina. His stomach bubbled. Church is where he could see her without the fear of speaking to her. When he would see her in school his mouth would dry so badly it would feel like his tongue had doubled in size. Occasionally, he could see her and she might glance at him in passing, but he would look away.

He knew, for now, she was always in tiny Myers but in his heart, she seemed on the other side of the world. In the church, he knew at least they were together in some small way.

During the Good Friday Mass, all the parishioners followed the priest outside in the darkness carrying candles. The priest, who chanted and carried the gospel above his head, started to circle the church to the left. Puppy swung the cantor, carrying the incense behind the priest and Nemo carried a large cross. The men of Myers carried a casket of flowers symbolizing the body of Christ right behind them. All the parishioners followed. They stopped at the back of the church at the spot where they had found the puppy. All the people circled the priest and the men with the casket of flowers. Puppy looked through the crowd. He could barely make out the faces, which were only lit with the candles in front of them. He saw Martha in the back. She was looking down at her candle, staring at the flame as it flickered in the gentle April evening. Her shoulder length black hair was covered on top by a white veil the size of a Kleenex. He studied her face as she studied the candle. She blended with all the other young women her age, but to him she stood out. He knew, somehow or for some reason, she had crawled into his heart and stayed on his mind. Suddenly, she looked up and their eyes met. He froze for an instant, as if he were taking a picture of her brown eyes with his eyes.

When the Good Friday Mass ended, Puppy Moses walked by himself down the path off Syrian Hill in the spring moonlight. He stopped on the bridge and listened to the creek run by. When he saw the moonlight reflect in the water, he thought of the candle flickering in Martha's eyes. His stomach started spinning as he thought, *I wonder if Martha is thinking of me now like I think of her?* He remembered how their eyes connected and thought, *I wonder if that is how you feel when your lips touch?* He looked up at the full moon and then, turning his head, he traced all the moonlight down to Syrian Hill and he wondered if Martha was looking up at the moonlight at exactly the same time.

Maybe our thoughts and dreams could cross paths in the moonlight, and she could know how I feel without me ever saying a word. He closed his eyes and listened to the creek and thought, *Maybe she will stop on the bridge and listen to the water run by and she will hear my thoughts repeated to her as the water flows over the rocks.* He stood alone for an hour and could have stayed all night, but he had been on his feet all day and the thought of serving midnight Easter Mass the next day sent him down the road past Abraham's grocery and tiptoeing into the Moses house. Only Takla listened for the footsteps, and once she heard them, she closed her eyes.

CHAPTER 10

In the darkness of the next morning, I lay half asleep and start to think of that day's practice. It will be the first practice in uppers (shoulder pads and helmets). Suddenly, Christian Washington, one of the most impressive young men I have met or recruited but never coached, shatters the front window and thunders into the silence of the living room in his uniform carrying a football. The moonlight shines on him as if it were his personal spotlight. His muscles flash like lightning as he charges forward. He cuts past the commode, stiff arms the wheelchair onto its side like it is a hapless linebacker, then lowers his shoulder as he heads toward me. I quickly sit up on the couch but keep my shoulders lower than his and reach out to wrap my arms around his waist, but he eludes me like a slippery halfback. He spins away from me and leaps over Casper, who is sleeping in his hospital bed, then knocks down the side living room wall and crashes out of the house.

I race to the hole in the wall and watch him bound across my yard with one mighty leap and onto Salem Ridge Drive. He leans his body to the left as he turns and sprints south on Route 85 toward the Academy. "Do not stop until you get to Kings Point!" I scream after him. "Let them try to tackle you!" By the time the sun rises, Christian Washington is gone from my dreams, but his stranded shadow still wanders around in my heart.

Christian is another example of the sacrifice military families make. I learned during my years coaching and teaching at the United States Military Prep School for West Point (USMAPS) that all branches of the military treat their members as family. A family member that lives in a military uniform not only risks sacrificing life but also sacrifices time, family time that is lost and never shared.

Christian had been enrolled in the Coast Guard Academy Scholars program and sent to a private prep school. The scholars program gave an extra opportunity to top applicants who had not received an appointment through the standard application process. In earlier years, the opportunity included a chance to attend NAPS, the Naval Academy Prep School in Newport, R.I., not far from New London. Now, the prospective cadets were sent elsewhere.

Admiral Stosz once asked me, "Coach why did they stop NAPS?"

I knew Tim Fitzpatrick, the athletic director, was pushing hard to get it back, but I thought before I said anything, *She must have all of the details. Why did she ask me that?* Maybe she just wanted to hear what I would say.

"I am not sure, but I know that a Coast Guard cadet was under the direct support of a branch of the military there," I answered. I wanted NAPS back more than anyone.

Admiral Stosz, who is a no-nonsense, get-the-job-done military leader, possesses the ability to listen intently to people and absorb what is said. She leads with a sense of compassion and understanding.

When we had championship teams at Coast Guard in the 1990s or ten years ago with Christian George's group, we did exactly what West Point did in the 1980s when I was at West Point Prep and what Navy and Army do now—fill up the prep school with top football players. We had one year with about eight NAPS-groomed players and a bunch of years with just a few. They entered the Academy ready for the military training, advanced academics, and ready to play.

Coast Guard admissions pushed for the move to private preparatory schools rather than NAPS, which was run by the Naval Academy. They also changed the policy for retention, removing some students who struggled after one semester if they felt the student would not improve. However, the athletic department was never notified of the policy until after the fact.

I once shared a letter with then-commandant of the Coast Guard, Admiral Thad Allen, regarding Christian Washington, who would attend one of the private prep schools provided by the Coast Guard. Admiral Allen was the definition of a Coast Guard officer; after Hurricane Katrina turned New Orleans into a disaster and recovery efforts failed, the city was turned over to Admiral Allen. It was Admiral Allen and the Coast Guard who led the rescue of New Orleans. As commandant, Thad Allen would occasionally send me a brief email about a game. After winning several close games in 2007, he sent me a one-line note: "*You continue to build character and take years off your life.*"

Admiral Allen visited the Academy with Congressman Elijah Cummings in an ongoing effort to increase minority recruitment and retention as well discuss racial challenges facing the Academy. After their visit, I forwarded the letter sent to Ray LaForte by Christian Washington, whom Ray had recruited out of Georgia.

Christian's letter was the most articulate piece of writing I have ever received from any potential cadet. Christian arrived at the Academy on a recruiting visit seeking more than football. He found it in the Corps of Cadets, describing the entire corps as welcoming young men and women who accepted him as he was. He was surprised at how football team members called each other "brothers," and never once did he hear unflattering comments about another person. Christian did not believe he would find this type of camaraderie at the college level. At the Academy, Christian belonged to something greater than himself.

Admissions sent Christian Washington to one of the new prep alternatives, which lacked the military support system offered NAPS. Without such support, students fended for themselves and many, like Christian, were disenrolled by the Academy's admissions department.

I was informed of that unfortunate decision by email from

Victory Base Complex in Iraq by Christian's father, Army Lieutenant Colonel George Washington III who was stationed in Iraq. Colonel Washington wrote that he was deployed to the Middle East on the same day his son left for prep school and, as such, he could provide no guidance to help his son overcome academic challenges at the prep school. Christian was, in fact struggling, earning C's and D's, while his father provided caring and worry for all of those sons and daughters under his command and in the direct line of tragedy.

Christian received his separation letter during the Christmas holiday break and contacted his father. Colonel Washington made no excuses about Christian's dismissal from the CGA scholars program. During Christian's first semester, he could tell in his son's early letters that Christian struggled adjusting to the lifestyle changes as well as the new academic system. As the semester wore on, the letters became more positive, and he was encouraged that Christian felt better about the next semester.

As soon as Colonel Washington learned of his son's dismissal, they talked by phone and Christian's response was that he had let me down, as well as Coach LaForte, and his own father. Colonel Washington finished his message to me by stating his strong belief in his son and, from the middle of a war zone, asking that God bless Coach LaForte and myself.

The following year, the Coast Guard Academy reevaluated and reversed its policy, returning to a more lenient and personal evaluation. Each student was reviewed on an individual basis depending on his or her situation.

CHAPTER 11

Wednesday, the first day of shoulder pads, goes smoothly and we actually look like a football team. The individual drills move quickly, and it is good to see all the players hitting bags with pads on. They have more excitement, and there is an Academy sprint from drill to drill. They feel the Kings Point game as much as I do, partly because I have pounded it into them, and because of the inherent, historic rivalry fueled by school pride.

By the end of Thursday's practice, the offense has a strong grasp of our no-huddle, run game and is ready to expand our passing game. After the practice, the freshmen and any upperclassmen who have summer leadership roles are sent to Chase Hall for the start of Sea Trials. It is the last time we will see them until Saturday at one.

During the six-week Swab Summer training, cadets learn about military leadership and teamwork. The Sea Trials are one final challenge to a group of eighteen-year-old young men and woman who have left home and already proven they are tough enough to attempt to become officers. The twenty-four-hour day will test each future officer with one problem-solving challenge after another, including everything from rescuing downed pilots in the Thames River to survival cliff climbing.

I am home on Thursday by eight and Hat has stayed longer to say hello to my brother Dan, an orthopedic surgeon with an undergraduate degree in mechanical engineering from Cornell University and graduate of Cornell Medical School.

Dan, Nancy, and Lila are sitting on the couch next to Casper.

"He slept all day. A couple of times I had to check his breathing, but he seems fine," Hat says as he gets up to leave. "When he woke up, all he wanted to talk about was that Spencer Tracy, Montgomery Clift movie about the Nuremberg trials."

"I'm shocked that gets stuck in his head," Dan says. "We all know how confused he gets."

"Uncle Dan is here to see you," says Lila, who is sitting next to Casper and spoon-feeding him tiny scoops of vanilla ice cream.

"Thank you, honey. I can eat it," my father says. He swallows like a baby bird.

"Dan, do you remember when we first saw that movie?" I ask.

"Not really," Dan answers.

"It was when we were in junior high, I think. We were in Myers in the house he grew up in. It was on TV. I remember Bobby Caliel, Dicky Solomon, Dad, Uncle Nick, and Uncle Otsie sitting there in the living room and explaining it to me," I say. "I kept asking them what sterilization was."

"I don't remember," Dan says.

"That is not what he is talking about though. He is thinking about a show with a girl with red hair in a concentration camp," I say.

"The movie *Schindler's List*, you mean?" Dan asks.

"I'm not totally sure but he brought this up a few times in the middle of the night last summer," I say.

Lila and Casper each have their own small bowl and a portable tray in their laps. Every third bite, Lila takes Casper's spoon from him and puts a small dab on his tongue. He opens his mouth and awaits like a man dying of thirst waiting for drop of water.

"It is good for you, Gido. It will make you strong," Lila says.

A tiny smile emerges, his eyes droop and stare at her with hope. He is alive for her. His face opens wide with shock.

"Was that her in that story today?"

"What are you talking about?" I ask.

"When we got off the train. That was her with the red hair," Casper sobs.

"What?" I say and glance at my brother and Nancy and their faces reflect the same confusion.

"We saw that movie again, Dad and I, two years ago, right here in this living room. Lila was two," I say. "But around the same time, we saw another movie about the trial of a Nazi leader."

Casper cuts me off. "She was four just like Lila. She had red hair. The Nazis sent me, Nancy and Lila one way and you another. You told me to take care of them and you watched us walk away."

"Casper," Hat interrupts. "You were sleeping all day. You must have been dreaming."

"What is he talking about?" Nancy asks.

"Dr. Martin Foldi, a survivor of the concentration camps, was on the stand," I say to Dan and Nancy. "The survivor describes how he got off the train and the Nazis sent his wife and son and four-year-old daughter toward the gas chambers. He told his son to take care of them. The man's four-year-old daughter had a red coat on, and he watched his family slowly walk away with the crowd. All he could follow was the red coat. He said he watched his wife carrying the child. Everything faded except the red coat. That was the last he had seen of his family. I remember thinking about Lila at the time. She was two, and now here it is, and she is four. It is odd, but I remember thinking about the red coat and Lila's red hair when the documentary was on. And now when she is four and the same age as the girl, he brings the story back up."

"Yes," Casper says. "That is what happened to Nancy and Lila and I."

"No. It happened to someone else, Dad." I explain the movie, but I cannot fathom why he brought it up.

"No, it happened to us," he says.

"It happened to somebody, but not us," I say.

"No. It happened to us." Casper pauses. "If it was not us, then it was somebody exactly like us."

"Stop it," Nancy admonishes. "You're creeping me out like Casper does sometimes with his talk about heaven and Lila. I do not want any talk of Lila and death or heaven."

Dan senses an uneasiness and interrupts. "I will get him into the bathroom." I hand my brother the red suitcase that my mother used for her and my father when they traveled to New London for the games.

"Where is Gido going?" Lila asks solemnly.

"To Uncle Dan's."

"Why?"

"He is just going for two days until Sunday," Dan says. "I will get to spend time with him for a few days and you can have some time with Mom and Dad." My brother Dan took Casper for a week in June and a week in July and, living only an hour and a half away, he is able to come to our house often to help.

After Casper is off the toilet and into the wheelchair, we start him out the door and into chaos.

"No! I do not want Gido to go!" Lila screams as she climbs on his lap. "He is not going to come back!"

"Yes, he is." Nancy pulls her off his chair and holds her tightly. Lila reaches back, trying to escape from her mother's grip.

"No, Gido should stay!" her face, in full terror, starts to scream in desperate panic. Lila's screams escalate as Nancy sets her down. She grips the wheelchair as it is wheeled outside toward the passenger side of Dan's SUV. As the wheelchair is turned to slide Casper into the passenger side, Lila erupts in full sobs of horror. She buries her head into his lap and grips tightly around his waist. Nancy bends to pull her off.

"Honey, are you okay?" Gido asks as he slides his wrinkled fingers through her hair.

Lila lifts her face in full fright with her silent mouth wide open and then screams. I am stunned. I not only did not expect this, I did not, even in my own selfishness, see it coming.

Back inside the house, I hold Lila tightly, but to no avail. The screaming does not stop. "I'm a little scared," I whisper to Nancy, "she's going to have some kind of breakdown."

"Take her back outside," Nancy says calmly.

Dan waits a few minutes and rolls down the passenger window. I slip Lila through the window. Lila grips Gido around the neck, buries herself in his lap, and weeps into his chest. As the minutes pass, her crying slowly subsides, and every few minutes she kisses him.

"*Ohhh,*" he sighs as he looks down at her. "She feels cold. Make sure you cover her up good tonight. It will be cold tonight."

I reach through the open window and touch Lila's forehead. "She is warm, Dad. It is a warm night, and she is warm."

"It will be a cold night, and in the morning it will be very cold," Casper says.

After ten minutes, her little body becomes worn from the emotional pain, emitting only whimpers when I pull her out of the car. Gido makes the sign of the cross. I can see him trying not to cry. We take her back inside and put her into bed in between the two of us and she cries herself to sleep. I listen to her tears as they turn to the heavy breathing of exhaustion.

The night does feel a little cooler, I think.

On an early Sunday morning in February of 1940, a biting, bitter wind blew down from Canada and past Buffalo and Rochester. When the wind reached the northern end of Cayuga Lake, it turned south and raced along the blue open water. Cayuga spit back the air in the form of giant white-capped waves, ignoring the sub-zero temperature, refusing to freeze no matter how low the temperature sank. As the cold blasts repeatedly swept into Myers, it left everyone in the valley and on Syrian and American hills frigid. The wood stoves and coal furnaces became alive both day and night, eating calories and breathing heat and life into the house of every immigrant. In the cramped basement of the Syrian Orthodox Church, Puppy Moses and Nemo Saleem stoked the church's coal furnace. They huddled close until the heat warmed them. Casper George sat next to them.

"Thanks for helping," Puppy said to Nemo.

"I guessed you would be here before any of the men to get the church ready," Nemo said. "Now that you still serve on the altar and I don't, with you being the oldest, the priest gives you all the duties," Nemo said.

"I know. And in this cold, I figure most of the men have to work in the salt plant every weekday in the cold, so here we are." Puppy looked at his friend and smiled. "And it was too cold for Casper to be alone up here."

They moved upstairs, leaving Casper next to the furnace in the church basement, and started lighting the candles. In the front near the altar, the candles were encased in dark red glass about twelve inches long. The long, dark glass magnified each flame as it flickered and turned in all directions inside the glass.

Suddenly, a blast of wind whistled as it hit the side of the church where they had found the puppy. Both boys stopped and looked at the spot where they heard the wind.

"I think of the puppy a lot," Puppy said to Nemo. "I know I should think of Jacko or the Solomons, but I think of the puppy."

"Why'd you bring that up now?" Nemo asked.

"Sometimes when I hear something like a gust of wind or see a flash of a shadow at night, you know, when you walk into a dimly lit room at night and you think you see something and then there is nothing there."

"And what do you think?" Nemo asked.

"I think I wish it were the puppy and he was trying to see me or tell me he is somewhere, maybe like heaven, but he could still be here sometimes and somehow. The puppy must be somewhere. I do not want to believe a little puppy could have just disappeared forever."

"You miss the puppy and want to see him again, don't you?"

"Yes, I miss him," Puppy answered.

"Is that why we believe in heaven?" Nemo asked.

"Yes," Puppy answered. "That is why."

"You know, sometimes I think maybe you could become a priest," Nemo said as they moved away from the altar and church entrance. A few feet to the left of the entrance door, just inside the church, they aligned thin, small candles on top of a flat, white tray that was six inches deep with white sand. The parishioners would light a candle as they entered and say a prayer to themselves.

"Are you kidding?" Puppy smiled. Nemo's comment began to free his mind of the deep thoughts of the dog. "You have to be sensitive but also strong in the face of tragedy."

"That sounds like you," Nemo said.

"Maybe, maybe not." Puppy paused and looked hard at Nemo as thoughts of the missing dog again surfaced. "I still think of the puppy far too much."

Nemo watched Puppy's eyes tear. "I know you do," he said softly.

"Besides, a priest also has to be tough, as well as forgiving," Puppy added quickly, trying to push the dog out of his mind.

"I could see you as forgiving. I'm not sure I could see you as tough on someone down on their luck. Besides, I'm not sure you have to be tough to be a good priest, and you would be a good priest," Nemo said.

"No. I am not going to be a priest," Puppy said as they both moved along the sides of the church. They started lighting small, red candles that hung in gold chains in front of the stained-glass icons of Biblical saints. When they lit the candles, the light would give life to the dark green and red glass of the icons and bring the saints they depicted to life.

"You know, in the Syrian Orthodox Church a priest can still get married," Nemo said.

Puppy thought about Nemo's sister, Martha, and for a split second almost blurted something out about his feelings toward her. "I know that in the Orthodox Church you can get married, but in the Catholic Church you cannot. The priest is always telling me that the two churches should not have split."

"Yeah, why is that? I don't understand it, but I hear everyone say they are very close," Nemo said, sitting.

Puppy joined him and gazed at the beauty of the church now resplendent with burning candles. "They split a thousand years ago when there was fight between Rome and Constantinople. As best I understand it, the Catholic Church wanted to follow the pope as a supreme leader, and we did not. Also, it has something to do with the Virgin Mary. The Catholics believe she is without sin, you know, a perfect person."

"Don't we believe that too?" Nemo asked.

"Not really," Puppy started to explain. "Religion gets translated sometimes by people who want us to think the way they think. We believe Mary is like us but that she was chosen to be Jesus's mother because she was such a good person. And maybe that is what religion should be, just be a good person, like Christ. Just love everybody."

"Like our mothers?" Nemo asked. "Mary was like our mothers."

"I suppose she is just like our mothers. I suppose she is like all the ladies in Myers," Puppy said. "I guess you could say she is like all ladies anywhere."

"Why do you say that?" Nemo asked.

"Women don't start wars—men do," Puppy said.

"That's confusing," Nemo answered.

"Religion should not be confusing. It should be simple, but it gets confusing to me too," Puppy added.

"It is confusing. All I know is everyone around Myers is always praying," Nemo said.

"Yes. Sometimes they are praying about some recent tragedy and sometimes they are praying to keep away the next tragedy, as if they know one will always come," Puppy said.

"They are two very different types of prayers," Nemo said.

"No. They are the same because they both carry some kind of hope," Puppy said.

"What do you mean, the same?"

"Both types of prayers want something to be healed or made better. One may get answered in this life, and one may only be able to be answered in the next," Puppy said. "Like you, if you go on to be a doctor, you will answer prayers that could be done here on earth."

"I am a long way from being a doctor," Nemo answered.

"No, you could go to Cornell and play baseball and become a doctor. Gehrig played baseball at Columbia. You could be like Gehrig."

"I don't know what a bigger dream is, going to Cornell, becoming a doctor or playing baseball for the Yankees," Nemo said.

"Yes. I would like to play just one game for the Yankees. Gehrig never stopped. He played every day," Puppy sighed. "Until last year. But you wait, he will be back with the Yankees this spring."

"If you played one game for the Yankees like Gehrig, like Gehrig did every day," Nemo said, "you'd run off the field in your Yankee uniform as soon as the game ended and take a train to Myers. You'd get off the train in your Yankee uniform and run from the train station past the Myers Grocery with your cleats still on, and for once in your life you wouldn't stop on the bridge and look at the world. You would just run across it. You'd dig your cleats into the path and sprint to the top of the Syrian Hill. Then you'd run between the Isaacs' house and the church and past John George's house and over to my house. You'd knock on the door and ask for my sister Martha."

Puppy's face turned red. *I might do that.*

Puppy's mind now moved to fantasy. *Yes, Martha would come to the door*, he imagined. *She would reach out and brush my hair as it stuck out from my Yankee cap and then her hand would move down touch my cheek. Then she would slowly lean forward with her eyes closed and kiss me.* He smiled slyly.

Nemo watched Puppy smile and left him alone with his thoughts.

"My, Puppy, how handsome you look in your New York Yankees uniform."

Suddenly a gust of angry air shook the side of the church and rushed inside as if it had been intentionally sent to extinguish Puppy's fantasy. His thoughts shifted, sinking his spirits. *I am not the invincible, handsome Gehrig.*

He stood and started back to the basement. "I need to help Casper put more coal in the furnace," he said to Nemo as he quickly disappeared down the cramped staircase.

CHAPTER 12

The morning routine without Casper seems strange at first, but we adjust as if life was never different. No nurses, no caregivers, no hospice aides and, oddly, no memory of the daily struggles. The mind has a selfish and humane way of moving forward.

Lila is quiet but not noticeably sad. On the ride to the Academy, I open the sunroof. "The trees are moving fast," she says into the rearview mirror. I watch her look up through the sunroof at the overhanging trees. "The clouds are bubbly again, Dad."

The cumulus clouds are full of life and move like giant faces across the sky. I think of Anna and wonder what Lila thinks of Gido.

"At night," Lila's voice cuts into my thoughts, "when we drive around and I look up, the moon follows us everywhere."

I glance at her through the rearview mirror again and see she is still looking upward. I wonder what Lila thinks of the world around her.

The Coast Guard Academy Sea Trials have created an off day for football, so the office is quiet as the coaches watch yesterday's practice tape and plan Saturday's practices. Every so often I stick my head outside the football office and watch the cadets with admiration as they march around in the summer heat with heavy backpacks.

In the afternoon, Nancy picks Lila up from the Academy child center and stops by to say hello. At four, we a ride to the village of Watch Hill in Rhode Island. We park and walk down the public pathway to the ocean. Lila and I wade on the shore for as long as her pale skin can take the sun. I look out into the ocean and wonder if we have not gone on enough little trips like this with Lila since Casper has been with us. On the way home, we stop for dinner out. Between football and Casper, this will be our last chance for a while.

The Saturday meetings come and, as expected, the freshmen sleep the minute the lights go out and films go on.

"I think Cody Bain is in a coma," Ray LaForte says about our fourth-class player from Pittsburgh as I walk by his meeting. He leaves Cody sleeping when the meeting ends. We finally wake him, leaving him with just enough time to get dressed for practice. The practice goes on with freshmen taking a knee most of the time. I am worried someone might drop from heatstroke or exhaustion, but we make it through another practice day in which we cannot maximize our practice time.

Sunday, we go to church. I go along since Nancy is taking Lila, and because I will probably skip going for the rest of the season, as the coaches will be in the office all day on Sundays. After church, we clean the house and wait for Casper. It is a free Sunday and the last one I will have, but we seem content to stay home. It would be tough to get Lila to go anywhere.

"When is Gido coming?" she asks over and over.

Lila refuses to go upstairs until he arrives. Luckily, the car pulls in at about eight. Lila jumps up and down like a cheerleader and races out to greet him in the same spot she left him.

"He was quiet the whole ride," Dan says, as he starts to get Casper out of the passenger side. "He just sat there and watched the world go by. Did not say a word for the last hour. He just seemed peaceful and content. 'I want to go back home and see Lila,' was all he said when we got into the car."

Casper is grinning widely when the door opens and he sees Lila. "Oh, honey," is all he says. His drooping eyes tear with joy behind his needless reading glasses. He reaches out to touch her as we shift him in the wheelchair, but his hand misses her. As soon as he is sitting, she climbs on his lap and wraps her arms around his neck.

I let them hold each other for two minutes and then interrupt.

"We have to get him into the house," I say as I pull her off.

Lila holds Casper's hand as we push the wheelchair into the house. The two worlds, *joy* and *sorrow*, squeeze through the house side by side.

They smirk at each other. "Oh, I am so glad to be back," he moans. "I missed her too much." They sit on his hospital bed and cuddle until bedtime. Lila becomes quiet as time wears on. She plays and seems to be talking to herself as Casper sits there watching.

When I stoop to pick Lila up to take her to bed, she leans out of my arms toward Casper, so I lower her, and she kisses him softly.

I turn the light out and his eyes still have tears, but this time they are tears of sorrow.

That kiss she gave him, I think, *Maybe it would ride with him to the next world. Like a good luck charm on the journey. Or maybe the kiss would be taken to the heavens to be shared.*

Nancy comes down and scoops Lila into her arms.

"Is there a war in Syria right now?" Casper's fading evening thoughts come alive in the darkness.

"It is a revolution. They are trying to overthrow the government," I answer.

"Jesus is over there with Anna. Did we help them?" Casper asks.

"Jesus is in heaven," Lila says.

"No, he is over in Syria with Anna, and they are dying. They are dying with all the little children who are dying in the war," Casper proclaims.

"No, they are both in heaven," I say. "It is time to go to sleep."

"No," he says with a slight tone of anger. He tries to sit up as if he is getting out of bed. "Did you give Jesus and Anna food or clothes or medicine or money over in Syria?"

"They are not there," I say.

"Yes, they are, and they are there with a lot of people and their children," he answers.

"Casper," Nancy interrupts, "I know what you mean. Jesus said,

'If you did not clothe or feed the poor or help the imprisoned and the sick, then you turned your back on me. Not helping them is the same as not helping me.' Remember what he said? 'Whatsoever you do to the least of my brothers, that you do unto me.'"

Guilt wracks me and I look up at Nancy. I can see her silent sympathy in the dark room say to me, *You have only really liked three kinds of people, those who have played for you, those who do play for you and those who will play for you.* She turns and takes Lila to bed. I fight off the guilt knowing that I really have not done very much at all for the rest of the world.

I watch Casper stare through the darkness at the ceiling with his eyes open as I go upstairs to bed with Lila and Nancy.

When I come down an hour later, I can hear Casper's voice.

"Immay," he calls out a few hours later in his sleep, using the Arabic word for mother. *"Immay,"* he calls out again.

"Dad, go back to sleep."

"Where's my mother?" His mother, Helanie, had died of a stroke in 1966 when Casper was thirty-nine.

"Where is Anna?"

"They are both in heaven," is all I can answer. I do not want him to get back on the topic of Syria. Guilt in the middle of the night is a hundred times more painful than guilt in daylight, and I do not want to examine my life.

"Oh, no," he cries. "Did I bet on horses too much?" He switches gears on me, as if his brain had been turned on and was being controlled by someone else.

"No, and then you stopped." I surprise myself, as I did not know I had the power to grant forgiveness.

"Did I spend too much time on betting horses and not the rest of the world?" he asks, almost crying aloud.

"No," I answer. "You always thought of the rest of the world." Then I say, "You know, Dad, you may have bet on horses, but you always put Mom and Dan and me first, and you did pay attention to the world. Hell, I bet on horses, too, and I don't pay any attention to the world. I think that the difference between me and you is that I would waste a day studying the horses, then a day betting, then a day mad at myself when I lost. Then I would stop for a while. But you just kept going and then you hit that long bad streak."

"Was I like that?" Casper asks.

"I don't know, Dad. I think we all have depression, but you had it your whole life and the horses were your escape."

"Oh, yes. Those boys in Myers. All those boys in Myers," Casper closes his eyes and cries softly. "And that girl. And my cousin. And their mother, my Aunt Atina. I was one of the first people to visit her."

It is my turn to keep my eyes open and stare at the ceiling in the middle of the night and wonder about the rest of the world for a while. Then I think of Myers.

"What do you mean one of the first people to visit Nemo and Martha's mother?"

Casper does not answer, and I do not repeat the question.

In the deceiving afternoon sun of a chilly Thursday in November of 1940, word spread through Myers about the death of Atina Saleem, Nemo and Martha's mother. She sat complaining of a headache and had a stroke. She lost consciousness and never awoke. Her sister, Helanie, raced up the hill, but Atina was gone within an hour. Word spread all around Syrian Hill, and from the grocery store to all of Myers and nearby Lansing. The flood was the first taste of tragedy and Mary Caliel was the second. Those deaths stuck sharp, painful daggers. Atina Saleem's passing was the first taste of natural death for the immigrants.

Puppy served on the altar for the funeral. He ignored everything but the mechanics of the proceedings. When the body was taken from the church and off the hill to the cemetery a half mile up Route

34B, he followed it, with the priest holding the incense. *This is my last time as an altar boy,* he thought. *I am in front of all of these people and all I see is sorrow.*

In quick glances, he would see Martha clutching tightly to her older sister, Mary, while they both wept. Nemo's father and brother wept openly, as well. Puppy would catch Nemo silently crying to himself. *It is as if he is letting the tears roll from his face because he cannot hold them in, but letting the rest of his feelings stay locked inside,* Puppy thought.

When the day was over and the sun had crossed Cayuga Lake and dipped beyond the far hillsides, Puppy stood alone and contemplative in the cool darkness on the Myers bridge. *It is odd,* he thought. *The night is alive with stars. They look like they are trying to jump from the sky and land on the earth.* Then Puppy noticed the stillness of the air and it seemed motionless to him, as if life had been sucked out of it. *The heavens are so alive, but Myers seems so dead,* he thought.

Puppy listened to the soft trickle of the creek and waited. An hour later, he heard a branch crack on the path down the hill. A figure appeared on the edge of the bridge and slowly walked toward him.

"I knew you would be here," said Nemo, still dressed in his suit from the funeral.

"I knew you knew I would be here," Puppy replied. "I knew you would come to find me here."

"How did you know?" Nemo asked.

"I could see it in your face all day," Puppy said.

"What did you see in my face?" Nemo asked.

"I did not see anything. Just your face and your tears. I could not see inside of you."

"They're all crying and I'm numb," Nemo started. "It's like an empty, scared feeling of the unknown. Like one world has ended and another one has started. A new, scary one. Do you know what I mean?"

"No," Puppy answered swiftly. Deep down, he thought of the flood and the puppy, but the guilt dared not have him compare his feelings. He thought of the time he saw the Isaac brothers on the bridge, staring at the creek with tears, and promised himself to never ask again about the puppy.

"Puppy, do you remember when we walked upstream that afternoon last May?" Nemo started across the bridge to the other side to look upstream in the darkness.

"Yes," Puppy said.

"We walked around the corner upstream, and we hit the long stretch halfway between here and the Ludlowville Falls."

"Yes, I remember." Puppy knew exactly where he meant. "We have been there a lot as kids," he answered, "where the long pools of slow, still water run past the green pasture."

Puppy thought about the long stretch of Salmon Creek where the water would glide slowly along through a series of shallow pools. The clear water glowed as the sunlight cut through to the gravel and turned the rocks into glistening diamonds. On the side of the stream was a long field with wild, green grass that always seemed to be covered in golden sunshine. At the edge of the field, a farmhouse stood at the bottom of Ludlowville Road as it entered the village of Ludlowville. On the other side of the water, the banks were steep with gray shale, which rose for ten yards, turning into a forest of pine trees, which reached up another fifty yards to the top of the tall bank where it leveled off. The pine forest stretched only slightly on the top of the bank, as it had been cleared and turned into a cemetery on Route 34B.

"Yes, I know, but do you remember what you said that afternoon?" Nemo asked.

Puppy remembered in silence.

Nemo choked back tears. "You said this is the most beautiful stretch of water in the world and you could sit and watch it for hours and forget about the world."

"I remember," Puppy answered.

"You said that there are people, like Jacko and the others from the flood, laid to rest in a cemetery forever, above the most peaceful stretch of water in the world. It was so they could listen to the creek forever, like Jacko," Nemo said.

"Yes, but I suppose that everyone could listen to the creek forever, no matter where they are buried."

"Yes, and you said one day our mothers or fathers or even one of us might be there," Nemo said. "And you said maybe one day we will both be there together or neither of us could end up there."

"Yes, I remember," Puppy answered.

"And Puppy, you said, 'We either die who we are or we die who we are not.'"

"Yes," Puppy answered. "Yes. I remember." He looked down into the dark water beneath him and he imagined the stretch of the creek that Nemo was talking about. He felt an odd sense of loneliness as Nemo repeated what he said a few months ago. He feared he may never be able to enjoy that stretch of water alone again, that he would have to be with someone.

"And Puppy, when you said, 'We either die who we are or we die who we are not... what did you mean by that?"

Puppy looked up at the sky and stars as if to ask the heavens for the right words. He said nothing but kept staring. *I wonder if the stars are alive?*

"Please, tell me what you were thinking when you said that," Nemo pleaded. The desperation in his voice brought Puppy back onto the bridge in Myers.

Puppy took a deep breath. "I think that we live our life one way, and if we are happy with who we are, then we die who we are, the way we have lived all of our lives. Like your mother, she lived her life to love her children, and that was who she was," Puppy said.

"And what about the flood and the Solomons or Jacko, who died so young? Did they die who they were not?" Nemo asked.

"No. I did not mean it to do with age," Puppy thought hard about what he had said to Nemo after the deadly Myers flood of 1935. "I did not mean it that if you died either way it was good or bad. I guess I was just saying that you can live your whole life striving for something and if you get a chance to make it happen, then you die who you are."

"And if we died now, right now, what would we be?" Nemo asked.

"Right now, we are who we are here in Myers. I guess we would die who we are not because we did not get to try to live our lives or change the world. But let's say the future took me and you for a crazy ride and we did things that made the whole world better, then maybe we would become different than we are now, and we would die who we are, who we had become."

"I'm not sure who I am or who I will become. I'm not sure about anything," Nemo sighed. "And I am not sure about my mother."

They stopped talking as another figure emerged from the darkness and appeared on the bridge, walking toward them.

"It's just me," Casper said. "I followed Nemo out of the house."

"Maybe, also if a person lives long enough," Puppy continued talking as if Casper had not arrived, "everybody gets a chance to change. They live life one way, then they change and become someone new or do something new, something better, something better for the world." Puppy took a deep breath and wondered if he should say anything else, but the words came out quickly as if he had no control.

"Maybe when I first said that I was thinking that if you don't get to do all you want to while you are alive you can still do something more when you are in heaven. I was a lot younger when I said that at Jacko's grave." Puppy paused and started to think about what he had been trying to explain. "Maybe I was wrong."

"What do you mean, wrong?" Nemo asked.

"I should have said we die both who we are and who we are not, who we have yet to become. I should have said *and* not *or*. Maybe what we don't finish here we finish in the next life."

Talk of Jacko turned Puppy silent, as a dormant dream he had about Jacko months ago flashed into his thoughts. He dared not tell Nemo about it now. In the dream, Jacko was standing on the bridge on the day they had found the little puppy, wearing white shoes. Then Puppy realized something odd about the dream and thought, *Jacko did not have white shoes on the day we found the puppy, he did not have white shoes until after he died. They bought him white shoes just to bury him in them. The shoes in my dream were not brand new either, like the shoes they buried him in. Jacko's shoes in my dream were worn and scuffed as if he had been walking around in them for months.* He shook his head, ridding himself of the mysterious dream and returning to the bridge in Myers.

Nemo stared into the night sky, still confused but mollified by Puppy's statement of living and dying. He turned to Puppy and said, "I need to go to the cemetery."

"Now?"

"Yes. Right now. I need to see my mother," Nemo answered with a sense of urgent fear.

"Let's go then," answered Puppy.

The three of them walked in the black night up the road, past Syrian Hill and up Route 34B and into the cemetery.

Atina's grave was bare, but the dirt was covered with flowers. They stood alone together. Puppy looked around in the eerie, black night as if to see if anything was left alive in the world.

Casper wandered in the darkness to the grave of Marion's mother, Mary Caliel, then looked back at Nemo and Puppy.

"I just cannot believe she is down there," Nemo said to Puppy, his voice cracking with sorrow. "I cannot believe my mother, who worried about me every second and kissed me every minute, is down there six feet under. She must be home. If I run home right now, I will find her sitting in her room brushing her hair in the mirror. She will see me in the reflection of the mirror and look up at me and smile."

Nemo started to cry as he realized his hopes and dreams could not change the past.

Puppy put his arm around him and felt Nemo's shoulders tremble. Nemo's body was coming alive with pain. Puppy looked out across the dark cemetery and into the still trees and listened to the echo of Nemo's sorrow. The pine trees that were nearest the graves whispered softly, like a sorrowful hymn, when a gentle breeze caressed their branches and wove its way through their pine needles. In the distance, Puppy could see the bare branches of seasonal trees that had been stripped of their leaves from the chills of autumn. *The trees of November always look so empty, like skeletons that are still alive somehow,* he thought.

To him, it seemed like the trees were watching the two of them standing in the cemetery, waiting for their next move. It was as if the whole world had stopped and was watching the sadness. *I wonder if this is the new world starting?*

Puppy felt the gentle breeze gain strength and turn itself into a gust, and as he looked up, he could see clouds illuminated by the moonlight behind them blocking out patches of the stars. *It is beautiful. I have watched the big, white clouds roll across a sunny, blue sky many days. But why have I never noticed the beauty of the clouds at night? It is as if the night wind is a magic wand, and it has brought the night's clouds onto the sky to be together with the stars and the moonlight just this one time.*

Suddenly, a pine tree thick with its needles shook louder with the arriving gusts, and his thoughts retreated from the sky. A twinge of guilt raced through him, as he had forgotten that Nemo was tucked underneath his arm and staring at his mother's grave. *The wind and the stars and the clouds and the moonlight are all together this one time, just for Nemo,* Puppy thought. *And he cannot see their beauty.*

CHAPTER 13

Monday morning comes just as early for Casper as it does for the cadets. Casper has been up and is back in bed by seven, after a quick diaper change and some water with his morning meds. Sadly, it has become a mechanical movement to get a dying man all set before we leave the house. I am not certain his brain is even awake yet. We have no choice but to provide this gritty level of care. Hat would wear down if he had to do anything but wait until the first hospice caretakers come every morning.

I am out the door by seven-thirty, and Nancy waits for Hat, then takes Lila to the childcare center as soon as he arrives at eight. It is the first day back at the Academy for the entire Corps of Cadets and it will begin with two days of the dreaded personal fitness exam, the PFE as it is called. Football linemen despise the test the most because their size hinders them. The test consists of seeing how long it takes to complete sixty push-ups, followed by two minutes of sit-ups, and then a mile-and-a-half run, which crushes the linemen. The test is administered every August and January to each cadet. The data shows anyone who weighs over 215 pounds suffers the most and has the lowest scores.

The coaches are demanding, watching for push-ups that are out of cadence or not deep enough. With the sit-ups, lost points come with a failure to touch the bent mid-thigh with the elbow or return the shoulders to the mat.

After Tuesday's practice, the Coast Guard football team limps off the field after two days of the PFE, and twelve hours each day of military training. The players' legs are tight, but their spirits remain high.

Thursday of the second week of practice adds another distraction with convocation at Leamy Hall. I march in with the faculty and relax until the third time a speaker says, "Beat Kings Point," words that lift my soul from Leamy and drag me back to the sidelines of the football stadium.

Friday gives us a chance to put in a normal college practice. On Saturday, we hold a non-tackling, intrasquad scrimmage.

When I walk in the house on Saturday at six-thirty, everyone is waiting for me before they start dinner. We move Casper to the dining room and say the Lord's Prayer. Casper is as vocal as he can be. Lila holds hands with him. I am surprised that he does not miss a word. In the living room after dinner, Lila has him covered and surrounded with stuffed animals within minutes.

"Gido has his bunny ears on," Lila jokes.

"I see," I say. The ears make his thin face look even smaller. Somehow, the cuteness of the scene is lost to me in the sadness of his fate. Stuffed puppies and a teddy bear surround him on the couch. His clarity and attention while praying at dinner now wanes, almost as if he is having trouble hearing. He sits content, however, knowing he is making Lila happy.

"Gido, you say 'How are you today?'" Lila instructs him to play. Regardless of whether he moves, she just keeps playing as if he was participating.

Lila sits on the floor in front of Casper who just stares at her. Every so often, he turns his head slightly to find her if she has moved away from his direct line of vison. He looks like a curious bird with a large beak as his hollow eyes squint at her.

"Gido, you pretend you found my lost dog and you have been taking care of him for me." She puts a small stuffed beagle on his lap. He holds it gently with his two hands for a moment and then reaches out with it as if to give it back to her.

"No, you take care of it now," she tells him.

An hour later, Lila is in her pajamas when we take Casper over to the bed.

"Here, Gido," Lila climbs up, puts the stuffed puppy next to his face and kisses him.

"She is from heaven," he says as his face leans against the stuffed toy. "On earth and in heaven," he mumbles. The meds are kicking in and he closes his eyes but he keeps speaking softly.

I turn to Nancy, who has Lila in her arms. "Take her upstairs and I'll be right up."

"No," Lila jumps in, "Gido is saying something to me."

Casper mumbles as he fights the Trazodone and Lorazepam. His glassy eyes crack slightly, he stops mumbling and he looks around in confusion, as if he does not know where he is.

"Go back to sleep, Dad," I order, upset that my work night is over, but I must keep going, like replaying a down after a penalty.

"He is not a machine. He cannot be turned off. Let him speak," Nancy instructs.

"If your mother is in heaven, what does she do in heaven?" he asks quietly.

"In heaven, there are angels, Gido," Lila answers as softly as Casper is mumbling his questions.

"What do they do?" he asks. "What does Anna do up there?"

"She helps people and makes the world better. That is what angels do," Nancy answers, as if she was trying to clarify it for Lila as well.

"That is what angels and people do, Gido," Lila adds.

Just as Lila's words hit me hard, Casper looks to me for reassurance and asks, "Did I help the world enough? Did I, Bill?"

"Yes," Nancy answers. I have the feeling she is also talking to me. "Casper, you are a wonderful person. You care more about people than objects."

"But I bet on horses," he starts to cry. "I spent too much time on me and not enough on everybody else."

"Not all the time, Dad. You spent a lot of time with the world, as well." I feel as if I am trying to reassure myself, not just him. Deep down, I believe it about him but not me.

"Anna was like that all of the time," he says. "What did she used to say?" he asks as he shut his eyes.

"She used the Jesus quote," Nancy says. "'What profit is it to a man if he gains the whole world but loses his soul?'"

The statement is made for me. I know she is referring to this year's Merchant Marine game, but it does not bother me in the least. It is as if deep down I truly do not care about anything else in the world.

"You worried about the world all of the time," I know Nancy is telling Casper, but the words are meant for me.

Nancy moves her mouth to my ear. "Make sure it is not too late before you worry about the world. You cannot start to *do good* five minutes before your time is up," she whispers as she takes Lila upstairs.

I follow them up and wait for Lila to drift to sleep and then I am back on the couch.

A few hours later, in the middle of the night, Casper calls out, "Bill." His voice is stronger than usual at night.

"Go back to sleep," I order like an angry football coach. The strength of his voice leads me to the conclusion that he is wide awake.

"I want to know about Nemo and Puppy. Why did I wake up thinking of them?"

"Go back to bed!" I yell like an irritated coach who must repeat himself too many times to the same player.

Casper goes silent in the darkness, but I know he is awake. It is as if something is trying to stay alive in his brain. He says nothing again for a while, but I know his eyes are open in the darkness and I can tell he is not falling asleep by the occasional ruffle of his bed sheets mixed with a whimper or a deep breath of air.

"Bill," Casper calls out in clear voice.

The strength of his tone surprises me. *Oh no,* I think. *He is wide awake.* I do not answer him.

"Bill, Bill," he repeats.

"Yes, Dad."

"What happened to our house? The house we all lived in in Glens Falls?" he asks.

I do not want to tell him I had to sell it to use the money to take care of him. I do not know what to say. It was a small one-level home on a small lot in a quiet neighborhood. You could walk in the front door and within three steps be through the living room and into the kitchen. The table where we ate all of our meals was five feet from the stove.

"Is the house still there?" he asks.

"Yes, Dad, it is still there."

"But we won't ever go back home again, will we?" Memories in the middle of the night are more painful than those in the light of day.

I do not answer him. It took me two years after Anna's passing just to abandon the phone number I had spent a lifetime calling my parents on.

"When I would come home late at night from bartending at the Blue Sky Restaurant at two in the morning, I would stand outside of your bedroom and I would think you and your brother came from heaven."

Came from heaven? I think. *He says that as if we were already up there. Already created and ready to come down.*

"Then I would think of Nemo and Puppy and I would start to cry. You know, when your mother and I were first married and you were a little boy, we lived above the Blue Sky Restaurant with George and Esther." Above the restaurant, there were four bedrooms where everyone lived. "At night, when I looked at you, I would think of those boys and the girl and cry myself to sleep in your mother's arms."

I stand and walk across the room and touch his forehead and his eyes look at me through the dark.

"The Blue Sky is gone. George and Esther are gone. Anna's gone, and those boys and those girls from Myers have been gone for a long, long time," he says as his voice starts to weaken with memories.

"Maybe that is just the way the world is, Dad."

"What do you mean?" he asks.

"Maybe it is someone else's world before we all get here, then we are here and we cross paths with the people who are here during our time, then we leave and it becomes someone else's world after we are gone."

"After we are gone, will we get to see everyone again?" he asks.

"You said it a few minutes ago, Dad. You said we come from heaven. So, we must have to go to back to heaven." In the hectic pace of life, I have forgotten about so much, but now I at least feel there is meaning in why he remains with us.

"Try to rest, Dad."

"Thank you, Bill," he says, as he stares at the ceiling. "Now I know I will get to see those girls and those boys again. Now I know I will see Myers again. I know I will see the lake like I could see it from the hill near the school, above the fields and tennis court."

On a mostly clear Saturday morning in March of 1941, Puppy Moses sat alone on a long hill across from Route 34B, where American Hill ended. He looked down onto Ludlowville High School, where Myers Road ended at the top of American Hill and crossed Route 34B and turned into Ludlowville Road. *I have plenty of time before I run on the track,* he thought. *Maybe I will follow Ludlowville Road down into Ludlowville and watch the falls. It is March and the runoff from the spring thaw will be heavy and the water will look beautiful.*

He remembered once standing underneath the falls on a clear day like this with Nemo and they looked up as they watched the spray of the water separate and fall over the hundred-foot drop. As they stared in the water with the blue sky and cumulus clouds in the background, he told Nemo, "The water looks like it is falling from the sky."

"It never stops," Nemo said.

He remembered how the powerful water raced over the falls on its way down the creek to Myers. Then the thought of the water rushing over the falls turned ugly, reminding him of his helpless puppy on the bridge in the flood six years before. *It seems like it was just yesterday, but it was not. I suppose nothing in life was just yesterday.*

Puppy turned to his right and, carrying the grief he had just created, walked up the hill toward the Ludlowville High track. When he was near the track, he turned toward Cayuga Lake and sat, lowered his head, bent his knees upward and put his face down. He pressed his eyes into his kneecaps to hide his tears. He cried softly for few moments, and when he stopped he lifted his head into the day in front of him.

Puppy looked down the hill from where he sat and saw the tennis court just below him, which was across from the school and baseball diamond. Just behind him, farther up the hill, was the cinder track where Ludlowville held its track practices. Puppy gazed out into the distance beyond the school where he could see over the treetops and out to the dark blue water of Cayuga Lake. The air was crisp but pleasant for March in upstate New York.

He was dressed in a gray, cotton sweatsuit that bore the name Ludlowville in yellow. He was holding his metal track spikes in his lap. He put them on the ground and pulled his hand up to his head, running his fingers through his full head of bushy, curly black hair. He kept his hair unusually long and he knew it separated him from the rest of Myers. He loved how his mother, Takla, would run her fingers through it with both her hands, then gently pull his face toward hers, and with the gentlest of lips, kiss him on the cheek like he was a newborn. Using the Arabic word for baby she would say, "My *habeba*. My teenage *habeba*."

Puppy watched a few low puffy white clouds start to roll toward Myers from the far stretches of the horizon, as if they wanted to join the scene just to add beauty to his view of the lake. He could see Nemo, Casper, Martha, and Dawn walking from Dawn's house, which was one of the only two houses to the right on Ludlowville

Road. Nemo carried two tennis rackets and a bag of balls. Puppy watched as they stopped on the court. Martha looked up and saw him sitting on the hill, said something to Casper, then walked alone across the court and up the hill toward him. His nerves attacked his stomach as he watched her approach. She was becoming a woman now and her thighs flexed forward and popped out from underneath her tan skirt as her legs took each uphill step.

As she got closer, he could see the dark curls of the hair on her shoulders bounce slightly on her red sweater. He watched her lips smile at him as she sat next to him. *It is a special smile meant just for me,* he thought, never daring to say anything like that aloud.

"I came to watch them play," Martha said. "I dragged Casper along. He was stuck in my house while his mother cooked with my sister, Mary. Nemo wanted him to shag tennis balls."

Puppy looked down at the whiteness of her legs, following them to the top of her ankle socks. Then he looked out onto the court where Nemo was serving and Casper and Dawn raced to fetch errant balls. Puppy had forgotten how frail Dawn had been looking.

"She is not well," Martha said. "That is why I came. To watch her. Nemo says they are checking everything."

Puppy blushed in silence.

"It does not look like they can even play today," Martha said, looking at Puppy and wondering what he was thinking as she watched him study the girl.

"Say something," she said.

He turned and looked at her. He wanted to say something about himself or about his feelings for her. And here she was, finally, as he had hoped for years.

"I used to watch Nemo glide across the court. I used to think he could become another Lou Gehrig, so handsome, so strong," Puppy said. "Dawn was the same way, so beautiful. People would stop to watch the two of them play. It was like they were dancing together and the whole world was watching."

"Lou Gehrig is not playing," Martha said, surprising Puppy with her answer.

"Yes," Puppy said. "He was the strongest. Invincible. Never coming out of a game. But that was yesterday."

Surprised by his response, Martha waited and thought about what Puppy had said. "And what does that have to do with Nemo and Dawn?" she asked.

"Nemo is still the Gehrig before Gehrig grew weak and sick. Nemo is still on top of the world. But Dawn looks like Gehrig looks now that he is weak."

"And what do you mean by that?" she asked.

"I guess that maybe we can all be strong sometimes, and we are all weak sometimes. Maybe we all possess some strengths and some weaknesses."

Martha looked over at him, mystified, perhaps, by the depth of his thoughts. He did not sound like any other immigrant on Syrian Hill. She watched his eyes as he looked into the sky, cuing for her to look up as well. The puffy white cumulus clouds had now rolled upward and were basking in the pale blue sky and sunshine. Martha stood when Nemo and Dawn started off the court and back to Ludlowville Road toward her house. "Bye," she said, watching him study the sky.

"Bye," he puffed out, still staring at the sky and not looking at her.

A few steps down the hill, she turned to him and asked, "What do you see up there?"

"Sometimes those pretty white clouds appear from nowhere, as if they escaped from heaven," he answered.

"Escaped from heaven?" She looked at his bushy hair and round frame and felt confused. Then she thought, *He has hardly ever spoken to me and now he is talking like some kind of priest.*

"Yes. Clouds are like us," he answered.

"And how are they like us?" she asked. She waited several minutes for him to answer as he stared at the sky. Just as she started to walk away he said, "I watch them move fast across the sky and I wonder if they are trying to catch tomorrow before they are left behind or get back to yesterday before it is gone forever."

Puppy leveled his gaze and saw Martha walking down the hill. *I wonder if she heard me.*

CHAPTER 14

On the second day of the academic semester, I stand up from the desk in my office minutes before the weekly offensive line lunch meeting. As I turn and look behind me, the giant picture of the 2007 offensive line, ready to charge forward at the line of scrimmage, hits me in the face. The picture hangs only a few feet behind me and above my head. The line looks dominant and powerful, the players in their football stances, ready to explode. Massive Texans Justin Brooks and Ryan Fox on the far side of the line are barely visible. Matt Krueger leads the way with his hands over the ball next to Nick Hartmann, the All-American from Louisiana. Closest to me is six-foot, four-inch Texan Charles England, who broke his leg in the second game of the season right after we beat Merchant Marine in the 2007 opener.

Peter Lewia, a senior in 2007, is not in the picture because second stringers, especially linemen, do not get their picture taken. Pete struggled like any person who dares take on the endless flood of challenges that face all cadets who enter a service academy. The challenges for Pete multiplied on the athletic field. He was a tall, chunky, slow of foot high school lineman who had to lose nearly fifty pounds just to meet the body fat requirements for entrance into the Academy. Then, like all linemen, twice a year he had to meet the requirements for the physical fitness exam. On top of that, once a month he would starve himself for a few days to meet the body fat requirements. Football was Pete's escape back into the real world. In most football seasons, a first-class lineman with Pete's skills would have been a starter, but during his years at the Academy, the talent pool was much deeper.

After England broke his leg in the second game of the 2007 season, Pete went in as his backup and played the last three quarters of the game. On the following Monday, I told Pete I had moved a player from another position, Dave Zwirblis, a sophomore backup at guard, as the starting tackle instead of him.

"Coach, can you tell me why?" he asked calmly while sitting across from my desk.

"You struggled when you went into the game. When I graded the game film, you knew all your assignments, but you struggled against the faster, more athletic defensive linemen," I said.

"I know but it was the first time I've been in a game in four years. I'll get better," Pete said. His voice was not strong enough to disguise the hurt he felt.

"I know, but I am going to give one of the younger guys a shot. Zwirblis has better feet, he is quicker, he has a little better balance when he kick-slides in pass protection." I rattled off as many reasons as I could to justify my decision.

"Okay, I'll keep working," Pete said as he left my office.

Pete did keep working like the officer he would become, helping Zwirblis and the team as a leader. Five games later, Zwirblis broke his leg. I moved Mike Fiori, the other sophomore backup guard, to play tackle. Pete remained second string on the offensive line anyway, but not in life.

In fact, Peter Lewia may have taught me more about myself and the purpose of the Academy than anybody I have ever coached. During the last half of his senior year in 2007, after he had already been passed over twice as the starter, I would often cross paths with him as he was racing down to the locker room in Roland Hall to change for practice. Somehow, I do not remember exactly how, but I started to ask him, "Who won today, good or evil?" Pete would answer in one word based on how his day had been. If anything had hindered or interfered with, in any way, progress toward his graduation, like a bad test score or a demerit, he would huff and say, "evil." If it had been a good day and nothing slowed his progress toward that final Academy day, he would smile and say, "good."

One day late in the 2007 season, I left the coaches' locker room and started on my way to the practice field when Pete raced down the long corridor in my direction.

"Who won today, good or evil?" I asked.

Pete did not miss stride as he rushed past me and said, "It was a tie."

I quickly turned and said back to him like a true football coach, "If it was a tie, then evil won."

Pete stopped and looked back at me and said, "No, but maybe every day is a tie... for us anyway."

I thought for a moment. Maybe he was right. Every day is a tie, for everybody, and we get the chance to change it, to make it good or evil. *But what does he mean by, "for us?"* I thought. *Is Pete saying something that tells me I am wrong?* In my head I was second-guessing myself.

"What do you mean for us?" I shouted down the hallway to him.

Pete stopped, turned back to look at me and said, "Every day is tie for us here at a place like Coast Guard." Pete paused for a moment and stared at me like he could see my soul. "I suppose there are people all over who do not have a chance no matter what they do. A lot of people wake up where they are and evil rules the day no matter what they do. I have a chance every day. They do not have the same chance as me." He turned and disappeared into the men's varsity locker room.

I stood stunned for a moment and then started out to practice and thought, *That's what they teach here, the age-old lesson of faith and charity. That's what they teach here. You just can't be good, you have to do good. They teach that your life is not just about you, it is about others. The Academy teaches all these cadets that they are defined by what they do, who they help, not who they are.*

By the time I reached the field I felt really good about Pete as a football player but disappointed in myself as a person. Pete never played the game "good or evil" again with me after that day. He would walk by me and smile with confidence as if he discovered the secret of the universe.

Lunch is delivered Tuesday to Billard, and the players grab it and head to their meeting rooms. Coaches Grant and Fleischmann meet with the defense in the main lecture hall in the engineering building. Coach LaForte meets down the hall with all the skill players; the offensive linemen meet in the small conference room outside my office.

The offensive line is an impressive group to have a football meeting with. Sophomore engineering majors JD Dunaway and Jordan Hart have put some weight back on now that Swab Summer is a year behind them. Last year, they both had to start as freshmen and had lost at least thirty pounds apiece during Swab Summer. We relied on them last year and they fought through being pummeled on the field. That is typical of college cadets who are mismatched physically and behind the learning curve as football players due in part to the massive load of twenty-two credit hours. Juniors Tommy Condon and Kevin Painten are clearly the leaders of the offense, and they are also clearly overachievers with a work ethic that matches their toughness. They know how and when to throw in a hint of humor to keep everyone loose. Rounding out the line at center is senior Keven Postiglione, who struggles to keep his weight above 200 pounds. Kevin may be the smallest starting offensive lineman in all of college football. Due to our lack of depth and experience, we had to move Kevin over from the defensive side of the ball. We needed a body, and his body was the only one we had to plug that hole.

The meetings are relaxed but serious, and we always spend part of it on the Kings Point blitzes, twists and defensive fronts. I can say the best part of my day is being the offensive line coach, more so in many ways than head coach. I am "one of the guys" in the meetings and in the practices. It's like I am back in time with them; I am nineteen again and playing football and not worried about the real world.

As the meeting starts, the freshmen eat and stay quiet, while the upperclassmen relax with a few jokes or comments.

On Friday, the day before we're scheduled to play WPI in a limited scrimmage, my cell phone rings.

"Billy, it's Hat."

"What is the matter?" I ask.

"Your father slept almost all morning." Hat sounds nervous. "When Debbie came by from hospice, he didn't wake up, so we let him sleep. I just finally woke him up for lunch and he doesn't know where he is or who I am. I showed him a picture of Lila, and he doesn't know who she is either."

"Is he saying much else or moving?" I can feel my skin crawl with panic.

"No," Hat answers. "He's just sitting there with a blank stare on his face. His eyes are all glassy and I'm not sure he can hear me all that much."

"Put him on the phone," I order.

"Casper, Casper," I can hear Hat's voice through the receiver. "I'm going to put the phone up to his ear."

"Dad... *DAD!*" I yell. *"DAD! DAD!"* I yell louder. I wait and hear nothing.

"He is just sitting there," Hat says as he gets back on the phone. "He had no reaction at all."

"I'll call the hospice nurses," I tell Hat. "He has had a stroke, I think."

I rush out of the office and call Amy, his main hospice nurse. "I'll head right over," she says.

I call Nancy and she senses the panic in my voice. "I'll pick up

Lila at the Academy children's center and meet you at home, if you want," she says.

"It might be better if we leave her there and you wait for me to call."

"I agree," she answers with a sense of sadness.

In my panic, instinct tells me she is the compassionate one and I am the business caretaker. I know it should be the other way around, but it is not and that is my fault. The panic crushes the guilt out of me as I race home.

I walk in the living room a few moments after Amy, who is kneeling in front of Casper. The afternoon sunshine fills the room from all sides. Amy takes his vitals and turns to me. "I think he has had a mini stroke."

Amy stands and I take her place on my knees in front of Casper. I can see his face clearly in the bright orange rays of sunlight flowing into the room. His face looks droopy, like it is beginning to melt.

"Dad, it's me, Bill." He looks at me with a blank stare. "Dad, it is me Bill, do you know who I am?"

His eyes study my face, which is very close to his. His gray eyebrows raise slightly. I can see his eyes try to see me as if they are looking at me from far away.

"No," he whispers softly.

"It is me, Bill."

He just stares at me, expressionless.

I grab a large picture of Lila off the television mantel. I put it within his line of vision. "Dad, do you know who this is?"

He studies the picture but says nothing.

"It is Lila," I say as I wait for him to say who she is.

"No," he mumbles.

The scenario repeats itself over and over for about thirty minutes while Amy doublechecks all his vitals.

"He seems stable," Amy says. "He is not in pain or any discomfort."

"He is in hospice care," she reminds me. "Just make him comfortable."

"Is he going to die?" I ask.

"Eventually. But if you want me to tell you when, I cannot. I do not have that answer." She looks at me with a soft, gentle smile that the whole world should have but only a hospice nurse possesses. "It is the never-ending hospice question that no one can answer."

I kneel in front of him again and he looks a little more alive. His eyes and face seem to have brightened.

Suddenly, Nancy rushes into the room carrying Lila who is clutching Nancy tightly around the neck. "Casper, how are you?" she asks.

He turns his head away from me and looks up at the two of them and smiles but says nothing. He looks back at me, sighs, and starts to speak but stops before he says anything.

"I think he's coming around a little," Amy says.

"Dad, it is me Bill, do you know who I am?" I ask again.

He studies my face. "You look a little like my son Bill, but Bill is a much younger, handsomer man."

The room is quiet. I wonder if he is lost in some other dimension, as if his mind is not with us. Or maybe he is here, and my ghost is here, the one I have been trying to catch. Maybe Casper is trying to get back to somewhere else or trying to go home again, maybe back to Myers one last time.

For five minutes there is an eerie silence that lingers around Casper's words, until Nancy decides to insert warmth. "I think I may have had a stroke too," she is referring to me. "I remember Bill as a much younger, handsomer man, too."

Laughter restarts the stalled day as Casper slowly comes around in the next two hours. I head to practice; the nurses leave, and Hat goes home early. Nancy and Lila take care of Casper and keep me posted as I return to football.

The Friday practice that afternoon is less than the normal two hours with a scrimmage looming early the next morning. We are lucky for now, as the dreaded four o'clock Friday parade drill, which all cadets participate in for no less than one hour and thirty minutes in full parade dress in the heat, has not yet begun. Lucky for now, but not for Merchant Marine week; the night before the Kings Point game will be the first one. It will be accompanied by an early morning drill practice each day that week as well.

After practice ends and I am walking off the field, Casper pops back into my thoughts, so I rush home to get there by seven.

"He ate a bowl of Cheerios," Nancy says, "but he has been quiet. Lila has been taking care of him."

"I gave Gido a shot," she says, holding up an empty plastic syringe used for children's medicine.

Casper looks up, but his eyes stay riveted on Lila, who quietly attends to him, thinking she is medically helping him.

"I suppose, in some way, she is helping his mind or something," I say to Nancy off to the side of the room.

"She is helping his soul or spirit. That is part of being healthy and alive. It is not all about the mind and body," Nancy adds.

"I think his brain works better around Lila. I think he has a separate love for her. Almost like the rest of him has died and a shell or a piece of him has stayed behind," I say.

"Sometimes he is here and sometimes he is not," Nancy says.

"Maybe he is going back and forth like he says. Maybe sometimes he is in the next life, and maybe sometimes the next life is here with him. Maybe they have contacted him from the heavens."

"Are you trying to rationalize his thoughts or your own?" Nancy asks.

I do not answer her question and I go to bed thinking about Kings Point instead of the WPI scrimmage the next day.

I wake up a couple of hours later and notice Casper is awake. I lean over him.

Casper looks up at me and says, "The big track meet is tomorrow."

"No, Dad, we have a scrimmage. In two weeks, we have a big football game."

"No, Bill, tomorrow is the big track meet. I told you about it already. The big race. I told you about it."

"Yes, Dad, you did tell me about the race. A long time ago you told me about it."

Casper keeps his eyes open but says nothing else, content that I know what he means.

CHAPTER 15

"It is raining for your race."

A nervous Takla Moses peered into her son's room on a cloudy, gray Saturday in June in the tumultuous year of 1941. She watched her son Michael as he sat on the edge of the bed dressed in his navy-blue tank top with a bright yellow stripe and matching shorts. The name Ludlowville was in bold white letters running diagonally down the yellow stripe.

Takla would pretend not to listen to the radio or to hear the brief talks of Europe and the South Pacific at Abraham's store. Like many, she wanted to make herself believe all was safe in Myers. To many, the changing world was far away, but it weighed on Takla who worried about her sons.

George and Joseph, her oldest, seemed like grown men, but not her Puppy—her little boy who wouldn't talk. She gazed at his bushy hair, thick thighs and meaty calves, legs that held up a solid, round frame.

"I wish it were sunny," he said dreadfully, as he lifted his head and his amber eyes locked with his mother's.

"You will run your mile well and win," Takla intentionally lied with a mother's love as she stared into his eyes. She walked across the room, reached down and ran her fingers through his hair and bent to kiss his cheek.

Puppy looked up and forced a smile.

I have not beaten one single runner in any race, he thought. *I have finished last in every mile race I have ever run. And now, of all days,*

I must run this last race and I do not know why. I do not know how I ended up being a mile runner. I do not know any of the reasons why things happen. He had felt like this before, as if some things in life were being driven by a greater force. *It feels as if something unknown is pushing me from behind toward the path I am supposed to travel.*

Takla decided she would walk up American Hill and watch his last race. She had not watched him run much lately; seeing her baby boy lose was painful. She hated to see him struggle; to her he ran as if he were in pain.

"Will you stop and see Dawn at her house before you race?" Takla asked.

"Yes, Nemo will be there," he answered.

Puppy and his mother walked together down the dirt road which led to Abraham's store. The muggy grayness of an odd June day was spitting sporadic drops of rain on them. When they reached the store, Casper George was leaning against one of the wooden beams, which held up the cover of the small porch. Takla looked at Casper and thought, *I wish my Puppy were a few years younger like Casper.* Takla kissed her son goodbye and walked past Casper into the store.

"Puppy, you're going to win today," Casper said. "You'll run a good race today."

Puppy looked at him and forced a smile, then walked past the store and up American Hill on his way to stop at Dawn Worsell's house.

Puppy crossed Route 34B and onto Ludlowville Road. He walked past the baseball field and the tennis courts, glancing above the courts to where he could see a few people on the hill around the track.

At Dawn's house, Puppy Moses circled around to the back, left his track spikes on the back porch, and went in through the kitchen. He walked through the living room and into an enclave off to the side. Dawn Worsell lay still in a bed, gently breathing and casually opening and closing her eyes every few seconds as if to reassure herself where she was. Nemo was at her side, holding her boney, fragile hand with his strong, muscular fingers. Dawn was whiter than he had ever thought skin could be, ravaged by leukemia. *She looks like a ghost,* Puppy thought, deeply frightened and stunned by the sight. He had not seen her since she came back from the hospital a few days ago. He watched Nemo bring her hand up to his face and gently hold it against his cheek, damp with tears. Martha sat a few feet away, fighting back tears of her own. Martha looked up at Puppy and they both looked back to the bed. Dawn had been sick for months, in and out of the hospital, and her fate now seemed sealed.

Puppy Moses was uncertain what to do or say or how to act. He looked over at Martha, not with nervous butterflies in his stomach, but instead with sorrow for her brokenhearted brother. Instinctively, Puppy walked over and put his hand on Nemo's cheek. Nemo turned so that his cheekbone was in Puppy's hand, and his tears dripped into Puppy's palm. It was as if Nemo had moved his face so that his tears would have a place to linger a few moments before falling on the floor and vanishing forever.

Puppy bent and kissed the top of his friend's head then turned to leave. He looked straight ahead as he left but he could hear Martha sniffling and he felt her crying eyes follow him out.

Puppy left the house and walked back onto Ludlowville Road toward Route 34B and then stopped and looked up to the gloomy sky and thought of Dawn and Nemo and Martha. The rain was spitting harder now but he ignored it. *I could turn around and walk down Ludlowville Road into the valley of Ludlowville and cut across the field at the bottom of the hill and walk to the creek,* he thought. *I could watch the creek roll by the shale walls that slope down from the cemetery. I could forget about the world and watch the creek roll by.* The raindrops piled on top of his bushy hair.

No. That part of the creek looks sad when it is raining and the water turns milky brown. Then he thought, *Maybe that is what life is really like; you have to take the good with the bad. The same spot is so beautiful in the afternoon sunshine but so sad in the dark rain.* Puppy moved forward toward the tennis courts and up the hill to the cinder-top track. Before anyone could see him, he ducked into a patch of the surrounding woods.

No one knows I am here. No one will even care if I run this race. I could disappear and, as this day fades away forever, no one will ever know or remember this day. No one on this earth would even care. It will just be another of a million forgotten yesterdays.

Now the rain that he had ignored interrupted his thoughts with its persistence. *I wish it were sunny and I could see the blue sky or the bubbly white clouds.* Deep down, he knew there was no escape from the gray day. Puppy moved slowly from the solitude of the damp woods and out into the world he was hiding from. Although he knew he was alone, he felt he was being watched from above by all those who had passed into history. Deep down, he knew that maybe he could escape the world that surrounded him, but not all of eternity. It was as if those in the next world anxiously awaited his next move.

Puppy watched the track meet start from his vantage point in the woods. He was unaware that he had drifted a few, slow steps out into the open, as if someone or something had gently nudged him from the obscure safety of the woods. He noticed the mile run was about to start and, instinctively, he moved forward and jogged out of the woods and to the track. He sat next to the starting line and put his track cleats on. He could hear the black cinders crunching beneath his feet as he jogged back and forth behind the starting line until he felt ready. Before the start, he touched his toes and studied the white line of chalk in front of his feet. He could feel a few tiny spots of rain from the gray day sporadically touch the back of his neck. He shook his legs a few times to calm his nerves.

When he stood, he twisted his hips and studied the other six runners, three on each side of him. They were leaner with tightly defined muscles, but he stayed positive.

No state champs or four-minute milers, he thought with relief. *Just this one time, just let me beat one runner, please God. Just one runner this one last time.* He pleaded rather than prayed. It caught him off guard, as he never prayed for victory or success.

When he saw the starter raise his black pistol, he glimpsed his mother off to the side. She looked stoic and worried. *It has become a way of life for her.* Then he noticed Casper standing next to his mother, grimly looking on.

I have to get out of the gate quickly. He readied himself for the gunshot. He had no footspeed, and all the races he had started slow ended with last-place finishes.

The starter's gun rang into the ears of the sparse crowd. Puppy started out two steps behind the six others. Every few steps, he would feel a wet cinder kick up against his face, the humiliation of being in the rear. Around the turn they went, and down the long stretch of the first side.

Puppy was still with the pack at the 220-yard mark, halfway around the first turn of the four laps of the quarter-mile track. It felt good running and, physically, he knew he might match up with this group, which stayed in a tight pack. As they finished the first lap, one runner jumped out five yards in front of the rest. Puppy did not care; he was hunting the weakest of the herd, not the strongest. Another runner had joined the leader but the other four were still only a few yards from Puppy. He stayed with them until they hit the half-mile mark and started on lap number three. His thick arms grew heavy, like they were bound with chains. He could feel the blood burn as it raced from his heart and rushed through his arteries. He felt the air push painfully against his lungs. He swung his arms and sprinted just to keep pace with the four runners who were now ten yards ahead of him. The two leaders were now twenty yards ahead of the group. Puppy swallowed and thought he tasted blood. He swallowed again but tasted nothing. Then the face of Mr. Smith, his English teacher who had introduced him to the mile, flashed in his head. *Where is he now? He could help me. He could make me not finish last.* Mr. Smith's face reappeared in his head but now as a mighty pilot ready to take off and fly into the Battle of Britain and down the throat of the Luftwaffe. The image of Mr. Smith dressed like a pilot lingered. *How do you just disappear?* he wondered. *One second you are flying planes and the next you are gone, missing, never to be seen again.* He inhaled deeply and left Mr. Smith behind, buried deep somewhere in the English Channel.

Puppy knew this was the weakest group he had ever faced, and this was his chance. As they hit the turn to the start of the final lap, he noticed the two leaders had sprinted off with a third close to them, all three over 100 yards ahead. His lungs burned and his thick legs began to swell. Now the pack of three trailers started to stride away from him, too. As he struggled into the far last turn for the last 220 yards, panic set into pain. As he swung his head upward and to the spot where he had stepped out of the woods, he saw Nemo sitting against a tree, his hands buried in his face and his head buried in his lap. Martha was standing next to him with her arms folded and watching.

Puppy thought, *All of Myers knows that Dawn Worsell has leukemia, but no one has ever mentioned it by name. It is as if the name itself is alive, like the disease, and if you mentioned it by name, the evil leukemia would become angry and retaliate.*

He rounded the last turn and saw only two runners out of the corner of his eye. His heart kicked into full gear, and he chased the two. With one hundred yards left, one runner was only thirty yards ahead of him and striding well. The last runner was just twenty yards ahead and weakening. With fifty yards to go, he had closed the gap to fifteen yards. He felt the strange taste of blood creep up from his lungs, but he pushed on. Then he felt both calves tighten and a sharp pain knife itself below his left calf, as if a wild animal had bitten into his Achilles tendon. He pushed the leg pain away and kicked on in anguish. But his brain was relentless. *Even the handsome Gehrig is gone,* he thought. *How could he play so many games more than anyone, how can he be the strongest one moment and the weakest the next?* Fatigue set into his brain and tricked him. *Please God, tell me they did not bury the invincible Gehrig.* Seeing the finish line thirty yards away surged energy into his muscles as he charged forward with all his might.

With twenty yards to go, he had cut the lead to ten, but his head felt like it was going to explode. He had cut the lead to seven yards when he saw the other runner fall across the finish line. Puppy staggered past him with his best time ever, but ending his career consistently last. He bent with his hands on his knees and sucked as much air as humanly possible. Then he started coughing frantically and spitting out mouthfuls of thin blood and white phlegm laced with lactic acid onto the wet cinder track. The red blood pooled and, with its white streaks, looked like peppermint candy. Puppy stared into the blood and thought of Nemo and Dawn and of Mr. Smith and of Lou Gehrig. He closed his eyes so his mind could go blank, but instead the face of the puppy appeared, and the image caused his grief to bubble up from his throat and mix with the blood in his mouth. He sunk his upper teeth into his lower lip so that he would not cry. Then he lifted his head and moved about as if only the race itself was on his mind.

CHAPTER 16

As both teams warm up for the scrimmage, I cannot help but think that in just two weeks, the Coast Guard will line up against the Merchant Marine Academy. They will be ready and well-prepared. I wonder if their coach, Mike Toop, is like me and is chasing his own ghost. Kings Point will have every player ready to go and lined up correctly in every situation. They will not make mistakes. I suppose every football coach is no different than me; they love their children, their families, their players, and they want something good to come out of their time on earth. Coaching football does not allow you to obsess over your opponents. It's about your performance, not the other teams'. Win enough, you keep your job; you lose too much, you don't. In NCAA Division III football, losing your job means losing your paycheck, not like Division I football where they pay you millions of dollars years after they fire you. Mike Toop has earned the most deference I am allowed to give him as an opposing coach in a massive rivalry—my respect.

The goal of the scrimmage is to rehearse and stay healthy. We start the scrimmage at ten in the magnificent sunshine with one-on-ones, each offensive line going against each other's defensive line, simulating pass protection and a pass rush. Our offensive line holds its own against their beefy defensive line, except for our center; he is just too small and gets shoved around. As the drill wears on, the center starts to move his feet more and adjust his balance. Our second team linemen lack experience but know enough to use toughness to match size. Even so, WPI eats them alive.

After that, it's a simulated game with a combination of ten-play drives using first and second team players against each other. All in all, we move the ball and hold our own on defense, but we limit the starters to twenty plays. We escape with no injuries.

I walk off the field sometime after one, thinking it is time to get ready for our opener against St. Lawrence.

As I pull into the driveway, I can see Hat and Casper sitting outside in the shade of the house holding hands. They watch Lila as she lounges in her tiny two-foot pool. Nancy has her feet submerged in the water as she watches Lila float back and forth on her belly. Casper's methodical stare signals contented happiness. His frame looks even hollower outside the closed dimensions of our living room. The world is alive, and it magnifies his decaying body while he still is breathing. Lila splashes the water against the plastic walls filled with rubber toys. There is almost no space for my feet as I step in. Lila looks at me and smiles. I am in another world—her world— and wonder if it is a world I forget about too often. The unit air conditioner hanging out of the living room window grinds an ugly tune in the calmness of the late afternoon. The routine moves forward as the hours pass, with either Lila playing or reading with Gido.

"He is like another stuffed toy to her," Nancy says. "He does what she wants. Sometimes he can barely hear her requests and he only makes sounds or says a few words back to her. And, like the toys, all he returns is love and companionship."

"Gido, you sit next to the horse and the monkey," Lila says as she lines them up next to him on the couch. "All right now, class, pay attention as I read you a story." The book pages turn, and Lila describes the pictures as if she were a teacher in a classroom. Her tiny fingers turn each page as she looks up at him, watching his face stare down at the page. She waits a few moments as he scans the page and then glances at her. Their eyes connect and her lips flash a soft, barely visible smile that Casper may or may not be able to see but somehow seems to understand.

Casper sits entranced and content. His body is drained, yet he is happy. He is living now and not dying.

"I want to watch Willie Wonka," Lila says after her game of book reading to her silent participants ends.

"No Willie Wonka, Lila," Nancy says. "It makes you cry, Lila." My sweet four-year-old looks across the room at me.

I know the original movie, with Gene Wilder, is somehow too old for her, yet she loves it and somehow is crying like an adult at the end. Maybe it is the grandparents all living together, surviving in a one-room apartment, that rattles her during the movie, reminding her of Casper. It is at the end of the movie, when the little boy is given the chocolate factory and he is riding around in the spaceship, that makes her sad. I wonder deep down if she hopes the world around her ends up that way also.

Lila keeps asking for the movie. I know her repeated requests will be granted.

The VHS tape is inserted, and Lila once again submerges into a time warp with three adults.

I get Casper up for a last trip to the bathroom and his meds.

We turn the movie off and slowly lower his tired body.

"I do not want you to get old, Daddy." Lila glumly looks at Casper and does not see him as one of the stuffed animals now. "He cannot stand up anymore," she says, sensing he is no longer a playmate. She rubs his arm, and he reaches out and touches her cheek. His eyes are watery.

At fifty-six, I appear youthful next to Casper. "I will not get old. I promise I will be young forever."

"Why did Anna have to go and I stayed?" Casper asks. His mind is once again bucking the sundown syndrome. "And those two boys, Nemo and Puppy, where are they now? Why did everyone go and I still stayed? Why am I the last one left from Myers?"

Nancy picks Lila up as the conversation deepens and holds her tight as I try to get Casper to fall asleep.

"I don't know." I tuck his blanket up under his chin so the air conditioner does not chill him.

"When do we know what time or why?"

"I don't know why," I mechanically answer. I stop and think for a moment. "You are here to be with Lila. When you go to heaven, everyone will want to know about her."

"When will I go? I don't want to go," he says with his eyes shut.

I say nothing.

"Did I do everything right?" he asks.

"Yes, Dad," I answer. Now I feel his words snaking their way into my brain.

"Did I love everyone like Anna did?" Casper asks.

Again, I say nothing but now I wonder about my own days. If I knew when my last day would be marked, would I waste the moment or would I ignore the calendar and live like I live now?

Nancy now leans toward Casper, still holding Lila tightly. "Casper, Anna used to repeat the Gospel of John. As God loved us, we too should love one another. As long as we love one another, God remains in us."

"Did I do that, Nancy?" Casper asks.

"Better than me," I answer before she has a chance to say anything. Casper never swayed from religion. *You treated everyone with kindness,* I think. Guilt cuts into my own consciousness. I have blended myself into the importance of my own days.

"'Come upstairs with me' were the greatest words ever spoken." Casper's words are now slightly joyful as if he is realizing he is a good human being.

I think for sure he is referring to the end of his gambling, when I brought him out of the basement to admit to Anna that he needed to borrow money from me to pay off a bookie. Then, something inside of me makes me think he might have new meaning for "come upstairs with me." It bothers me that this thought has popped into my head like a dormant message waiting to be opened.

"Bill!" Casper's frail call takes me away from my thoughts and brings me back to him.

"What, Dad?"

"Do you remember the first time I told you and Dan about Puppy Moses? Do you remember what I said?"

"Yes, Dad, I remember. But I do not want to talk about it."

"That's okay, Bill. I just wondered if you remembered." Casper closes his eyes. "It was about kissing a girl."

In the middle of a steaming day in late July of 1942, Puppy Moses stood in the middle of the bridge in Myers and looked downstream beyond the trestle and out into the lake. The creek was low but the wide, deep pool just above the railroad trestle was always swimmable. A tall, steep rock embankment had been built on top of the rocks after the flood. It turned all the water back to the stream's path before overflowing. The new, steep embankment created a slower, deeper pool just above the trestle. Today, the swimming hole was empty.

Puppy watched Casper, carrying a fishing pole, walk across the railroad trestle, stop in the middle, and waved Puppy to come with him. Puppy signaled for Casper to keep going. He watched Casper cross the tracks, walk down to the bank of the creek and follow the creek bed toward the lake.

Maybe she will pass today. She must pass today, Puppy thought as he stood waiting in heat of the summer sun. *I am running out of time.*

When the mail truck stopped at Abraham's store and dropped off the mail for the town, Puppy would sometimes wait to see if Martha would be by to fetch her family's postage. Sometimes it would be her sister Mary during the day or her father after work at the salt plant. Puppy shifted the strategy of his cat-and-mouse tactics to the afternoon, hoping he would at least see Martha walk by. He had not thought about what he would say, or if he would say anything at all. He knew only that, *I am running out of time.*

The sun, and his nerves, attacked, drawing sweat that soaked his bushy hair and moistened his forehead. He wondered if he was destined to a life of toil in the salt plant, or if he was headed out into a new universe. And what would become of he and Martha, if anything.

His heart jumped when Martha appeared out of the path. Just before she stepped on to the edge of the bridge, she stopped and waved to him. Puppy waved back but said nothing as he watched her carefully walk down the embankment to the flat, rocky side of the creek. Martha moved a few feet downstream to a spot where quicker water ended just beneath the bridge, and the water stilled into the softest of swimming holes as it rolled to the trestle. Martha smiled at Puppy, again, and kicked off her sandals and peeled off her blouse, revealing a one-piece red bathing suit. She rotated her neck and shook her shoulder-length black hair in a circle to loosen it, and gathered it in her right hand and tucked it into a white bathing cap. She slowly put her left foot, with its red, painted toes, into the water. She looked back up at him and waded a few steps out into the shallow water.

"Whew," Puppy Moses took a deep breath as he watched Martha, clad in a swimsuit, gingerly move out into the creek until the water was at her knees.

Puppy's eyes stayed glued as she waded deeper, and gently slid her body into the creek. Martha turned in the water, glanced back at Puppy on the bridge and slowly floated on her back, like a carefree swan, to the trestle.

"It's perfect and it is better than our heat box on the hill," she shouted up to him, referring to the swelling summer heat trapped in all the shoebox houses in Myers.

He was stunned and, as usual, too shy to engage in conversation. He could feel his insides swell with emotion as his sweaty forearms broke out with winter goose pimples in the July heat.

Puppy silently studied her as if she were a ballerina on a stage. He watched as she would slowly raise a leg out of the water as she floated downstream. He knew she was no longer a little girl, but now a woman.

"You look like an angel on a cloud floating through a beautiful blue sky," he blurted, spontaneously, instantly wishing he could retract the words. *Where did that come from?*

When Martha reached the trestle, she turned and slowly waded upstream against the weak current. When she reached the pool, she rose out of the water and waded thigh-deep into the shore. She removed the bathing cap and shook her hair free until she could feel it run across the back of her neck and the tie of the suit.

Puppy watched the water run onto her legs and could see her cleavage against her wet suit. She stopped and started to towel herself off.

Puppy felt pure joy, the fright vanquished, the emptiness dissipated. *This blue sky must stretch forever,* he thought as he tilted his head, stood on his toes, and stretched his calves as if his legs would lift him off the bridge like a rocket. He then focused on Martha as she finished toweling off.

After she put her clothes on over her wet suit, Puppy watched her walk up the embankment, mesmerized. When she reached the end of the bridge, she smiled at him. "Thank you, that was a very nice thing to say."

She looked at him for a moment, again seized in silence. *Please say something. I should say something, but what?* He could feel his tongue being locked shut within his clenched teeth.

"Happy birthday!" he shouted.

Martha jerked her head back sharply and smiled. "How did you know it was my birthday?"

"July 26 is your birthday, right?"

"Yes," Martha answered. "But how did you know? My brother did not even remember."

"Because it is my birthday, too," he answered softly.

Puppy felt like he was on a cloud.

"Your birthday, too?" she asked, almost giddy.

"Yes," he said. He let his eyes pore into hers as if he knew he could talk no more and now had to let his eyes speak for his heart.

Martha looked back into his eyes and froze for a moment, trying to feel what was in his eyes.

"You were born on July 26, 1922, and I was born on July 26, one year later in 1923," Puppy said.

"I never knew that," Martha said. "You knew my birthday and I did not know yours. How long did you know we had the same birthday?"

"A long time," he admitted.

"And you never said anything until now?"

"I never had the chance until today," he said. "It is one of those things that must be told at a specific moment, or it does not mean as much. If I told you about it any other day, it would not have had the meaning that it did today."

"Next year, I will be the one who says it is both our birthdays," Martha said, waiting for him to say something. But all she could see was his gentle smile. As she studied him, she could tell his eyes looked watery. "And the following year, you will remind me, and we will take turns every year."

She turned and walked toward the path at the bottom of Syrian Hill and disappeared into the path. Every few yards, he would catch a glimpse of her between a clearing in the bushes of trees. When she reached the top of the path at the edge of the grass between the Isaac house and the church, she turned and looked down at him for a moment and waved. Then she turned and disappeared toward the middle of Syrian Hill.

Puppy stood on the bridge, alive as he had ever felt. He kept gazing at the top of the path on Syrian Hill. Her wave eased the pain he felt toward himself for years of failing to speak to her more.

Puppy remained on the bridge for over an hour more watching

the water flow and, in his mind, repeatedly watching Martha. Every moment, every glance, every movement, and every word were now trapped forever inside of him, pounding at his heart. *Maybe,* he thought, *someday I will kiss her.* He closed his eyes, parted his lips, and slightly ran the tip of his tongue across the inside of his lips, trapping the moisture on the inside of his mouth, as if he had trapped a kiss from Martha.

One week later, just before the hot August sun had risen to scorch Myers, Nemo stood in the dew on top of the path near the Isaac house and the church. He could see the thickness of the trees covering all of Myers like a blanket, as if to hide it away from the rest of the world. He was happy and excited. He looked down to the empty space of the bridge and saw one lone figure. He scurried down through the thick brush, a path he knew by heart.

"Puppy," he said as he approached his friend on the bridge. "It's just after five. What gets you up this early?"

They stopped and turned when they both heard the door of Casper's house open. They waited for a moment in silence as he walked on to the bridge.

"It is so hot, I can't breathe," Casper said as he stood on the opposite side of the bridge, hoping the pathway of the creek would allow a breeze to travel through.

"I couldn't sleep either," Puppy said. "This muggy heat is tough. The air is even thicker in our house than outside. What about you?"

"I'm taking Dawn for a swim in the lake when she gets up, but I could not sleep."

Dawn's leukemia had abated, miraculously, after several attempts at experimental blood transfusions, and she was feeling better with each passing day.

"You should wake her up and take her to the Ludlowville Falls,"

Puppy said.

"Now? Why?" Nemo asked.

"Now is perfect," Puppy said. "The sun is not up, and even when it starts to rise, the light from the sun will help you see, but the heat of the rays will not get into the valley of Ludlowville until it rises higher. It is like going back in time."

"Back in time?" Nemo asked.

"Yes," Puppy said. "It will seem like spring under the cool water before the muggy air and the heat of the sun change the day back to August."

"Yes! Yes!" Nemo repeated. "I'm going to wake her up." He turned and bolted, sprinting down the road past Myers Grocery, leaving Casper and Puppy behind in the heat of the valley. He continued his excited pace up American Hill, across Route 34B, past the school and down Ludlowville Road to Dawn's house.

As Nemo approached Dawn's house, he could see her sitting on a large, black, wooden rocking chair. She tilted it so slightly back and forth along the wood porch that not a sound could be heard as its legs moved. She curled her petite, pale body into a ball and she glowed against the oversized rocking chair. She lit up and smiled when she saw him.

"What are you doing up? I thought I was going to have to throw a few rocks at your window," Nemo said as he stood at the bottom of the porch steps.

"I was so happy. I just woke up. I was so happy I feel so good," she said as she uncurled her legs and gently placed her soft white feet on the porch and slid off the rocking chair. "I am alive again."

"I feel the same. I feel so wonderful now that you are all better," he said. He watched her tiptoe across the porch and gently walk down the steps until she stood right in front of him.

"Can I kiss you?" she asked.

"You can kiss me anytime you want," he said.

Dawn stretched her legs up on her small toes, tilted her head back and moved her chin forward as Nemo moved his face to hers. When their lips met, each parted slightly, and the tips of their tongues touched and washed against each other. Nemo wrapped his arms around her and she kissed his neck and rested her head against it.

"I know I am in love with you," Nemo said to her.

"I can think of nothing I could dream of that would make me feel better. I have been in love with you for years," she replied.

Dawn flipped on her sandals, and they walked hand in hand down Ludlowville Road, past the green pasture stretching to the water, where in the springtime the long, still pools rolled past the gray shale that crept from the far bank up to the Syrian cemetery; but now only a trickle of water flowed through the dry creek beds.

As they walked, he thought, *I am in love with the most wonderful girl in the world and she is in love with me. I am the luckiest man on the face of the earth.*

When they reached the waterfall, they kicked off their shoes and Nemo took off his shirt. Dawn grabbed him by his muscular bicep, and he led her to where the water gently sprayed down on one side of the falls.

Puppy was right, Nemo thought. *The water is cool. It is like the spring, not the heat of summer.*

They let the cool wetness refresh them and kissed again, this time with wet lips and wet faces.

"Maybe we could stay here forever, just like this," Dawn said as she held him tightly. "We could let the water keep moving past us, but we would never have to move."

I wonder if Puppy can tell me a way to stop time, Nemo thought.

CHAPTER 17

Before I walk into the football offices Sunday morning to meet with the coaches and start preparation for our opening game, I stop at the entrance to Cadet Memorial Field. My eyes fix on the engraved names at the small monument just to the left of the entrance. The monument is shaped like a headstone. Cadet Memorial Field is named after cadets who passed away before graduating from the Academy. Some died in the line of duty for the Coast Guard, some in the natural path of life that we all travel, all before they completed their destiny here on earth. *Life is short, even for Casper,* I think, *but so much shorter for so many others.* I gaze out at the beauty of a stadium where I play like a child forever pleasantly trapped by a game. What a beautiful playground to spend my never-ending youth—the stone wall on top, the giant oak trees, the wide river below. This, the most beautiful football field in the world, is a giant memorial.

In the office, we grade the scrimmage and finalize our plans for the opening game against St. Lawrence, a team that was 8-2 last season and has all its players returning. They have one of their best teams in the last twenty-five years and are as good as any NCAA playoff team and our first test before facing our rival.

The practices go smoothly, and the players stay focused on St. Lawrence, yet by Thursday they look Academy tired, and during practice they drop more balls and jump offsides more than any practice yet.

The Friday practice turns out better. The team is loose and excited about finally playing a game, even though the Academy has already emptied for the weekend.

I walk into a quiet living room early evening and watch Casper's tired eyes drift open and shut.

"He was excited when I first got home. He knows Dan and Regina are coming for the game," Nancy says, referring to his brother George's daughter, who grew up at the Blue Sky along with her brother Gary, and is like a daughter to Casper.

"He will have fun at the game tomorrow," I say.

Nancy has been fretting about getting Casper to any games, and she looks at me with a smirk. "He is a very weak man, and it will be hot. He is susceptible to anything."

"What else does he have?" I counter.

"He has Lila," she answers.

Lila climbs up on the couch next to him clutching a white teddy bear in her arms as if it were her baby.

Casper opens his eyes to look at her, then turns to me. "Is the door locked?"

"Yes, why?"

"If the door is locked, how will Anna get in when she gets home? She will be locked outside all night." His weak voice cracks with worry.

He buries his face in his hands and starts to cry softly. "Please forgive me," he says realizing Anna cannot walk in the door.

He lays on the couch with his eyes shut and I bring Lila a small piece of vanilla cake with vanilla frosting.

"Get Gido a piece of cake," Lila says to me.

"No, he's tired and it is late for him to eat."

"I will give him some of mine." She walks to the two of us with a handful of cake.

"He's been coughing at night lately, so I'm going to stop some of the late-night treats," Nancy says.

Lila keeps the cake in her hand and bends to kiss her grandfather on his gaunt, wrinkled face. Casper opens his eyes to the kiss as if he has been awakened from a deadly coma. He smiles at her and asks,

"Will I be locked out?"

"What do you mean locked out?" I ask. "No. No one is locked out."

"Locked out of the house?" Lila asks.

"I think he means heaven," I say, as Nancy looks down at Lila and smiles.

"No one is locked out of heaven, Gido," Lila answers.

Maybe we lock ourselves out, I think. *Or maybe we lock heaven out of ourselves.*

Casper blankly stares at Lila's face. His eyes droop as if to shut but his subconscious mind is working hard. Lila bends her head forward and the frosting touches her lips, smiling as the sugar hits her taste buds.

"Maybe she can get me into heaven if I am locked out," Casper says.

"Casper, I think you mean she came from heaven," Nancy adds calmly as she tries to save Casper before his confusion goes off the deep end.

"She came from heaven," he says with his eyes shut. "Like all of us, she was sent from heaven."

My mind drifts as I lay his head back. Lila is entranced with her cake with vanilla frosting. *Maybe she really was sent from heaven,* I think, but dare not say it aloud. *Maybe we all are. Maybe I was once on a path to save the world and I let it all go astray. Maybe I could save just a little of me or the outside world. Not all the outside world or all of me or all of every day but just a little piece of something.*

I watch a little four-year-old with orange hair dive deeper into her cake and wonder if maybe it is every child who is here to help the world, not just her. The thought pops into my head that Casper is now sleeping or dying or both, but either way he is somehow on his way to heaven.

"Bill," Casper says.

"What, Dad?"

"Will I get to ice skate in heaven?"

"From cloud to cloud, Dad. You will get to skate across the sky."
"Are my ice skates up there already?"
"Yes, Dad, they are already there."
"I love you, Bill."
"I love you too, Dad."

On a bitterly cold day in the middle of December in 1942, Nemo Saleem and Puppy Moses stood on the bridge in Myers and watched the snowflakes filter from a sky ladened with winter clouds. At first, the flakes seemed small and floated sporadically, but as the minutes passed, they descended faster and larger. As the intensity of the snowflakes fell, they formed a thick white fog over the frozen creek. Together in silence, Puppy and Nemo listened to a solitary skater glide up from underneath the railroad trestle on the ice and through the foggy snow. The ice was as white as the clouds in the sky and the ice grew silent when the skater stopped. Puppy and Nemo stared silently off the bridge and into the white fog.

The silence was cut by the sharp scrapes of the black skates as they dug into the ice and turned with the skater's churning legs. Fifteen-year-old Casper Abraham George moved with the ease of a ballet dancer, his arms at his sides and legs floating as if he was walking on water. His jet-black hair was covered with a crown of snowflakes atop the most beautiful face in all of Myers. Casper started to swing his arms as he took each leg and crossed it in front of the other, sometimes with lightning quickness and sometimes with long, gliding strides. His body shifted wildly from side to side, but his balance was never in question. As he moved upstream, closer to the bridge, he abruptly spun halfway around and started skating backward. He leaned his shoulders forward and let his hips navigate his body. After a few strides backward, he looped slightly, and looped again, carving the figure eight into the ice. He retraced the backward eight once more, and a third time. Then Casper turned, flashed his chest forward, and with his black skates firing like rockets, he instantly disappeared underneath the bridge up the frozen creek. Nemo and Puppy kept staring straight downstream together, neither saying a word, but both waiting in silence for another twenty seconds for the skater to reappear. Suddenly, he shot out from underneath the bridge like a bullet speeding downstream. Halfway between the bridge and the trestle, where the deep swimming hole started and the ice grew wider, he leaped into the air, his arms and legs wrapped tightly together as he spun his body around. He landed on one leg and bent his chest forward and extended his arms to his sides, like the wings of a graceful swan, and glided underneath the railroad trestle toward the lake and away from Nemo and Puppy.

They could barely see his silhouette as he skated around in circles on the thick ice below the trestle. They stood as motionless as the frozen solitude of Myers in winter. The white smoke from the rows of chimneys of the Myers houses heated only by coal blended into the white skyline. Deep down, they both knew the world was different now and the solitude of Myers was not as far away from Pearl Harbor or Europe as it had once been, certainly not for boys who were about to turn nineteen.

"Will you still try to go to Cornell?" Puppy asked Nemo.

"Yes. Cornell or maybe Syracuse. That's a good school, also," Nemo answered. "If I don't go right away, I suppose I'll wait and work at the salt plant." It had been hard for him with his mother gone and with all the pain of watching Dawn fade in and out of good health. Sometimes, not often but sometimes, he felt as if he was starting to breathe again.

"The salt plant is okay for me, but not you," Puppy said.

"It's not that bad, but I cannot cure the leukemias of the world from there," Nemo's voice had a new determination in it. "It will take me years, but I'll get there."

"I believe you. I believe you will become a doctor someday," Puppy said.

"Yes. A doctor. A doctor who cures leukemia. I thought for a while about being a researcher who studies in a laboratory, but no, it must be medical school," Nemo said.

"Or maybe Lou Gehrig's disease," Puppy added.

"Yes. All the ugly leukemias," Nemo said.

"Where do you think you might go to medical school?" Puppy asked.

"I don't know. Cornell Medical School, maybe after college," Nemo answered.

"Yes. The movement of time will take you there," Puppy said as he watched his white breath in the cold air carry his words.

"Yes. I think about time," Nemo wondered aloud. "Some days it seems like we have a lot of it and some days it seems like we don't."

"Yes, Nemo, I know what you mean. I think time moves like the creek below us."

"What do you mean moves like the creek below us?" Nemo asked him.

"Time moves like the frozen creek. The water under the ice is moving but we do not see it. Every day we just see the ice and think that time is not moving. But time is moving like the water that is running below the ice. That water below the ice is gone forever."

"Puppy," Nemo asked cautiously, "do you think they have time in heaven?"

"I do not know. No one has ever been there and back to tell us."

"What do you mean?" Nemo asked.

"All the Syrians in Myers pray and talk about heaven, but it is the one place no one on earth has ever been," Puppy answered. "Even the smartest person on the planet cannot tell you if you are right or wrong. No one has been there and back."

"I think about my mother. Will she be the same age she was when she died?"

They stopped for a moment when they heard the door to Abraham and Helanie George's house open. Nemo and Puppy turned their heads to the porch and watched Marion George walk out to the street and stop and look at them.

"Do you think his mother is in heaven and is still young in heaven waiting for her baby?" Nemo asked. "Do you think time stopped for her?"

"I do not know," Puppy answered. "I just know that time is moving for all of us here, time is moving like that frozen creek."

"Where's Monk?" Marion shouted to them, referring to Casper.

They both pointed downward from the bridge to the ice-covered creek.

"Tell him the *good cat* went to the store to get some candy," Marion said.

Marion walked in the opposite direction toward the store, and they turned their stoic faces back to the frozen creek. Then, through the snowflakes, they turned away from the creek and looked deep into each other's eyes, said nothing, and gently smiled goodbye to each other. Nemo parted up to Syrian Hill, and Puppy toward Myers Grocery and his house.

Casper ceased his ice dancing downstream, well below the trestle, and with an explosion, took off upstream. His head was down and his legs in unison like a locomotive without tracks. He picked up speed just above the trestle in the wide pool until he glanced up at the empty bridge. He stopped, slowly gliding in the open space just below the bridge, then he bent forward and put his hands on his knees and watched the white breaths that his lungs were churning out quickly disappear into the solitude of Myers. Casper watched a drop of perspiration fall from his forehead and land on the ice. Next, he faced upward and felt the snowflakes wash his face like cool water. The snow was still falling fast, nearly blinding Casper as he stared upward at the empty bridge.

CHAPTER 18

I lean over the concrete on the top of the stadium at eight Saturday morning and look out onto the Thames River. The dark water reminds me of my first game. *It's strange, the constant motion of the football office is about strategy, game plans, film, players' meetings, coaches' meetings. Practice is the same way. Football locks your mind.* I push my thoughts aside until today's game drifts away for a few seconds.

As I stand with the emptiness of the field, alone, I drift to another day. I am back in 1999 on a Friday night at nine before my first home game, and the third game of the season. I am standing on the drawbridge in Mystic, Connecticut, a few miles from the Academy, staring into the blackness of the night water. I can only see hopelessness, not the reflection of any lights from the nearby buildings.

Chuck Mills, the former athletic director, had offered me the job the previous April. Ray Cieplik took over as athletic director three months later, the same time Ray LaForte and CC Grant arrived to fill two vacant faculty coaching positions. Together, we had to build a program that now had four different head coaches in four years, me being the fourth. Our numbers were down, and we spent the August PFE recruiting every cadet who looked like an athlete. We only had two quarterbacks, and one was a freshman. Our starting nose guard was a diver on the swim team.

In 1999, we lost our first two games, one to the only opponent the 1998 team had defeated. In the second game, Rensselaer Polytechnic Institute, RPI, was running the clock out in the middle of the second quarter so as not to embarrass the Coast Guard Academy, or maybe to make sure we came back out of the locker room after halftime.

That night before the 1999 home opener, I worried. *Tomorrow, we play perennial national powerhouse Springfield College, a constant NCAA playoff team, on Parents Weekend.*

Springfield's triple-option offensive attack leads the nation in every rushing category, and we are last in every defensive statistic in the nation. We have only made a handful of first downs with our inexperienced line, I thought. *How are we going to make it through this disaster?*

"Coach!" A hand slapped me around the shoulder and an arm wrapped itself across my back, pushing my ribs into the metal railing of the bridge.

I turned and, inches from my face, a giant smile shouted, "We're gonna win tomorrow, Coach." It was Brian Smicklas, a first-class running back from Ohio. He was not flashy and did nothing particularly special on the field. But he was tough and could take a beating.

It was Brian's smile that I always seemed to notice. It was wide, bright, and lively. His smile jumped at you as if it were leaving his face to join yours, to spread joy or just make you feel a little better even for a moment. *Maybe that is what a smile is supposed to do,* I thought, *leave your own face and join a smile on another face. Yes, that is what a smile is supposed to do, but I am not a smiler.*

I looked deep into Brian's face. *Springfield will knock that smile off,* I thought. *Maybe these Coast Guard people believe too much in themselves for their own good.*

The next day in front of 4,000 people, we handed Springfield College their most embarrassing loss in school history. We threw the ball, we caught the ball, and we ran the ball. The diver on the swim team, and rest of the skinny defensive guys shut down the number one Division III running attack in the nation. The defense stayed completely disciplined, not missing a single option responsibility.

The only game we won in 1999 was against the best team on our schedule. That was the only game we won on the scoreboard, anyway. We never quit, we never stopped. When people went down, others stepped up. The 1999 team taught me to smile now and again, how to be a football coach, and, most importantly, they taught me about the resilience and pride of the United States Coast Guard.

The team buses from St. Lawrence filter down through a near-empty Academy. Unlike Parents Weekend, homecoming, or the Merchant Marine game, only the football team remains, left behind as the last line of defense against an overwhelming enemy.

Coast Guard holds its own and plays extremely well until about midway through the third quarter. We trail 21-14, driving deep into St. Lawrence territory with a chance to tie it when an interception stops us cold, shifting the momentum and flipping the game upside down.

I look out into the Thames for an instant and then subconsciously glance up to the handicapped section. I can see Casper sitting in his wheelchair basking in the sun. The final score is 45-14, a rout by a team that looks playoff strong. Their size has worn us down and we have melted in the heat.

I return home after the game at seven and the house is eerily quiet. By the time I reach the living room, I can tell why. Casper is sound asleep on the couch. His face is bright red with sunburn.

"He is out of it," my brother Dan, the doctor, says. "I got to the game late and brought him home early. Just a couple of hours in that sun and his body reacted quickly."

"Is this it?" I ask. I had not thought about the fact that he was in this house so much that the outside world is so much different, and I left him vulnerable to the elements. I wonder if my neglect has killed him.

"I do not know, no one ever knows. He bounced back a bunch of times," Dan answers. "I think he is just wiped out."

"Do we call hospice?" I ask.

"Maybe just to explain the situation. He ate a few bites at lunch and had plenty of water, but that sun beat down on him and Hat through the whole first half, and with no sunscreen," Dan adds.

"They are coming Tuesday to recertify him. He has been on for over a year, and he is thriving as they always tell me. His two nurses, Amy and Jessica, always do all they can to get him recertified. They know we will never make it through the season without them."

"Maybe it will be a blessing that this happened," Dan says.

"Not if it ends up killing him," Nancy says. "You spend so much time thinking that he needs to be in the stands for the Merchant Marine game, you forget how fragile he really is." She had told us not to bring him in the heat.

I catch Lila in the corner of the room sitting quietly and playing with a few cars. "Lila," I call.

Lila does not look up. She just keeps rolling the cars back and forth in her hand. I walk over and pick her up and she rests her head on my shoulder. I kiss her cheek. I can feel the cars, still in her hands, against my back.

"She is ignoring or is blacking out the situation, but she knows he is not well." Nancy takes her from me and they start to leave the room.

"Gido's face is red like Santa Claus," Lila says.

Nancy stops and we both look at Lila as she is almost crying. "Only Santa Claus should have a face that red," she whispers sadly as she puts her head on Nancy's shoulder.

We call hospice and end up letting Casper sleep. Lila sits on the floor beneath him with a stuffed bear. She keeps playing with it quietly and glancing back up at him. She never says a word but seems to be looking to see if he will wake up and say something to her.

After a while, she looks at me and says, "Gido tells you stories about Christmas Eve like you tell me."

"Yes." I'm thinking she must remember Casper telling me a story about Christmas Eve a few days ago.

Nancy finally carries her to bed.

I keep him on the couch and sleep on the other couch. In the middle of the night, Nancy tiptoes into the living room. "How is he?"

"He is breathing. Sometimes I think he is not, but he is okay," I say.

"I know you're worried," she says.

I wonder why I pray now and not always. I wonder why I worry at times, and other times I go about my merry way. *I guess I am.*

"You are like that reading by Job," Nancy says.

"What reading, a Bible reading?" I ask.

"Yes, we are all like that until something hits us hard. We just plow through each day, working to get to the shade at the end of the day, with no thought but of wages. When we can't sleep, we sit up and wait for the day to come, but when the day is here, we cannot wait for it to end. We are like Casper, days are passing and vanishing, too. Life is but a breath." Nancy bends to kiss Casper and walks back upstairs.

I sit up and watch Casper breathe slowly as he sleeps. Every couple of minutes, I lean over him and wait to hear a faint wisp of air either going in or out of his listless body. I start to see myself in his face and my worry about him compounds as I start to wonder about my own vanishing days, as well.

Then I think about the Christmas Eve story Lila was talking about.

On Christmas Eve in 1942, Puppy Moses stood alone on the bridge in the quiet darkness of Myers. The still air was chilly but not bitterly cold. *Nothing is moving,* he thought, which struck him as odd. He reached into the pants pocket of his gray flannel suit; like all of the immigrants, he wore his only suit on occasions like Christmas. His fingers fumbled and found a thin, gold chain, long enough to put around a woman's wrist. He felt along the chain until he reached one gold piece about the size of a dime. He pushed it deeper into his pocket and nervously rubbed his two hands together. He had not worn gloves. He looked up to the top of the path on Syrian Hill, preparing himself to get to the church for the Christmas Eve services. There were only a few inches of snow on the ground, just enough to make it seem like Christmas, but a little too much to walk the path and ruin his only pair of good shoes. He looked up to the sky and the millions of stars then heard what he thought was a quick, sharp whimper beneath him. He looked down to where the fast water had frozen as it ran over the jagged rocks but saw nothing. After studying the silence for a few moments, he raised his head and gazed downstream to where the creek grew wider underneath the railroad trestle. The slow water near the trestle was covered with a smooth blanket of ice. Beneath where he stood on the bridge, he heard the sharp whimper again, and a moment later he heard it a third time. *It must be the ice cracking or maybe the ice starting to come alive.* He waited until he heard the ice again and thought, *the ice sounds like it is alive, it sounds like it is crying.*

Puppy knew he was already late for the Christmas Eve service. When his family had walked over the bridge on their way to church twenty minutes earlier, he stopped on the bridge and told them, "You go ahead. I will catch up."

"No, you come with us. You will be late," his father, Daniel insisted.

"No, let him stay," Takla said to her husband. "He is not like the rest of Myers." She thought of her other two sons, Joseph and George, who were already preparing for war, and the fear it caused made her move quicker across the bridge and toward the church. "He is a deep thinker," she said as they walked. "You and I and all of Myers only need to survive through each day. I am not sure that is enough for him."

"But he will be late," Daniel protested.

"Let him be alone and think," Takla said. "Church may not wait for him, but something tells me the world is waiting for him."

"Waiting for him? How?" Daniel asked his wife.

"I do not know. I just know." Takla took her husband's hand and led him away from Puppy and toward Syrian Hill.

Daniel shrugged and followed his wife's lead.

By the time Puppy tiptoed into the church, Christmas Eve Mass was almost half over. He quietly slid to the right where the men sat and stood with many others who did not have seats. His eyes immediately scanned the church, and he instantly recognized the back of Martha's head. He reached into his pocket and his fingers touched the gold chain. *I have got to find a time to give it to her,* he thought. *It has to be tonight. It has to be a friendly Christmas gift to Nemo's sister. I can give it to her that way.*

Puppy's father had given a gold bracelet to Takla, with eight gold pieces the size of a dime on it, that he brought from Syria. It was her only piece of jewelry besides a thin, gold wedding band. "My daughters can have it when I die," she told everyone, but she took one of the gold pieces off ahead of time and gave it to Puppy. "I want you to have this," was all she said.

When the Mass ended, he waited in the back of the church, and when Martha walked by she smiled at him. "Merry Christmas," she said.

"Merry Christmas," he smiled back and stared into her eyes. He pulled his hand out of his pocket, but the crowd in the tiny church closed in on the two of them and his moment of privacy was gone.

After everyone left, Puppy Moses stood on the snow-covered ground on the side of the church where they had found the puppy so many years before. He thought of the puppy and, at first, it made him sad, but then he thought about Martha. *I was close, closer than I have ever been.* It made him feel proud that he had a plan and had tried. He walked to the front of the church and past the Isaacs' and Solomons' houses and cut through John George's yard until he stood outside of the Saleems' house. In the darkness, he could see their Christmas tree through the light of the windows. *I could put it in a Christmas card and leave it on the door,* he thought. *No. This gift cannot come in a letter. It has to go from my hand to her hand, from my heart to her heart.* Suddenly, he decided to leave, as if something inside his brain told his heart to stop chasing hope and risk disappointment.

Puppy stopped in the middle of Syrian Hill. He noticed how empty and silent it was, only a short time before having been filled with people leaving the church. After a few moments of standing alone, he moved off Syrian Hill and stopped on the bridge in Myers. There, he took a few moments to study the stars, noticing how brightly they glowed. *It is as if they are alive and they are all jumping up and down and cheering for me,* he thought.

CHAPTER 19

I watch Casper intently the next morning and have never seen him sleep this deep and long. Nancy and I sit him up and his eyes open and look straight ahead. He shifts his head back and forth slightly to take a quick peek at both of us. I put a cup of water to his lips and he sips it down, so I give him another cup. Nancy and I lay him back down, roll him over on his side and change his diaper on the couch. The diaper nearest his body is dry, so we sit him back up and give him a third cup of water.

Lila climbs up on his lap and places a cool washcloth on his forehead. "Thank you, honey," are his first words of the day. They smile at each other. It is obvious they are both filled with joy, while Nancy and I are filled with relief. Lila kisses Casper on the cheek and his eyes open wide. He keeps staring at her as if he wants to fill his newly awakened brain with nothing but a vision of her.

An hour later, I am watching our game against St. Lawrence and Nancy walks in. "Tell me again how this internet film has made life easier for all of us. You still go in at noon on Sundays and get home at ten at night. Now you skip church to watch film at home. Your daughter is playing with your father, who is barely alive. Now that he looks like he will pull through for the precious Merchant Marine game, you don't need to pray anymore?" She puts *The Day*, New London's newspaper, down on my keyboard. "Read what Mike DiMauro wrote."

"What about Vickie?" I ask, referring to Vickie Fulkerson, who is the beat writer that covers Coast Guard football.

"Vickie wrote in her special way of making the world of Coast

Guard like the Land of Oz. She knows you have to rally them back for next week," Nancy says.

Mike DiMauro is the local sports columnist with a reputation of being one of the top writers in the state. In his article, he suggests that the Academy should drop football. Mike said good things about the coaches, but how the team doesn't match up competitively. "This week, St. Lawrence, next week Merchant Marine, then Hampden-Sydney. The Academy needs to give the coaches and players a chance."

Nancy and Lila head to church, and when they return I turn into a football coach and head to the office, leaving Casper in their care.

In the office, the Sunday routine kicks into high gear. The first four hours are spent reviewing offense and defense from Saturday's game. Then we review special teams and vote on player recognition awards for the game. We send out for a quick bite for dinner and start in on Kings Point film when the food arrives. We've already spent a great deal of the summer looking at the previous two years' games, but we review them again. The offensive coaches even go back six years to see how Kings Point's defense will line up to our offensive sets. We pore over film, knowing that their defensive scheme will be the same and may have some repeating characteristics, unlike the triple-option offense which is only a few years old for them. The defensive coaches spend all their game-planning time on schemes to stop Merchant Marine's triple-option attack.

I arrive home at ten and the house is silent, with everyone sleeping soundly. I feel like I have disappeared from the planet, not just escaping the rigors of Casper but hiding from the world in the football office.

I check on Casper who's still but is breathing regularly. When I lay down on the couch next to his, the Merchant Marine game film rewinds in my mind and starts to play. In week one, Kings Point played the Apprentice Builders, located in Newport News, Virginia, and won with two blocked punts. Jim Butterfield always told me the most improvement in a football team is from week one to week two. I was hoping their victory had them overlooking their mistakes, while we were living with ours. I had spent the day worrying about Kings Point, and Nancy had spent the day worrying about life and death. Nancy had kept pace with the day as it kept surging to get ahead of her.

I wake up Monday and check on Casper who seems to have bounced back. Then I'm back to Planet Football, leaving the worrying to Nancy and Lila.

We have a team meeting in Mac Hall at four, and the tone is set to pick it up after the crushing onslaught in the last quarter of the St. Lawrence loss. I wonder if my words have set in, and if we will plow over Merchant Marine to win the coveted Secretaries' Cup. When the team meeting breaks, I take the offensive line down to Billard to watch the St. Lawrence film and start on the Mariners. I can see the intense, serious look on Tommy Condon's face, and all the room picks up on it and joins together. The team hits the field for a full practice. With only one full game film this early in the season, we are ahead in our preparation. I spent all summer watching every snap of the previous two years of Mariners film over and over. Every possession, play after play, step after step. I head home cautiously optimistic and tired.

Nancy meets me at the door at ten on her way upstairs with Lila on her shoulder. "Casper is sound asleep again. He is clean, fed and has his meds."

"How was he?" I ask.

"He was fun," Lila says, as she lifts her head off Nancy's shoulder.

"He is slowly coming around, but he still has a way to go. And you have his recertification tomorrow. I will be gone early so you have them both in the morning."

"How could I forget?" I moan.

I wait until everybody is sleeping and watch the afternoon practice tape again. We always win in practice. No one works harder than the military.

The next morning, the Tuesday before the Mariners game, Hat

Fengar, our caregiver, comes in and starts to get everything ready for the visit from the head administrative nurse at hospice. Casper looks sickly, as if he is dying, not "thriving" as the nurses have contended.

I have all the commodes, bed pans and walkers set up, along with any other medical equipment I can display.

"We will not even make it to the game, let alone the rest of the season, without hospice coming in once a day to clean him and the nurses checking him out a couple of times a week," I tell Hat.

"I'll call you if they call ahead," Hat says.

"I hope hospice comes early in the morning so I can get back for the noon, offensive line lunch meeting," I tell Hat.

"If not," Hat says, "I'll play it up."

I drop Lila off and I'm in my office at nine when my cell phone rings.

"Billy."

"Are they there already?" I fire quickly at Hat.

"No, but I fell down," he moans.

"Are you all right?" I ask in a panic.

"Yes. I tripped over one of the medical things we never use but you put out for show. I just can't get up. Luckily, I fell near the phone. I can only crawl a few feet."

"What do you mean you can't get up?" I ask.

"I have no shoulders or solid knees. You see me wiggle side to side when I get off the couch."

"How the hell do you get Casper up?" I wonder aloud.

"I get him to sit up, put his feet on the ground, grab the walker and I pull him up by the pajama waist."

"You have got to be kidding me," I say, completely bewildered.

"No. But enough of that now. You'd better get home before the certifying nurse walks in or you're screwed. They will say you are not taking good enough care of Casper if they find me like this."

I race home and find Hat on the floor near Casper's hospital bed. I lift him to a sitting position and hoist him up to Casper's walker. I am in the house getting Hat on his couch just in time. Debbie walks in to clean Casper at her usual time of ten, with the recertification nurse following on her heels. The head nurse comes right after. She is all business, not like the loving daily nurses, Jessica and Amy. We wake Casper and Debbie cleans him from his standing position. They check him over from head to toe. He is still tired looking from the long day in the sun at the St. Lawrence game.

I leave when they do, but without an answer.

In the middle of the offensive line meeting, the phone rings. "Billy," it is Amy. For some reason, she calls me Billy too. "They recertified Casper for three more months. That will get you through the season." She is as happy as I am. They all loved gentle Casper.

After Tuesday's intense practice, I race home and enter the house relieved.

Lila races in from the living room. "Daddy," is all she says, but it is said with deep love in her voice and she hugs my waist as I bend down to kiss her.

At least one black cloud has been lifted, I think.

I wheel Casper back to the bed and lay him down. He looks up with the tiniest of faces. Lila walks over to kiss him. I cannot help but notice how a child's face is so small but full of life and ready to grow, while Casper's face is bony, as if the muscles have already started decaying.

"Was Anna with those three ladies today?" Casper asks. Nancy and I look at each other, stunned. Not only has his mind perked up, but he remembers something about today.

"They were the nurses. Those are the ladies you saw today."

"The nurses take care of you, Gido," says Lila, as Nancy tries to pick her up and cart her off to bed.

"Anna is in heaven, Dad," I add.

"With the three ladies?" Casper asks.

"No, those were the nurses. You're tired. Time for everyone to sleep."

"Do you know the three ladies in heaven that are with Anna?" Casper asks. "Please tell me who they are."

"He's back," Nancy chimes, as her failed effort results in Lila back on Casper's bed. My poor wife is exhausted, again.

"Please tell me who those three ladies with Anna were?" he pleads.

"I do not know, Dad."

"Jesus's mother, Mary," Lila says. Her mother has taught her young mind compassion.

"No, honey. Bill knows but he won't tell me," Casper says to her.

I search my brain. The only religion that sticks with me are the speaking parts of Christ in an Orthodox Bible study book. The words are highlighted in red.

"You better talk to him. He is getting upset," Nancy says.

In a soft, tender voice, Lila speaks with the gentle love of one of the hospice nurses, "It will be all right. Go to sleep and dream a fun dream."

"Help me, I cannot think." His little boy eyes plead with me as they start to water. "Tell me who the three ladies were. Jesus wrote about one of them. Anna told me from heaven."

Nancy says, "You told me once that when you were around ten years old, Anna said, 'The world will never be full of love and fair until at least half of the politicians and half of the generals are women.'"

"I know she said that," I answer. "But I don't think that is what is on his mind."

Then I remember that my mother would talk about the three ladies and tell my brother Dan and I the stories at night. "He's talking about stories my mother would tell us. I'm not sure what he means by a story Jesus wrote about a lady."

"I know what he is talking about. Your mother told me too," Nancy says.

"When?" I ask.

"When you were too busy with football," Nancy scolds. "Casper,

I know what you are talking about," she says. "He wrote only once and I think it was in the ground with his finger."

Casper looks at Lila, who is rubbing his head as if to help him think. "Yes, that lady is with Anna in heaven. Who was she?"

"She was about to be stoned for some reason and Jesus wrote in the ground."

"What did he write?" I ask Nancy, amazed that a selfish football coach cannot remember, better than his wife, a childhood story his mother told him.

"No one knows. He may have written down the names of those about to stone her or he may have written, 'He who is without sin cast the first stone.'"

"Yes, that was one of the ladies. What about the other two who were here today and are with Anna?" Casper asks.

"Tell him," I say to Nancy, embarrassed. "I am as confused as Casper. Were they here or in heaven?"

"I don't want to figure anything out. I just want the poor soul to get some rest," she answers. "The second lady washed his feet with her tears and dried his feet with her hair. And all the people told Jesus that he should not let her touch him because she was not a clean woman. Then he told all the people in the room something about loving people who need love the most, and forgiving those who needed it most. I don't really know, some parable about people who need the most love and help are who he was there for, not the people who needed love and help the least."

"I am not sure you have that completely right, but it sounds good," I say.

"If you know it better, go ahead," she says.

"No. I do not," I say shaking my head.

"Yes. That lady who washed his feet with her tears is with Anna," Casper chimes in as he clutches Lila at his side.

"The third one, Casper, I think was the lady who poured expensive oil on his head and all the Apostles said it was a waste of good oil. And Jesus said to them that she wanted to do something good for him, and what's wrong with that? Then he told the Apostles it is better to live a life of kindness and goodness. It is better to live like that, giving love and kindness rather than to know everything about religion but not practice its teachings."

I didn't know if Nancy was trying to convince me or Casper about what she was saying.

"Yes, those are the three ladies," Casper says, finally content. "They are with Anna in heaven. Yes, those are the three ladies that were here today. They left for heaven after they came to visit me."

"Maybe hospice nurses do come from heaven," I say. "Maybe a lot of people come from heaven."

"Bill," Casper says. "Did I ever tell you about when Puppy Moses and Nemo Saleem left Myers?"

"Yes, but tell me again, Dad," I say.

CHAPTER 20

Early in the morning on the third day of February in 1943, the temperature on the bridge in Myers stood at twenty-five degrees. The sky was a dark gray that seemed motionless, and its stillness created the feeling that there was no movement to the earth. It was as if the night had left the world, but the brightness of the day had forgotten to arrive. On the bridge, Puppy and Takla stood hugging each other as they stared silently onto the frozen creek. They could feel each other's insides shake with fear. On bright days, the big rocks along the creek carried the shine of the winter sun. In the darkness this day, even the rocks seemed to have hibernated. The trees and bushes on the side of Syrian Hill and all through Myers stood like wiry brown statues in the still air.

"If I could not hear your heartbeat, I would think we were in the middle of a winter painting," Puppy whispered loud enough for his mother to hear.

Takla looked down at a beat up and patched suitcase next to Puppy's feet. "That suitcase came to this country from across the ocean to Myers and now it goes back." Her voice cracked with pain from her sleepless face. Her sons Joseph and George had left for war and now she held onto Puppy as if he were all her children together. *He was the sickly one,* she thought. *He was not supposed to live past a year. And when he lived past a year, he did not talk until four more had passed.*

Takla was struggling to speak, so she tried choking every word out in a painful gasp. A fear paralyzed her, the kind of desperate fear that told her life was changing for the worse and she was helpless to stop it. "I thought when your brothers left it would all be over soon, and I never thought it would still be going on when you were of age."

Puppy kissed the top of her head. Panic caused her throat to swell with sadness and she could not reach his face to return a kiss. She pushed her neck upward against the sadness as if trying to free her neck from a noose.

When her lips finally reached his cheek, Puppy could not help but notice the pain and desperation in her eyes. "I will be fine," he smiled to put her at ease.

Nemo Saleem emerged from the bottom of the snow-beaten path on the side of Syrian Hill. Martha followed two steps behind him in silence. Nemo's father, Abraham, followed them all a few minutes later. He had sent his son, Sam, off to war and he knew what the Moses family was feeling. When Nemo, Dawn, and Martha all reached the bridge, they looked at each other but not a word was said. Takla sniffled quietly to herself as she wept, trying to hide her pain. Then the four of them walked past Abraham's store, where they met Puppy's father, Daniel, and his sisters, and to the bottom of American Hill. They all stopped at a small, wooden platform and waited for the train to stop.

They were early for the eight o'clock stop but there were already a few people gathered to wish them well. The train hardly ever came that early or to even pick up passengers, but this was a special run, and in a town like Myers they would pick up young draftees on their way to boot camp. The train was only used for the salt plant deliveries but had stopped one day before it normally would have just to pick up Puppy Moses.

"We all got cheated out of a day," Martha said to them.

Dawn looked over at Nemo. The youthful beauty of her face could not hide the fear that it showed. *This is going to happen to Nemo soon.*

I just know it is, she thought. Her eyebrows rose and her face quivered.

Nemo looked at Puppy. "Say something to Martha," he whispered. "You are going away. You may not come home for a while."

Puppy waited for Nemo to flash his boyish grin, but his face was frozen like a portrait.

Helanie and Abraham, the grocer, had joined them with Marion, Otsie, and Nick. Then, behind them, Casper emerged slowly, walked toward Puppy and stopped when he was a few feet in front of him. Casper trembled. He felt like he was choking so he took small gasps, trying to force air to his lungs.

Puppy reached out to him with his right hand and gripped him on the shoulder, then moved his hand up along Casper's cheek and onto the top of his head. "Keep hitting home runs, Monk."

Casper smiled back but not strong enough to convince Puppy his words had soothed him.

"And don't catch all the trout in the creek or down the lake at Mile Point," Puppy added. "Save some for when I get back."

Casper faked a smile but said nothing as Puppy Moses smiled at him and turned toward Martha and Nemo.

"One day," Puppy started to say. "What if we all only had one day in Myers? How we would treasure every moment of it. We all watch so many days go by like the flash of a moment."

Martha looked at him somewhat deeper than in the past. She had noticed at times that he seemed to have a crush on her, but she had always thought of him as Nemo's little friend. On a rare occasion, he would say something that would stick in her head for weeks and then make her think about him.

WOOOOOOO!

The sound of the train echoed from Mile Point, a tiny plot of land jutting into the water on the other side of the railroad tracks running along Cayuga Lake.

It is past Mile Point already, Puppy thought. Helpless fear fought with homesickness in his stomach and made him want to throw up. He remembered when the boys of Myers would camp out on Mile Point right after the last day of school when he was thirteen or fourteen. *Oh, if I could just go to Mile Point and hide from the world,* he gasped to himself. Again, he felt like vomiting but held steady for his mother's sake. *It will be past the salt plant in minutes, then over the trestle and at my feet.*

"I am hopping on," Nemo announced. "I'll ride with you to Ithaca and catch a ride back somehow."

Dawn heard him and said nothing. *If I cry it will be for Nemo and that is not fair. It is Puppy's time to leave.* The thought of saving her tears soured her stomach. She turned and slowly walked up American Hill toward the Ludlowville school and her house.

Nemo's words had given Puppy a reprieve, but no solace came to Takla. Puppy kissed a weeping, clutching mother goodbye. She could say nothing and squeezed so hard he had to wrestle himself away as the boarding of the only two passengers leaving Myers that Sunday began. He said nothing more, not even goodbye to Martha.

The loud churning of the coal engine kept the noise level high when they sat on the train together and they looked out into the small crowd, growing with some of the Syrians of Myers. Suddenly, from the crowd, Martha jumped onto the train and ran to where they were sitting. She looked deeply at Puppy, but neither of them said or did anything and as she started to turn and leave Puppy yelled, "Wait!" and handed her an envelope he had planned to mail to her. They looked into each other's eyes, his with deep love; she looked back with curious bewilderment.

Puppy watched her waving the sealed envelope in her hand as the train started rolling along Cayuga Lake to Ithaca.

The train rolled south along the shoreline to Ithaca. The gray sky had laid a coat of dark navy blue across the lake, making it look like a bottomless ocean. To Puppy, the lake still held all of its beauty and he watched it, hoping it would stretch all the way around the world alongside him.

As the train left the edge of Cayuga Lake and started its way into the city of Ithaca, Nemo spoke with confidence, as if he was within arm's reach of saving the world from disease and suffering. "I'll study medicine, maybe I can become a doctor," he said. "I have to get my grades back up. They dipped when Dawn was sick. Now that she is better, I think about her too much in English class."

"If anyone from Myers could become a doctor, it would be you," Puppy said.

"Take care of yourself, Puppy," Nemo said as he stood up.

"Take care of Myers," Puppy answered as he watched Nemo take a few steps, then turn and smile at him before he disappeared off the train.

In Myers, the few people at the train station had slowly filtered away back toward Abraham's grocery store and some up to Syrian Hill. Martha and Takla were the last to leave.

They crossed the bridge without stopping, as if it would have been too lonely to stand there without Puppy. They entered the nearly empty church. The air inside was cold and damp.

Martha sat next to Takla in silence until Helanie and Casper entered the church and stood in the back. Helanie took out a brown jar with twelve ounces of holy water. She unscrewed the cap and dipped in a red rose. She walked down the middle of the church, leaving Casper alone in the back. When she reached Martha and Takla, she waved the wet flower. As the drops of holy water hit them, they sat motionless.

Martha felt the cold and sorrow of the church moisten the chapped skin above her lips. To escape the sorrow, she went outside, to the left of the church, where they had found the puppy so many quick years before. Martha looked into the deep blue water of the lake and gently opened the sealed envelope.

Dear Martha,

I know this should be said in words to one's face, but I did not possess the courage to speak.

I hope someday to be able to say what I think.

I do not know if another person has lived in my thoughts as much as you have.

I would stand on the bridge and wait for you to walk by. Some days, I would wait in vain and just watch the creek flow to the lake. I would spend my time looking at beautiful, white clouds and think that you were on the Syrian Hill watching the same white clouds that I was looking at. In the summer, I would see the big, white clouds cover parts of the blue sky as they bubbled up in all different shapes. I would think the sun was playing hide-and-seek behind them. I felt like all of Myers was connected to the sky and I could walk right off the bridge and onto the sky. I would study the horizon across the lake where the treetops would meet the sky and think it is off in the future somewhere. In that future, I would be able to tell you how I really feel.

Wherever I am going, I will be looking at the clouds and thinking of you. I will always wonder if you can see the same cloud I am looking at. If we are too far apart from the clouds, I will think it will travel to you, and when you see the beauty of the cloud, you will think of me.

I will think of you always and especially when I see the future of a horizon or the beauty of a cloud.

Puppy Moses

Martha felt a small touch of warmth calm her nerves. She did not understand it, but it felt good, and she wished everyone in Myers and in the church and in the year 1943 could feel as comforted.

Michael Saleem followed Michael Moses off to World War II. He enlisted on September 1943, just three months after his high school graduation. After basic training, he returned to Myers, and on his last day, donning his uniform, he walked around Syrian Hill with Dawn quietly tagging along at his side. He tried to capture every memory, every sight, everything that gave him a sense of home. Every smile from every face on Syrian Hill crawled into his memory and hid away as if it might need to be called upon in another place and time. His mind tried to trap everything, but boiling nerves would sometimes erupt and tell his brain not to feel too much. Outwardly, his face showed his ever-present soft smile and the gentle eyes covered by his wire-rimmed glasses. He would walk in the clear weather, showing Dawn, who stayed quiet, his confidence. Dawn, however, could not hide her desperate feelings as tears escaped the corners of her eyes. When they reached the closed end of Syrian Hill, they stood next to the church near the Isaacs' house and said nothing while they looked down to the long blue water of Cayuga Lake that stretched to Ithaca.

Dawn wanted him to say something, but Nemo couldn't find words. Dawn kept looking up at him with glances that would last a few moments as he took his time gazing out at the lake, burning it into his memory.

All the time I have been around him, she thought, *I have always felt so different than I do now.* The new emotion scared her. *I have always been in love with him.* The new emotion worried her; it felt like half worry and half sadness, and it created a fear inside her that made her forget about love. *I remember years ago when I followed him around and he thought of me as a little kid,* she thought. *Oh, I hate this feeling I have now. I am sick to my stomach.*

Nemo sensed her anxiety. "Hey, everything will be over soon and we can pick up where we are now," he said.

"I'm scared. Very, very scared." Dawn's voice trembled.

"I will be back before you know it. Do not be afraid of anything,"

"You are going to war," Dawn cried. "And I hear the stories. The

Germans and the Japanese, they butcher everything they touch."

"I'm not scared, and nothing will keep us apart." He took her in his arms and, as she lay her head across his shoulder, he could feel her heart racing against his chest.

Dawn tilted her head back. "It is as if there is something, some evil force or giant monster that is trying to keep us apart. First there was the leukemia, and then comes this war that will keep us apart."

Nemo took her hand and they walked halfway down the path to the bridge with him leading her by the hand. In the middle of the path when they stopped, he turned to her and stared into her blue eyes and thought, *They are as blue as a robin's egg.* Then she closed her eyes and he leaned forward until their lips met with a gentle embrace. He heard her sigh slightly and after a few moments he could feel her tears rolling onto his lips as they kissed.

An hour later, Nemo, Dawn, and Martha stood together at the train station in Ithaca for Nemo's departure. They had drifted slightly away from the other Syrians who had come with them. Martha had always been so close to Nemo; he was the baby of the family and she felt more than an older sister, especially after their mother had died. After he boarded, Martha hid the sorrow of the moment by playfully jumping on the train as its engines grew louder. Nemo played along and together they would take turns hanging out the doorway, holding the train with one arm and leaning their bodies out. When the train finally departed with only Nemo buried in its belly and on his way to war, Martha stood silently and watched the last traces of it disappear as if it were venturing into another universe. She could feel the pressure swell into her head. She wanted to collapse but she could not. She wanted to cry but she could not. It was as if a horrible monster had decided to take shelter in her body. When she looked back at the train one last time, she saw Dawn's face staring down the tracks at the disappearing train, frozen and as white as snow.

CHAPTER 21

Pat Bennett, co-captain of the 2010 Coast Guard Academy football team, was born with a physical abnormality. His heart was where his brain should have been, and his brain was where his heart should have been. Pat knew how to think with his heart and create compassion with his brain.

On Wednesday at noon, I stare at a life-sized photo of Pat as he ran the opening kickoff back against Merchant Marine in the 2010 game. It hangs in the stairwell between the Academy's library and the only entrance to the admissions office. Every prospective cadet, parent, officer, or any other visitor entering the admissions office comes face to face with it. Pat jumps off the picture just as if he is running right past me on the sidelines. One hundred and seventy pounds of muscle thunders toward you with his feet off the ground, moving with the power and speed of Secretariat. The picture is silent, but my memory hears the earth-shattering eruption of the crowd, raising goosebumps on my arms. Pat scored Coast Guard's only touchdown on the first play of the game. On one of the last plays of the game, a two-point attempt by Kings Point, Pat was in the defensive backfield when the play failed, and we secured the 10-8 victory with only seconds left.

If Pat knew how to think with his heart, then I suppose many of the Coast Guard people have that ability as well, but it was instinctive with Pat, who defied failure. It could be seen on him like it was part of his uniform, not a pin or medal but a look in his eye. A walk, a smile, a pat on the back to others when his own life was upside down. An attitude that said, "*I am here for you. Watch me and learn. Watch me run sprints. I won't quit. You won't either. I'm on this earth for you to lean on.*" Pat never yelled or showed anger or self-pity, pressuring himself more than anybody else. He spent his Academy life constantly studying, and at the same time constantly under the pressure of academic dismissal.

I met Pat in April of his senior year of high school, and fittingly in the end zone at Cadet Memorial Field on a warm, spring afternoon as we were about to start a team workout. I could feel the confidence in his handshake and see the warmth in his eyes and smile. I watched as he easily mingled with his future teammates. Pat had been offered a spot in the Academy Scholars program at New Mexico Military, so we encouraged him to visit.

CC Grant had been recruiting him and said, "Bill, he's the best defensive back I've seen on film since we've been here. He's visited some strong football schools."

He knew the road ahead at Coast Guard would be tougher than his other options, but Pat viewed challenges as opportunities.

Pat plowed through prep school, just making the academic cut. At the Academy, he was always on the border but he never quit or wavered.

Dr. Kurt Colella, the dean of academics at the Academy, personally tutored and supported Pat, as did the entire Academy faculty. Pat took an entire season of football off to concentrate on academics. During another season, the coaches eliminated Pat from practice twice a week so he could have extra time for academics, enabling him to remain on the team. Thanks in part to Pat, we beat Fitchburg State that year 19-7, just a couple days after my mother died.

The car was packed when we left after the game. Lila was seven months old and slept through the three-hour trip to Glens Falls, where my mother would be buried. All I kept thinking about is that my mother died two days ago, and I wondered what it would feel like in the future without her. I watched the cars rush past in all directions, wondering where all the people were going. Maybe they were moving to a new town or house to start a new life. Maybe to a wedding or on vacation or to visit friends or family they had not seen in years. Or maybe it was a once-in-a-lifetime trip to their mother's funeral.

When we were about thirty minutes from Glens Falls, Nancy broke the silence. "Number two was the best leader I have ever seen."

"Number two? You must have the wrong number," I said. "That is Eric Gerken. He is a young pain in the ass with an attitude. He thinks he is better than everybody, and he thinks he knows more than anybody."

"No, you're wrong." Nancy snapped back. "He is a leader."

"You must have the wrong number. The number two on my team has a lot of growing up to do if he is going to become an officer," I said.

"No, it was number two. He was running up and down the sidelines all game telling the guys, 'We have to win.' He rallied the team all day long. He could feel your pain. He wanted to win for you."

"You sure it wasn't Pat Bennett?" I asked.

"No. It was not Pat," Nancy said quickly. "But it was somebody who acted just like Pat. It was somebody who followed Pat's example."

Eric Gerken was never a pain in the ass again after that Fitchburg win in 2010, and, as Nancy so aptly suggested, Eric morphed into a leader. Pat had mentored him well. That is how it works at the Academy; cadets pass the goodness they have learned out into the world.

With the current Merchant Marine game just days away, Wednesday's practice is sharp, but it seems to go by quickly and it leaves the coaches wondering if we have missed something. Even when Coach Grant pounds them with conditioning at the end, the team is upbeat and crisp. The cadets are flying around practice just like they are flying around the Academy. This week, every squared corner, turn of the foot or spoken word is accompanied by a cadet screaming, "BEAT KINGS POINT!"

The coaches spend the morning scrutinizing practice film. Time is closing in on us, and Thursday morning is gone as quickly as it came. The scouring of the practice film rolls into more Merchant Marine film. There's no time for major adjustments. The game plan is done.

While Coach LaForte is finishing the practice script, coaches Grant and Fleischmann are once again drawing the last triple-option cards. They have drawn every Kings Point blocking scheme imaginable. Our offense, scout team, and starters have run the plays a thousand times already. I am in my office with a reporter from the *Boston Globe*, Kevin Paul Dupont. The Academy has dedicated the game to Jimmy Crotty, captain of the 1933 football team. After graduation, he was working with a Navy command involving minesweeping in the South Pacific and was captured by the Japanese when the Philippines fell. He died while imprisoned during the war in a Japanese POW camp. His family didn't find out until after the war.

"Tell me your thoughts," Kevin asks me from across my desk.

"Two things keep running through my mind," I say. "Both have to do with a beautiful day like today."

"What two things?" the reporter probes.

"I mean, if you walk outside and stand in the middle of the Cadet Memorial Stadium and look up, you cannot see a cloud in the sky. Does a POW look up and see the same blue sky while he is dying in a heinous place? Did Jimmy Crotty ever think about the sky hanging over Cadet Memorial Stadium? Did he ever try to escape back here in his mind when he looked up?" I ask.

"And the second thing?" the *Boston Globe* reporter asks, without looking up, as he scribbles in his notebook.

"What about his mother? She takes every breath with a son who is listed MIA. She is frozen in some kind of living purgatory. Does she walk out to the mailbox every day like a nervous wreck and look up into the sky and wonder about her son?"

"Huh," Kevin says, as he keeps writing for a moment, then looks up and smiles and moves on.

I start to do the same and at two o'clock my phone rings. It's Nancy. "You know it is Hat's birthday. You didn't forget, did you?"

I draw a blank. I want to say I forgot but that would be a lie. I can't recall anything about Hat's birthday. I hang up and make another quick call, race out of my office and across the Gold Star Bridge into Groton. I zig-zag my way through the crammed streets along the Thames River to a duplex. Outside on the steps, an old man sits waiting for me. I say "old," but he's the same age as me, but no teeth, and the years have treated him harder than me. I have visited him once before with Hat, wandering through a tiny apartment filled with antiques, collectibles, toys, and baseball cards, but not much else. It looks like he ate and lived with his prizes all in one room. It was the life of many seniors living on their own, with no money, poor health, and not wanting to part with anything.

He looks up when I pull in and get out of the car.

"I'm not giving it away, Coach," he says, flashing a 1955 Ted Williams baseball card at me. "No money, no deal, Hat or no Hat."

When I visited him once before, I tried to buy a few old toys for Lila and old cards for me. He had come to a few games with Hat last year.

"I don't have much time. How much?" I ask.

"One twenty-five." He hands me the card. "One twenty-five and not a penny less. It's a beautiful card."

I look at it, bent on the corner with plenty of creases. It looks like it has been in someone's back pocket since 1955. All in all, Ted Williams' face is still clear, and it is not all that bad, but it is far from beautiful. That's why the old guy wants only one twenty-five.

"A hundred bucks. It is all I have on me."

It suddenly hits me that I haven't bought Nancy anything worth a hundred bucks for her birthday or Christmas in ten years.

"One twenty-five," the guy insists.

"A hundred. It's for Hat. Your buddy," I say calmly.

"I'll tell you what," he starts. "If you throw in some coaching gear, one of those nice warmup jackets and a Coast Guard football hat—"

"I can't do that. I can't give away gear."

As I am reaching for my wallet, I make one last bid to sweeten the deal. "I'll throw in some tickets for the big game Saturday."

"Ha," he laughs. "What would I want them for? I'm not crossing the Gold Star Bridge for the Merchant Marine game. You're gonna get your asses whipped."

His words bring me back to reality. I have just wasted five minutes and now I am fired up about time, about the game, and now about him. I look at him sternly.

The toothless man looks at me guiltily, knowing he has just told a coach he does not think his team has a chance to win.

"All right, a hundred bucks."

Thursday's practice is in uppers, shoulder pads, helmets and shorts. It includes an in-depth review of special teams. We run a quick team pass and a two-minute drill before we break into offensive and defensive groups. The practice looks sloppy, and it is over in a flash. The Kings Point buses will roll down the hill to Cadet Memorial Field in less than forty-eight hours. I stand in the shower after practice and let the fast water spray into my face.

Water and time, I think, *are a lot alike. They come at you fast and they both seem plentiful, but they are not.* One year has now shrunk to less than two days and I can feel my nerves tightening like coiled wire.

I walk into my house at eight and know Nancy has fed Hat dinner with Lila and Casper and kept him around singing happy birthday with a small cake. Now they need the special gift. I hand it to Nancy in the kitchen and she wraps it quickly and hands it to Lila.

When we walk into the living room, Casper looks up at me with tears.

"They took our land," he sobs. "They took our land."

"He has been crying on and off since we came home," Nancy says.

Lila races the present over to Hat, waiting for him to open it. "Hurry up, Mr. Hat," she giggles.

"They took our land," Casper cries out again.

"What are you talking about?" I ask.

"We watched a couple of western movies today and he cried through both of them," Hat answers as he opens the gift.

"Hurry up, Mr. Hat," Lila is gravitating to the present and ignoring Casper's sorrow.

"Are you crying because your brother Nick liked westerns and you were thinking of him?" I ask.

"No," Nancy answers, "he is rambling on about something he saw in the movies."

"They took our land," he sobs.

"What land?" I know he is confused but I must ask.

"The Syrians' land. They took our land," Casper says.

"No. They took the Indians' land. That is what you saw in the movies. The Syrians all came here on their own."

"Oh," is all Casper says, as if he now understands. He stares straight ahead, his face drained of life and wilted from confused sorrow.

Hat opens the gift.

"Ted Williams, 1955 Ted Williams, the card I always wanted, the only card I ever wanted." Hat grins widely, but it is a fake grin he displays to deflect away from his eyes, which are watering.

Lila looks at the card curiously and Nancy peeks, leaning over her shoulder. "It is a baseball card. It has a picture of a baseball player on it," she says to Lila.

Lila scoots across the room and opens a small doll house she keeps underneath Casper's hospital bed. She pulls out a clear plastic envelope, which encases a baseball card. "Like this one," Lila says as she walks back into the main part of the living room.

"*Jackie Robinson!*" I yell, as Lila hands me the card.

"There is your missing card!" Nancy exclaims.

I had one baseball card to my name in the house. I had always wanted a 1949 Jackie Robinson. It was a portrait in his white uniform with a deep blue Brooklyn cap with a white *B* in the middle. The background was red. It looked like the American flag. I always wanted that one card, as if I was a little kid, and some years back I bought it over the internet.

I show the card to Casper. "Jackie Robinson, Dad. You remember him."

Casper looks down at the card and studies it as if it lit a match in his head. He turns his face toward Lila and looks up at me. "Were the Syrians slaves? Did they come to America as slaves?"

"No, Dad. They came on their own. Mom's parents ended up in Glens Falls and yours ended up in Myers."

"Were they slaves in Syria?" he asks.

"No, maybe two thousand years ago when the Roman Empire ruled Syria. But not when they came in the early part of the last century," I answer.

"Are there slaves in Syria now?" Casper asks as his crying starts to fade.

I don't respond, but look around the room at Lila and Nancy and think, *Maybe there are slaves there now. Maybe they have a family that is held hostage so they have to be slaves and do what a controlling army tells them. Maybe that is why people do not risk their lives or revolt or escape. It is not just their own life but lives of their loved ones who are held as collateral. The love they have for others keeps them captive.*

"Tell me how we got here, Bill," Casper pleads. "Tell me, please."

The birthday party has gone awry. Hat goes home with his baseball card. Lila and Nancy go upstairs, and Casper settles in to sleep.

"Tell me how we got here," he keeps pleading in the darkness. "Tell me how you got here."

"Me?" I ask.

"Yes, me and you. There must be a reason why you are here." His face and body melt into the night, weak and tired, but his voice stays desperately strong.

"Dad," I plead from the couch, "go to sleep."

He rolls and turns and keeps calling to me. "Billy, Bill, I need to talk to you. Please, talk to me."

"Shut up and go to sleep!" I scold. I sit up and move toward the hospital bed in the corner. "I have a big game in two days. Go to sleep. Don't say a word."

"He wants to talk to you." Nancy appears alone in the far entrance of the living room. "Talk to him."

"You talk to him," I snarl.

"He is not my father. You are all he has left to his past, to his life," she answers calmly.

I calm down. "I don't know what to say."

"Just talk to him. Maybe he just wants to hear your voice," Nancy turns and goes back upstairs to bed.

I walk across the dark room and lean over his skinny face. I can see his eyes glistening in the darkness, looking back at me like distant stars that are almost too far away in the night sky to see. He seems to be calmer now that I am nearer.

"Did Anna drown when she was little?" he asks.

"No, she hit her head when she fell. When she was old," I remind him.

"Oh. Yes. Who drowned then?" he asks.

"She had a brother who drowned when he was five, before Mom was born." I pause, but think I should keep talking or the questions will just keep coming. "Her father, Mike Toney, was dropped off in America with his brother Jimmy when he was fourteen. When he was eighteen, he married Mom's mother, Mary, when she was fifteen. They had a little boy, and he was not supposed to go down to a canal near where he lived, but he did, and he drowned before Mom was born. Mary, Mom's mother, was six months pregnant with another child and she went into shock and the baby was stillborn the next day. They had to keep their life going. I guess they had the will to go on. In the end, they had five girls and a son."

"Why did God choose him and not your mother? Why did your mother live and not her brother?" he pleaded.

I stammer, but have nothing to say.

"What about me? Didn't I have a sister?" he asks.

"Yes."

"How come I never saw her?"

"She died in Syria before you were born." I look down at him and can see he is waiting for more.

"Your father came to this country and had to earn enough money to send for your mother, your older brother, George, and your sister. He came over on the *Lusitania* and went from Ellis Island to the salt plant in Myers. When the *Lusitania* headed back across the Atlantic it was sunk. That started World War I. No one could travel, so your mother, brother and sister were stuck in Syria for five years. And your sister died when she was five, before you were born."

"How did she die?" he asks. "I remember something bad."

"Her heart stopped. That is all I know, Dad. Her heart stopped." *Eventually everyone's heart stops one way or another,* I think, *including mine.*

"Did my brother George get killed by a bomb when he was a little boy?" Casper's voice is weak and tearful.

"No. He lived to be over ninety. He came to Coast Guard games with you and Mom all the time. He died ten years ago. In Syria, when your brother George was five, he and another little boy found a bomb and they started playing with it. The bomb exploded and the other boy's body was blown apart. The boy's finger went into George's leg so deep they had to cut it out."

"Why did George live and the other boy die? Who decided that?" he asks.

"I do not have those answers, Dad. No one does."

"Why did Anna's brother drown and not her? Why was my sister born ill and killed by a dog and not me? Was I supposed to do something more because it was not me?"

"I do not know, Dad." I look at him in the darkness. I become scared for myself more than him.

I start to think, *How could his brain be so alive all of a sudden? Was he asking me these questions or was someone else? Who was inside of that mind, inside of that skull barely held together by the skin?*

"Please, Dad, go to sleep." Now it is not my anger or impatience that wants him to stop, but fear.

"Those boys, why do I think of them? Puppy and Nemo? They had to leave Myers. Did they have to go back to Syria?" he asks.

I say nothing.

"There is a war in Syria right now?" Casper asks.

"Yes, Dad, a revolution. There is a revolution in Syria."

"You are helping, right? You are a good boy, Bill. I know you are helping the children in Syria who are dying in the war over there. I know you are helping the world."

I sit for a long time and watch him sleep and wonder what I am supposed to do with my time. I know I have done nothing for the world so far.

CHAPTER 22

On a dry, desert morning on the coast of North Africa in 1943, Puppy Moses dipped his soapy razor into his helmet, which was filled with water, and swirled into a tiny whirlpool of soapy foam. As he lifted his head, a few drops of sweat rolled from his scalp and lodged in his eyebrows. All he could see were soldiers like him mingling in and out of dark green tents, all moving slowly and quietly like they were content in the present with no interest in entering the future. He looked back down at the whirlpool in his helmet and watched the water fade to a stop. *They must all feel just like me*, he thought. *They must all miss Myers, like me.* A jolt of pride pushed his homesickness aside and he began to feel pleased that he made it through basic training so well and had gotten this far.

Basic training went quickly for everyone because they felt like me, he thought. His nerves had pushed him through with ease. He knew being a hapless mile runner in high school had steeled him. *It is so strange*, he thought. *I hated every minute of being a mile runner. Now I do not feel the shame of being last in every race, but the pride of struggling and finishing.* He looked back around at the multitude of faceless soldiers just like him moving all around. *I wonder if they are just like me? In Myers, they feel one way about life but in Casablanca, they feel differently about life.*

Puppy took a deep breath and swirled the razor again around in the soapy water. The white puddle reminded him of Myers in the springtime, when all the buds are popping and all the leaves are alive. The bushes and trees are coming alive. *If there is a heavy, fast downpour in the spring, all the puddles in Myers will look just like this. Puddles will be covered with buds and foam from the trees will be all around Abraham's store all the way to the bridge and all around the Syrian Hill.*

Instantly, a hard slap on the back of his left shoulder shook him away from the spring rain back to Africa and the Department of the Army.

He turned and stared into a face that seemed to appear from the other side of the world. "Gus Isaac of Myers!" he gasped, trying to catch his breath.

Their eyes radiated with excitement, but Gus's were subdued.

"All the way from Myers to North Africa! All the way from the house on the top of the path, next to the church on the Syrian Hill to North Africa! Maybe it is a smaller world than I thought," Puppy huffed.

Gus said nothing. His eyesight froze in a stare at Puppy's soggy helmet. *Shaving,* he thought. *Shaving.*

"Gus . . . Gus . . . Gus, " Puppy said, getting his attention.

"For a second, I was back at Mile Point, camping out and shaving in the lake on a hot summer morning. When I saw you from behind, I thought we were staring out from Mile Point and looking down the lake to Ithaca," Gus said. "Happy memories."

"Yes, happy. What about Nemo, have you heard anything from him?" Puppy asked. "Or your brother, Mike?"

"I haven't seen either. Not a thing," Gus answered. "What about Myers? Anything change?"

"No. A letter here and there. But nothing much changes."

"Gus, what do you think of when you think of Myers?" Puppy asked.

"I guess, getting home," Gus answered.

"Gus, do you miss Myers?" Puppy asked.

"Yes," Gus answered. "Sometimes I forget. But at night it comes back to me."

"What do you think about when you think of Myers?" Puppy asked a second time.

"At night, a lot of nights, especially after a long day, I have the same thought. I am in my house on a hot summer day, and I kiss my mother and father and then walk outside. It is hot weather, kind of like this," he said, referring to North Africa. "I start down the top of the path and then I stop and I look back and see Mother next to the church, and I watch her staring at me. I can tell she is crying. I walk down the path behind my house, stop on the bridge and look at the dry summer creek for a minute. Sometimes, when I am on the bridge I think of Jacko and sometimes I do not. When I think of Jacko, I cry too much, so I try not to think of him while I am so far from Myers. After I stop on the bridge, I walk to Abraham's grocery and I buy an ice cream sandwich. Sometimes I buy a cherry vanilla frost stick. I don't open it. I walk back across the bridge and up the path. I stop in the middle of the path and lay down in the bushes and open the melted ice cream and eat it. That is what I think of over and over and over again, every night of this war. I don't know why but that is what I think of."

There was a sad silence and then shy Puppy started to talk. He could not understand why he started to talk about his thoughts. Maybe he thought Gus was as close to Myers as he could get right now. Puppy began to open up.

"I am always standing on the bridge in summertime. I think I see my puppy down underneath the trestle, struggling to swim upstream back to Myers from Cayuga Lake. Back to me so I can hold him and kiss him while he licks my face." He paused and fought back tears. "I am standing in the middle of a war with someone who has lost their brother and I am about to cry over my puppy that's been gone for ten years."

"Leaving home and going to war can make you think of anything and everything and sometimes nothing at all," Gus offered. "You and I will see things that make us forget we are alive."

"Have you seen any action yet?" Puppy asked.

"No. Have you?"

"No," Puppy answered.

For a moment, there was a chilling silence. Then, Puppy felt he had to tell somebody from Myers his deepest thought.

"Sometimes I am standing on the bridge and I think of Martha Saleem and she walks past me to go to Abraham's to get the mail or groceries. On her way back up the hill, she takes my hand and leads me up the path and, in the middle of the thick brush where we cannot be seen, she kisses me. I mean a real kiss, where I can feel our faces melt together. Then she pulls away and looks at me like she has the biggest crush on me and walks away. Every few steps up the path she turns and looks at me and smiles. I can see that smile on her face over and over again."

Gus looked at Puppy with the hopelessness that only a war-weary mind could summon. "I sort of always thought you had a crush on her. You should have kissed her when you had the chance."

"I was too scared back in Myers," Puppy answered. "I was too scared sometimes to even say hello."

Suddenly, Gus wanted to know nothing more about Myers. He could not think of love or his parents or the church or the people on the hill. "I just want to be alone on that path with an ice cream."

"Yes, I know what you mean a little. Sometimes I think maybe I would walk up past the high school and down Ludlowville Road to where the creek runs along the green pasture with the farmhouse. You know where the creek slows and the still water stretches and rolls slowly in long pools along the gray shale? You can be alone there and hide in one of the most beautiful spots in the world."

"I know where you mean. Where the water runs over the shiny gravel in one slow pool after another slow pool," Gus said. "Beneath the long shale wall with the pine trees above the wall, right below the Syrian cemetery."

"Yes," Puppy said. "And when the sun shines through the clear water in April you can see the gravel sparkle. Where the rainbow trout from the lake come to spawn on warm spring days."

They stared at each other in silence for several minutes, each feeling their own sadness separately. After a short while, they felt time carrying them away, as the pace of World War II charged closer and stole their fleeting moment of time.

"I will see you back in Myers, Gus," Puppy said. "We will share an ice cream."

"Yes," Gus Isaac said as he started to walk away and then stopped and looked back at Puppy with his natural smile.

Puppy smiled back at him but said nothing.

Gus turned and headed back to the war and farther away from Myers and Puppy.

Less than a year after that chance meeting with Puppy, on June 2, 1944, in Italy, George "Gus" Isaac, of Army Company L, 30th Infantry, 3rd Division, watched the 339th Field Artillery Battalion of the 88th Infantry Division trudge past him. His eyes pored through the dust, which rose like clouds from the dry earth. The dust filled his eyes and turned the passing troops into walking ghosts. Every human went by as if lost souls drifting farther from safe havens like Myers. Gus studied the features with quick glances as he searched for his brother from Syrian Hill, Michael "Decker" Isaac. The faces, however, scared him. *I keep seeing Jacko,* he thought. *Everyone looks like my thirteen-year-old brother Jacko standing on the bridge in Myers just before he was washed away.* His eyes swelled, but he did not cry. *They will think it is the war, not Jacko I am crying for.* He knew the war had hardened him and now it pushed his thoughts away from Jacko and back to the war.

Gus had already been wounded and left for dead. "Get his dog tags," he'd heard the medic say. "He won't make it." But he did, recovering from shrapnel in his head.

When Gus returned to active duty in Salerno, Italy, his patrol was pinned down in a long gully by machine gun fire. The soldiers were spaced five feet apart so that if a shell or machine gun fire hit a spot, it would only kill one of them at a time.

"Isaac," the young lieutenant called from down the gully.

Gus scooted down on his knees and stopped a few feet away from the officer.

"Isaac, the machine gun burst is coming every few minutes and then they stop and wait. The next time it stops, can you time it up to stand and throw two grenades?"

"Sure," Gus answered without hesitation in his voice but with fear in his heart.

"They might not wait. They might fire right away. This could be it for you."

"I know," Gus answered. He put his rifle down and readied himself with his two grenades, one in his right hand and the other in his left.

Gus waited, his nerves rattling but his hands steady. He heard one blast, then a pause. *How much time was it?* he thought. His mind tried to keep a mental clock. *A minute, maybe two... I can't wait to time it too many times. They could change their pattern or even kill someone.*

PIP! PIP! PIP!

The machine gun ripped and then stopped.

Gus stood instantly, pulled the pin with his left hand, which held the other grenade, and threw the live grenade. He then shifted the second grenade to his right and pulled the pin with his left hand and threw the second grenade. He heard two quick explosions. The gunfire stopped. He had hit the German machine gun nest.

"Isaac, you will get a medal for this," the lieutenant said. But by the end of the day the lieutenant was dead. There would be no medal. Gus knew the millions of events of war died with the people who performed them.

The troops in front of him marching toward Rome kept moving, with no one from Myers that Gus could identify. One soldier walked by and looked him in the eye. *He looks thirteen, like Jacko, he looks like he has never even shaved yet.* Gus thought back to that day when he had seen Puppy shaving in North Africa. *Shaving,* he thought. *Not everyone here even shaves yet. Shaving.* His spinning mind took him back to the fighting again.

Suddenly, the face of Decker Isaac appeared in front of Gus, and World War II ended. They stared at each other for a moment, then joyously hugged.

"Have you seen Nemo?" Gus asked.

"No. But wouldn't it be nice to run into him?" Decker answered.

"I saw Puppy Moses in North Africa when we first came overseas," Gus said. "But I'm not sure where he is now."

They shared that night together and, the next day as they were parting, they decided to write a letter home. "Let's make it real gentle," Gus said. "Nothing about the war. You write half and I'll write half. We'll stick a hundred-lire bill in it with our names on it."

> *June 2, 1944*
>
> *Dear Mom and Dad:*
>
> *We have the greatest surprise for you as yet. I bet you can't guess who is sitting next beside me. Well it is brother George. We finally met and honest ma he sure looks good. And we were surprised to see each other.*
>
> *I was looking for George and he was looking for me. I left to look for George and he left to look for me. And the best part of it is we are only about a half mile apart. We were together all last night, and we are together today. But now we will try to see each other as much as possible. We are going to try to look Mike Saleem up and we will finally see him.*
>
> *Hello Mom and Dad. This is George. Well we have finally met. Were we ever glad. It was hard to believe I knew him*

right away. He changed a little. He is putting on weight.

You know what Ma? George is bigger than me.

We are going to write Sue and Roda now. So Good Luck and God Bless you and Dad. Loving Sons

Mike – George

CHAPTER 23

On Friday afternoon, I shut my eyes in the silence of my office. The Academy is motionless except for the parade field. It is as if a magnet is placed there when a drill is scheduled and every cadet, officer or professor is drawn away from their own life to the parade field at the entrance of the Academy. It's around four, and I am waiting to start football practice, and feel like I'm circling the stadium like a plane that has nowhere to land. Then Victor, someone I have not seen in more than a decade, appears as a vision. I open my eyes to see if Victor has returned to Billard Hall, but Victor is not there; nothing is in front of me but emptiness.

I am confused. I rub my forehead in distress. Should I be angry that Victor is not in front of me. Or should I be angry that my football team is not in front of me?

Victor is a challenged adult who was part of the work crew that would come to Billard Hall and clean every day during my first two years as head coach. *Victor was fifty-six years old the last time I saw him*, I think, *the same age that I am now.*

Victor was bald with big eyes and big glasses. He always wore a shirt buttoned to the collar and never took his jacket off, as if he was waiting for disaster to arrive at any moment and leave him homeless. His was slim, like a person who goes through life missing more meals than eating them. He moved slowly, as if each step he took might lead to danger.

Victor always appeared instantly. He would bypass the elderly Billard Hall secretary, Vi Oliver, who noticed everything. I would look up at my desk and there he was staring at me.

"Hi, George," he always started.

"Where did you come from?" I would say.

"Is that you, Victor?" Vi would ask. "I did not see you come in."

Sometimes I would be watching film in Coach Grant's or Coach LaForte's office. I would look up and he would be looking over my shoulder. I would look up and think, *How the hell did he tiptoe in here?*

"Can Coast Guard beat them?" I would ask.

"No, George. Too big, too strong," he would add as if he had been watching film of both teams all week.

Victor would appear like an angel. In and out as if there was more to him than what was in front of me.

"What's the story on Victor?" I once asked the young lady who was his supervisor and drove Victor's work crew in every day in a van.

"You know the rules; I'm not supposed to talk about the clients," she said.

"Yeah, I'm not supposed to do some of the stuff I do with remedial PFE or the football team or my classes, but I do what is best for the cadets."

The young lady wanted to tell me about Victor, as if it was important to know and not important to be kept a secret. "He was institutionalized for a quarter of a century, around half of his life."

"Why?"

"No reason. He is as gentle as a butterfly. He just slipped through the cracks. I guess they didn't have a place for everybody," she shrugged. "So, people like Victor just got drugged up and put in a room. He spent most of his life alone. It is a lot different now. Eventually, he ended up on the outside in assisted living and now in this clean-up program."

After September 11, 2001, Victor, because of his gentle demeanor and the new security clearance rules, was sent to work at the naval base across the Thames River in Groton. I never saw Victor again.

As I wait for the team to finish the Friday parade, I think, *Maybe*

Victor was an angel. He could appear and reappear from nowhere, like a cloud or a ray of sunshine. That's it, he was locked away by himself and while the world spins, he sits alone. No one knows about him, so no one cares about him.

Victor has become the old friend, the distant cousin, the human life I should be in touch with and talk with; instead, Victor is like the others, the human being I have forgotten about.

I want to keep thinking about Victor, but Kings Point has started practice and we are still in military drill formation, and the thought irritates me enough to forget about Victor once again.

Fridays at the Coast Guard Academy, whether the game is home or away, can be a disaster for our football team. The team is up at six and has drill practice in the morning, then attends a full day of classes. The worst is that the team must dress in full drill uniforms and march with the entire Corps of Cadets for the Academy parade at four in the afternoon.

It's just after five, and the coaches sit waiting, killing time with nothing to do. "It's hot and muggy," LaForte looks up at me as I walk by his desk and lean over his shoulder. I can see the offensive game plan on his screen. "I'm just double-checking the script on what plays to run today in practice." At most schools, Friday is nothing more than a walk-through, but at Coast Guard you need to have extra capacity. The cadets' brains have been filled with math, science and government all day, along with the two separate marching sessions. The Thursday night study habits of engineering majors hit the team the hardest. The coaches once tried extra meeting time on Fridays to reprogram the brain with football. That backfired with everyone falling asleep, so it was back out on the field for the reinsertion of football into the brain, with the body moving and blood flowing into the brain.

"The Merchant Marine team would be done with their Friday practice while we were still marching. And Kings Point did not drill at six this morning." Coach Grant complains as he, Coach Fleischmann, and Coach Driscoll watch a few last clips of film that they have seen a thousand times before. Meanwhile, CC and Jay are glued to the big screen, and Dana has his face buried in a laptop. Mentally, they are exactly on the same page, but it seems like they are worlds apart. It is like they have already split away to the sidelines and the booth, almost as if they are practicing how they will coach the game.

The cadets finally trickle down, but it is almost six o'clock before we start stretching with an already tired bunch. The thought of Kings Point stepping on the field invigorates them, and by the time we finish the warmup they are ready. Practice is crisp and sharp, unlike the day before.

They have honored the Crotty family at the Friday drill and so, after our practice, they join us on the field. There are twenty-five of Jimmy Crotty's descendants of all ages, with nieces, nephews, great-nieces, great-nephews and cousins. I feel somewhat relaxed talking to them, as the team takes a knee in a semicircle. It can be odd to think that the main enjoyment of Jimmy Crotty's brief life may have been on this field. After practice, the team shakes hands with his family members in a reception line, and the family searches every player to see who looks the most like Jimmy's old photos. The Crotty family studies every face carefully, as if they are looking for Jimmy, as if there is some time warp and he still may be here, as if he had never left and was twenty and getting ready for the Merchant Marine game and they have come to watch Jimmy play.

"This one," a lady of about forty says. "This one. This is him." They choose Blake Thompson from Texas, the quarterback we had benched last year in favor of Derek, and who is now one of our starting wide receivers.

I stand him out in front of the team, which is now back on a knee waiting for my final word about Kings Point. The Crotty family stands together behind the team. "Jimmy Crotty could be any one of you guys," I pause and watch all of them stare in solemn silence. "Someday, one of you guys will be Jimmy Crotty," I add.

At nine, when I walk in the house, Casper is on the couch and immediately he looks up at me. "Am I going to the football game?" he says, as if he knows the last game almost did him in.

"Oh, you are going," Nancy says as she walks in with Lila, who leaps from her arms onto Casper's chest. "Your son might kill you, but he is going to have you at that Merchant Marine game," she says quietly so that Casper and Lila cannot hear her.

"Dan will be here, and he and Hat will have him in the handicapped section in the shade and with sunscreen." Then I add, "They are going to keep him hydrated."

"Sure, after all, he is just a good luck charm. What could possibly go wrong?" Nancy asks, worried.

"I can't hear Gido's heartbeat," Lila says as she presses her ear into the center of his chest.

Nancy readjusts Lila's body and head so that it might be in a better position. Casper looks down with his eyes and rubs her head.

"I still cannot hear Gido's heartbeat," Lila repeats.

"Here, let me find the spot." I move Lila off and lower my left ear onto the center of his chest. I can barely hear the faint beat of his heart. As I listen, fear grips me as I think his heart was beating so strongly all those years of my childhood and now it is fading. I wonder if my own heartbeat is fading.

I lift my head off his chest and Lila crawls up past me. "Gido, can you hear my heart?" she asks as she puts her chest right onto his face, almost smothering him.

"Just a minute," I say as I lift her off his face. She slides down to his side between his body and the couch. "Dad, turn your head to the side."

Casper sits in silence as if he does not hear my instruction.

"Turn your head, Gido," Lila says as she gently turns his head away from the back of the couch so that the right side of his face rests on the pillow. Lila then lowers the center of her chest on to his left ear. "Can you hear my heart?"

"Yes, I can hear your heart," he says. He does not know exactly what she means, but he does give her the answer she needs. "They can hear your heartbeat all the way to heaven."

"Who can, all the angels?" Lila asks.

"Yes, and Anna and Papa Wes," Nancy says, referring to her father.

Nancy's father, Wes McGraw, who passed ten years before, would sometimes grow quiet and his eyes would get glassy, and you had the feeling he was not in the room with you. Wes's legs had walked away from the forgotten battles of the Korean War, but the bloodshed had stained and silenced his memory.

"Do they have heartbeats in heaven?" Lila asks.

"Sure, they do," Nancy says.

Lila says nothing, just staring into Casper's face. Her stare lingers as if her mind is trying to figure something out.

"What are you thinking about?" I ask.

Lila looks up at me with a content smile, but she says nothing. It is as if she has the answer to my question, but she will not share it with me.

Just after midnight, when the nerves of the game are throwing me all around the couch, Casper calls to me from his bed. "I am nervous. But I do not know what it is about."

"I know, Dad. Just get some rest." I was more patient than usual.

"How come Jesus yelled at God when he was dying on the cross?"

"I don't know. Because he was human, I guess." I had never really thought about it.

"Oh," is all he says as he closes his eyes.

I rub his cheek gently, like he is a baby, hoping he will fall to sleep. The guilt of how many nights I was not this patient rolls down my spine like an ugly snake.

Casper's eyes open slightly and his lips move as if he is trying to tell me something, but no words come out. He closes his eyes and says, "Jesus lost."

I don't answer.

"Jesus lost," he says again with his eyes still closed.

"What do you mean Jesus lost?"

Casper's eyes crack open slightly, as if some force is trying to shut them. "He died. He lost. He couldn't teach people to love and be kind and help people who needed help. He stopped living. He stopped talking to people about God and telling everyone to be kind and help the sick and poor. He lost."

"He died, but he did not lose," I answer. Then I sit silently, thinking in the darkness of the living room.

"Keep talking to me, Bill," Casper says.

"I guess he won because people are talking about what he talked about two thousand years later," I continue. "Maybe he won and lost at the same time. I don't always know what winning and losing really are. Especially in this case."

Casper's eyes are barely cracked open but looking at me as if he can see through my soul. "Yes, you know," is all he says for ten minutes, until, "I told you about when Puppy Moses took a trip to France, didn't I?"

"Yes, Dad. The very first time you told me about Puppy Moses, it was about his trip to France."

In the gray dawn of the first week of June in 1944, Private First Class Moses felt the wet salt air of the Atlantic Ocean filter through his nostrils and settle uncomfortably in his stomach. The steel landing craft, packed with soldiers, lurched forward and rocked from side-to-side as it moved within two hundred yards of Utah Beach off the coast of France during the Allied invasion of Normandy. The early waves had already successfully landed, and Utah Beach was somewhat safer for the following troops. Puppy could feel his charging nerves draw anxious sweat along the back of his neck at the bottom of his hairline. The sweat mingled with droplets of spray that had bounced up from the Atlantic and chilled his neck with fear.

The angry Atlantic did not evoke memories of Cayuga Lake as he was focused solely on the smoke ahead on the beaches of Normandy.

Puppy squeezed both hands tightly around the handle of his rifle to bring his numb arm back to life. His back tightened and his knees started to buckle. "Whew," he exhaled long and hard to compose his body.

When the landing craft flung its doors open, he jumped out into knee-deep water and paid no attention to the water or the sand swallowing his boots. Instead, his eyes focused on the few bodies scattered on the beach forty yards ahead of him. Puppy slipped for a step and felt his knee hit the sand, but he quickly recovered and lifted his round body upward and moved forward onto the beach, burdened with heavy military gear. All along the beach, American soldiers scurried away from the Atlantic. The soft sound of the shore and the lack of gunfire did nothing to calm Puppy's nerves. He quickly noticed a body covered from the waist up with a blanket. The fatigues on the legs of the soldier were soaked with blood as they protruded from the blanket. As he drew closer to the body, he saw the tops of the legs, which looked like ground, bloody meat, and realized they were not attached to a body; they had been separated at the hips. At the bottom of the blanket, he could see the footless stubs of the ankles. Under the blanket, there was no more of the soldier's body to be found. Puppy instinctively moved his eyes away as if to protect himself from the sight of a mangled human being the same age as he. Word had spread that the Allied landings at Omaha Beach had been a horrific slaughter, and Utah Beach had taken less of a hit and had gone smoothly, but nothing mattered now except what was in front of him.

Puppy followed the single-file movement of the troops and headed to a small patch of dunes on the other side of the beach, which lay just beneath a short patch of beach grass. Beyond the dunes, much farther inland, were flooded fields. When he reached the sand dunes at the end of the beach, he looked down and saw something an inch long sticking out from the sand. "Is that a land mine?" he said aloud.

"No," another soldier answered.

"It looks like a piece of flesh or finger," Puppy said.

Puppy bent and pulled at it and out came a three-inch piece of flesh torn from the outside of a human foot. The skin of the foot was still attached to a baby toe. He wondered if it was from the pair of legs he had seen or if it was from another boy. Then he thought of his mother and all the times she would count his toes when he was a child and he pretended to sleep.

I wonder if this boy's mother counted his toes when he was a little child, he thought.

He placed the small piece of flesh on top of the sand and scooped out a hole. Puppy gently lay the toe in the hole, covered it and made the sign of the cross on top of the sand with his finger and then blessed the grave.

The unit moved inland and stopped in a ditch alongside a dirt road. Each soldier was spaced five feet apart as they crouched. Along the gully, American soldiers waited in silence for the order to be given to scurry across the road. There had been no movement for almost two hours. On the other side of the road was another ditch, and just beyond that was a hedgerow of thick brush. Beyond the hedgerow was a field of about fifty yards. The Germans had flooded the fields just inland from Utah Beach, but this one had been spared. An order came down the line to move across the road to the other ditch. Puppy scurried for ten quick steps, fighting panic.

BOOM!

In a fraction of a second, a powerful explosion flipped him upside down and backward toward the ditch. He rolled his round body slightly sideways. At first, he felt nothing, and was deafened by the explosion.

He sat in the silence and waited, drifting as if he was floating away. He felt as if his body and soul had separated. Part of him was still the little boy in Myers, and part of him was the soldier in a brutal conflict. For a fraction of a second, his mind lifted him from the battlefield. He wondered if his mother, Takla, was still alive or if she was gone forever.

No, he thought, she is alive and well just two houses up from Abraham's grocery store in Myers. He was angry that his brain had brought the Nazis to Myers. He looked up and down the road at the boys who were just like him and wondered if they thought about their own Myers.

BOOM!

Another explosion.

Puppy was knocked out again for a few minutes, and when he came to his silent numbness was fading and he could sense the chaos of war around him. He no longer felt separated from his soul. His mouth was filling with blood, which was dripping from his nose. He could feel the jagged bones of his broken ribs poking into his lungs and he gasped for air.

"Whew. Whew." He tried to spit but he could tell that his jaw on the left side of his face hung shattered just beneath his ear, no longer connected to his skull.

Just then, a hand reached beneath his armpit and started to drag him across the road.

BAM!

A German bomb ripped open the insides and through the beating heart of the soldier lifting Puppy onto the sand. They both fell back to the ground, their faces just inches apart. Puppy stared into his glassy, lifeless eyes.

BAM!

Another explosion.

I have got to get out of this road, Puppy thought.

He tried to clear his throat as the blood choked him. He could feel the grains of the sandy beach scraping against the inside of his mouth.

He crawled on his belly for a few feet and then stopped.

I have got to make it farther. I have to go farther.

He kept crawling. When he reached the edge of the road, he slid face first into a small ditch and beneath the thick brush. The pain was excruciating, and he could not feel the solid, attached structure of his face and skull. He took a breath every few seconds until he fell unconscious.

Puppy was unconscious while they lifted him from the ditch two hours later. They shipped him on a transport boat back to England and into a hospital, unconscious and barely alive. His blood loss was heavy, his rib cage shattered, and the round definition of his unique face grossly distorted.

It was as if he was the pudgy teenage boy of Myers who was chasing life, just as he had chased runners. Suddenly, his heart stopped, and a spark ignited his brain. His glassy eyes opened from his fractured face. He looked straight ahead and, from his bed in an English hospital filled with soldiers exactly like him, he could see two thin clouds shaped like angels' wings against the blue sky of June 14, 1944. The wings of the angels were touching, as if they were holding hands. He saw the faces of his mother and Martha on the angels. Then, just below the two clouds, he saw Myers, as if he was floating above it on a sunny, warm June day.

First, Puppy saw his house and then his father and Abraham standing in front of Myers Grocery. He could see the bridge and the soft water of the creek roll underneath it and to the lake. He saw the path and Syrian Hill. And he saw the green-shingled church overlooking the lake and the never-ending horizon beyond. And in front of the church, he saw the puppy napping. The puppy lifted its head, opened its eyes and looked upward as if it thought it had noticed something in the sky. Seeing nothing clearly, it yawned and returned to its nap. Then the sunshine turned gray and the two clouds holding the faces of Martha and Takla were lost in the darkening sky as all of Myers disappeared.

Moments later, a nurse walked in and brushed her hand softly down his broken face and closed his eyelids over his hollow eyes.

One week later, right after she had finished her lunch, Martha Saleem walked across Syrian Hill from her house toward the path between the Isaac house and the church. The sunshine soaked the sky, but she couldn't help but notice the bubbles of black clouds rolling down from Lake Ontario.

Maybe the clouds will stay north and not turn south, she thought. *Rain would ruin such a nice day.* She wanted to walk along the lake in peace. Like all of America, the Normandy invasion had jolted her nerves. The battles and death tolls mounted daily in Europe and the South Pacific. Martha knew that every day was the same, but some days she could pray her fear away.

This is a perfect day for a walk along the lake if that rain stays away, she thought.

At the top of the path, she stopped and looked down on all of Myers. *I wonder if this is like any village in France. I wonder if Nemo is eating lunch right now in some little place like Myers.*

From her vantage point, Martha saw a long, black sedan stop in front of Abraham's store. The car paused for few seconds, then inched forward past the street which led to Puppy's house and crept toward the bridge with its wheels barely rotating.

As it moved onto the bridge, she noticed the four flags, one on each corner of the car. "Oh my God! Oh my God! Nemo!" she screamed. She turned and ran back to the Saleem house. When she reached the house, she was too scared to enter and tell her sisters or father what she had seen. She wept but worried they would hear her. Martha raced to the corner of the road, which led to Syrian Hill, and looked down the road for the car.

Maybe it is for Gus or Decker, she thought, hoping it was another Syrian who had died. *Oh, how horrible a prayer.*

Her heart pounded as she waited for minutes, which seemed like years. *No car coming up the road,* she thought.

She started down the road, back to her vantage point on top of the path. She caught sight of the car turning out of the two-house street of the Moses family and drive past Abraham's grocery and up American Hill on its way out of Myers.

"*Oh no,*" she cried softly. "*Oh no.*"

Martha slowly walked down the path. She was crying as her fear had forged into gloom, her heart melting in her sorrow. Halfway down the path, Martha removed her sandals to pick up her pace. She ignored the brush of the path and the cinders of the road as she moved toward Abraham's grocery. Everything in Myers seemed frozen, as if the world had stopped and it would never start again. She ran along without a person in sight.

Martha stopped at the end of the street next to Abraham's store, which seemed empty until Casper stepped outside onto the porch. He looked at her and smiled, then stepped off the porch and said something undiscernible. A jolt of fear cut into her. *What if they circled back to the main road and were going to my house from the other direction?* The sky was sunny but, beyond the church, the storm clouds seemed closer to the hill as if they hovered, awaiting instructions to devour the sunshine.

Suddenly, a scream cut the frozen time of Myers.

Martha Saleem turned and saw the thin, graying body of Daniel Moses dressed in a black suit, trying to run but only quickly hobbling toward her. His hands were in his hair, pulling handfuls of gray patches of hair and skin away from his scalp. She looked over at Casper, whose eyes were white with fear and his mouth gasped for air. Instinctively she reached out and grabbed Casper and pulled him to her.

Daniel Moses screamed again, pulling more patches of bloody gray hair from his scalp. When he reached Martha and Casper, he froze, his eyes wide open in horror, his hand full of his hair and his scalp bleeding. Then his mouth opened wide in silence like a baby, which had lost its breath but was about to scream at the top of its lungs.

"AAAAAAAAGGGHHH" he screamed, as he caught his breath.

The door of the store flew open and Abraham George leaped off the porch, got behind Daniel Moses, and wrapped his arms around his waist, dragging him into Myers Grocery. Screams echoed from inside the store like a violent animal trying to free itself from a cage.

"Go home!" Martha screamed at Casper and shoved him down the road in Myers toward his house near the bridge. Martha raced down the street the thirty yards to the Moses house and walked in. Takla Moses sat in silence, her eyes wide open and glassy. There were no tears or sobs. She did not look up at Martha.

"Takla," Martha said softly. There was no reaction. "Takla," she said again. Again, Takla Moses sat as frozen as Myers.

Casper raced with fright down the street to his house where his mother, Helanie, was cooking and he told her what he had just seen.

"Stay here with Marion," Helanie told Casper, as she bolted out of the house and raced to the Moses house.

Shock had frozen Takla, as it had frozen so many families in the world.

Helanie kneeled in front of Takla, then gently touched her knee. There was no reaction. She rose from the floor and whispered, "Your children need you."

Takla stared through the white lace curtains.

Helanie turned to Martha. "Go home to your family."

Martha did not react.

"Martha, go home," she ordered. "Go home and take care of my sister's family."

Martha reached the bridge when the clouds engulfed Myers. The first drops of rain hit her face at the top of the path. She walked the rest of the way home with the rain and tears mixing on her face.

CHAPTER 24

I slide off the couch at six on game day. Kickoff is at two-thirty, so I have time to let Casper rest until I clean him before he heads to the stadium.

He awakens and looks up at me with the saddest of eyes. Then, he lowers his head to see Lila, who has snuck in and stands at my waist.

"We are going to the game, Gido!" she shouts.

"I am going with you to the game," he whispers weakly. "Oh, I am so happy." Casper reaches his arm, which looks like a dying branch in late autumn, out to her. Instinctively, she leans forward so he can touch her cheek and run his fingers up to her temple. He stares at her in silence and closes his eyes, but it is too late for his eyelids to trap one tear, which rolls down the side of his face.

"Is he crying?" Lila asks.

"No," Nancy whispers behind me. "That is just some mucus in his eyes from his sleep."

Nancy leans to me and whispers so that Lila does not hear. "He is not a good luck charm, and another five-hour day outside in the sun could kill him."

"But if we win, what a way to go," I quickly joke.

"And if you don't, what a way to die," she sighs.

Before I leave, I go to Casper's hospital bed. I do not say anything, as he has fallen back asleep. I notice that above his head is the only photo of football in our house. It is a large photo of me in 1996, the year I met Nancy. I was coaching linebackers at Ithaca. I look at the photo, *I must have been thirty-eight years old,* I think. I was thin and, some might argue handsome. I looked confident and strong. *I need to be like that today,* I think. I look down at my father. *I am even past the middle of my years now. I am closing in on old age. I cannot see it, but I am changing and, like the photograph on the wall, I will change and not notice until time has long passed without me knowing it. I am like everyone else. I will not see the world around me until time has left me behind.*

I look around at more pictures, a few of Nancy's family and a few of my brother Dan's kids. *No Anna!* I think. I search the living room and find nothing in sight.

"What's the matter?" Nancy asks.

"I was looking for a picture of my mother," I say.

"What picture?" she asks.

"Any picture. We have no pictures of my mother up," I say back sharply.

"They are all buried away in every closet," she answers. "I asked you twenty times since we moved Casper in here four years ago. You always say, 'No, it will bother him.' He was so dependent on her for everything."

"I guess," I say.

"You guess what?" she answers. "He wants to survive. He cries but endures the pain and pushes on. He cries and it bothers you. But you don't cry."

"I cry," I say.

"You have not even cried for your mother. You loved her but you have not mourned her. You have not even cried for her yet. Before Lila was born, you would kiss your mother a thousand times before we would leave and head back to Connecticut. You would hold her tiny, little face and kiss her cheek a dozen times. And she would just stand on her porch on her toothpick legs with her eyes shut and just smile. Then, after we left, we would have to turn around and drive back so you could kiss her some more. No, you have not mourned for her. You have blocked her death out."

"I have mourned," I repeat. "I have thought about her. We have a lot going on. A baby and taking care of Casper. Our jobs."

"You do not think about her enough. You used to spend a lot of time with her. In fact, I think you used to go to church just to sit next to her."

"What does that mean?" I ask.

"I know you love and worry about Lila. And I know you are determined to go the distance with Casper so you will not let Anna down." Nancy stops for a moment, then says, "You have to put things in perspective."

"Like what?" I ask.

"You have spent thousands of days just to beat Kings Point once every three or four years. Now you think it is your last chance because of the changing tide at the Academy. I guess what I am saying is you need to spend a few minutes being thankful for all of the good you have."

"What do you mean by all of that?" I ask.

"Win or lose," she looks me straight in the eye, "the world will go on. The question is, win or lose, how will you go on with the world?"

I turn and head out the door. I am thinking of Kings Point on the ride in—not Anna.

When I arrive at the Academy it is still early, so I take a quick walk around the field and toward Billard Hall. A car pulls up. "Coach, good luck today," Admiral Stosz says from the driver's side. "This is Admiral Helis, the superintendent of Kings Point."

We exchange greetings. *How easy it must be just to go to a football game without having to worry about anything,* I think. *Then again, they, and everybody else, have their worries too.* I think about what Nancy said. She was right. Life does go on for everybody.

Inside the football office, I sit in the corner near a window where the defensive coaches meet. I can feel the butterflies, but I want everyone to see me as cool and calm. The team has finished the training meal and is now getting ready for pregame position meetings. A handful of linebackers has gathered around the big screen, looking at film and waiting for Coach Grant's meeting. Off to the right, in the corner, Coach Driscoll sits at a desk and pores over the Kings Point offensive sets one last time. He looks up at me but says nothing. I watch a few offensive linemen trickle by me and head to the other side of the offices. Their faces are hard and serious.

I am about to get up when I look out and down the Thames River. I am astonished to see an odd, thin cloud hanging just above the Gold Star Bridge. I watch it for a few moments and think of Anna. The sun is out but the forecast for the rest of the day says it's going to be cloudy. It brings me a moment of calmness. *Maybe the cloud is an angel,* I think. *Maybe the cloud is Anna. Maybe it is another angel. Maybe it is Victor tiptoeing around the football office like a cloud that cannot be seen.*

The thought catches me off guard. *I do not even know if Victor is still alive.* The guilt of not knowing about Victor brings me back to reality. As I head back to the offensive meeting room to start the offensive line meeting, the football adrenaline is pumping again.

The pageantry of academy football glows throughout the warmups and continues through the march-on by both Corps of Cadets. After the team goes through warmups, we return to the Billard Hall gym, our pregame and halftime area. Ten minutes before we go out onto the field, we take a knee and join hands, as one of the chaplains comes in and leads us in the Lord's Prayer. I suppose we break every rule about praying at a government facility, but sometimes common sense takes the place of rules that no one wants. We prayed at Ithaca with Jim Butterfield when I played and coached, so I just kept it going here.

We race back out onto the field with cadets of both academies lined up for their teams. Cadet Memorial Field stands are packed and loud for the start of the game.

Tyler Henning, one of the best kickers in the nation, puts the ball down near the five and inside the numbers, but our coverage breaks down. I watch the Kings Point returner race by me and I think how easy it is to dream of all the perfect things and how reality is not like you plan it. We, luckily, drag him down at the twenty before he can bring the ball all the way back for a touchdown. With our backs to the wall in the first minute, the defense comes out strong on the first two plays. On third down, MMA fumbles and we take over on the fourteen. Our sideline goes nuts.

We take over and drive to our thirty-eight, but on third-and-six, Derek throws an interception on an easy, short crossing route.

I can sense the doubt of the seniors who do not believe in Derek as he walks off the field.

Merchant Marine takes over the ball and one play after another for five plays, the speed and precision of our opponent's triple-option attack slices through the Coast Guard defense. On the sixth play, they find the end zone to go up 7-0.

After the following kickoff, the Coast Guard offense takes over at our own thirty-three. Derek connects three times on the next drive, including a touchdown pass from the nineteen-yard line, to tie the game at 7-7. I feel good, not just about the score, but that the game is flowing naturally, with us avoiding what could have been two disasters.

We hold Merchant Marine's triple-option attack on the next drive and force them to punt. The defensive victory is short-lived, as we fumble the punt and another turnover gives them another short field. Our defensive players, many of whom were on the punt return team, stay on the field without a breather. This time, the triple-option gives the opponent a quick score to make it 14-7. We do nothing on our next possession, and neither do they. After an exchange of punts, Merchant Marine mows us down. The speed of their cut blocks is much faster than anything we could have prepared for in practice. Their running game is now in a groove and, in no time, they have a 21-7 lead.

We fight back with a nice drive and, after a few first downs, our tailback, senior Jacob Wawrzyniak from Toledo, takes a pitch and sweeps past their cornerback, who is being blocked, then he cuts inside another defender and races into the end zone—a thirty-eight-yard touchdown run to pull us within seven at 21-14.

Merchant Marine answers with another long drive. Their offensive line is pushing us around and they are running the option handoffs as smooth as butter. They take back their fourteen-point lead.

With the score 28-14, we drive sixty-two yards with a picture-perfect spread option, no-huddle series of run-pass option plays. Derek reads everything perfectly; if the linebacker drops, he hands the ball off; if the linebacker fills, he hits the short passing route. The line blocks the run each time. The three-yard cushion, under the NCAA rule that enables a lineman down field on a pass, baffles the Kings Point defensive players. We end up on their three-yard line with a fourth-and-goal.

"Go for it!" Ray screams through my headset. "Go for it! I have the perfect play!"

I fight against all my Coast Guard principles and decide to go for it instead of kicking and getting the sure field goal points. I know, deep down, smaller players have a tough time in the red zone, where the field is compressed, and we cannot spread their bigger defense out. *We have the best kicker in the East, maybe the country,* I think.

With three minutes left in the half and fourth-and-three on the goal line, the pass is incomplete. I feel sick to my stomach. *I just cost us the game,* I think. *We could have gone in at the half down 28-17. Now we have nothing and we are down by two touchdowns.* I look over at Mike Toop, the Merchant Marine coach. *He would never have made that call. He would have kicked a field goal with three minutes left.*

I am on a knee, and I stare down at a leaf which has blown down onto the sidelines from one of the surrounding elm trees. It lies there, out of place. The field was cleaned before the game and is immaculate aside from the leaf, which must have blown down after the start. The leaf is rich and green, as if it were still alive and attached to the tree, as if it did not know its life was over and it had to turn brown. I have seen the stray leaf a few times at my feet but now it seems to be following me, like I am its only friend in the world. Maybe it is my only friend now.

With first-and-ten at their own six-yard-line and three minutes left in the half, Kings Point's triple-option attack can just run the ball into a two-touchdown lead at halftime. Merchant Marine has yet to attempt a pass in the half.

I stay silent on the headphones. I am too embarrassed to talk to the other coaches. *They will just run the clock out,* I think. *They have not thrown a pass yet. They are not going to throw one now.*

On the first snap, they drop back into their own end zone and throw an out pattern on the far sideline. Eli Maurer, another senior of ours from Ohio, steps in front of the ball to intercept and sprints twenty yards into the end zone. I cannot believe my eyes. The place goes ballistic. Football is a game of emotions, but never have I felt so down and wracked with despair and had my feelings brought back so quickly. I suck in air as if I have been rescued from the bottom of the ocean. My body shakes with relief as the extra point team pushes past me and onto the field. One of the players bumps into me on his way out and it spins me in the direction of the handicapped section. I quickly look across the rows of wheelchairs and I think I see Casper and Hat, but I am not sure as I turn back to the game.

The players charge off into the locker room down 28-21. I follow them and when I reach the end of the stadium exit and turn toward Billard Hall, a hand slaps me on the back.

"Keep showing up, Coach. They're making plays today. They'll make some more," says Pete Barry, who had retired as the Academy basketball coach five years earlier.

He turns and walks away and does not hear me say thank you.

Keep showing up, I think. That is what he would say when he came into my office during my early years, when I was losing a lot more than winning. "Keep showing up, good things will happen," he would say. He hardly knew me but treated me like an old friend. *What a way to go through life,* I think, *treating everyone like they are your family.*

I turn away from the early years and hustle into Billard.

CHAPTER 25

At halftime, LaForte recharges the offense while Grant and Fleischmann scribble every triple-option adjustment imaginable in just ten minutes. Watching a cadet change plans while exhausted and at the height of emotion is exactly why sports help prepare future officers. We charge out of the locker room the same way we came in. The late score at the end of the first half has given us a new life. The weather shifts in the second half, as a gray sky blankets the sunshine and spits out a misty drizzle. I am hoping it will stay dry, as a wet day will help their running attack and hinder our throwing game.

In the middle of the third quarter with the ball at our own thirty-seven-yard line, Collis Brown, our senior captain from Texas, takes two steps back from the line of scrimmage and Derek hits him with a backward pass. Collis winds up and throws downfield to the Jimmy Crotty look-alike, Blake Thompson, for a thirty-two-yard gain. I have told LaForte all year to use the trick play against Kings Point, either in the middle of the second or middle of the third quarter. LaForte designed the play, then drilled it to perfection during practices.

On the next play, Derek hits Collis for a thirty-one-yard touchdown. The game is tied and now our defense faces the test. Tyler Henning, whose punts have hung in the air all day to help our field position, pins them tight with a perfect kickoff between the painted numbers and hashmark. Kings Point comes out firing and drives with short, churning gains, as senior defensive linemen Joel Wyman and Aaron Black, both tall, muscular, and built like tight ends, make stop after stop. The secondary of James Rizzo, Maurer, and Joe Rizzardi keep it tight on the perimeter. After a penalty on first-and-goal from the nine puts Kings Point back five yards, it gives us a chance. On third-and-goal from the thirteen, they kick a field goal to take back the lead at 31-28. We are still in reach with two minutes left in the third quarter and the defense is getting used to the game speed of their attack.

The kickoff is a touchback, so we start the drive on the twenty with a two-yard run. Three short pass completions and we are at midfield. That is when Derek finds Jordan Groff, a smiley, laid-back but tough-as-nails senior from Pennsylvania, for a touchdown. Jordan had been a running back in high school, but we shifted him to receiver. He had a knack of always sleeping during meetings, but whenever we could wake him up, he was money in the bank. He has been silent thus far in the game but now he is awakening. He dodges a few Kings Pointers and we have a 35-31 lead. The score has no effect on me as I feel like we're trailing by twenty.

In the fourth, the Coast Guard defense stops them twice. We have the ball on our own thirty-two-yard line with seven and a half minutes left in the fourth quarter. Derek hits Groff twice for gains of fourteen and five yards. With the ball on our own forty-seven and five minutes left in the game, we face a third-and-three. LaForte calls a run-pass option, with Groff running a short slant pattern in from the left to the middle of the field. Derek throws the ball well behind Jordan but, somehow, he reaches back without changing his forward stride, grabs the ball, shakes a tackle and splits the seam of the defense. He scoots down the middle of the field for a forty-seven-yard touchdown.

With Coast Guard leading 42-31, Kings Point returns the kickoff back to midfield and they are alive and fired up. We hold them on a fourth-and-eight on our twenty-seven. They have one more chance after we punt it back and they drive to our twenty-one. Down by eleven with a fourth-and-ten, they have two choices; go for the first down or kick a sure field goal and try for an onside kick to get the ball back. They need a field goal, a touchdown and a two-point conversion to send it to overtime. We had lost in double-overtime at Kings Point a few years ago. That was a few months after my mother's sister, Jenny, had died and I kept saying, "Help me out, Jenny."

As Merchant Marine lines up for a potential field goal, I am screaming up and down the sideline, "Hands team! Hands team!" for our onside kick team to get ready. I keep screaming and stop only for a second to watch the line drive kick. "Hands team! Hands team!" Out of the corner of my eye, I see a few defensive players jumping for joy. I'm caught off guard by the field goal attempt which goes wide. The game is over. All we have to do is take a knee.

It is over. I feel relief, not the jubilance of the players and the crowd. I look up and try to see Casper in his wheelchair in the handicapped section, but I cannot see him. I take a knee to catch my breath and watch the seconds tick away.

Beneath my knee is that same perfect, green leaf that I had seen earlier. *How odd*, I think. *This leaf almost seems like it has been following me around today.* I put it in my pocket as I head across the field to shake hands with the Kings Point team.

After the ceremonies and celebration, I spend time with the reporters and record a video for the Coast Guard website, and then I leave. As I always do, I stop in the Academy chapel and sit in the second-to-last row. That is where Anna and Casper always sat at St. George's Orthodox Church during my childhood. I think it odd that I am only in the Academy chapel a couple times a year. I am just thankful no one was seriously injured in today's game or worse. I watch the dusk darken the stained-glass icons and think of all the relatives who are gone.

At home, I put Lila on my lap and an arm around Casper on the couch. I sip on a glass of straight whiskey and chase it with a beer until it is time to put Casper to bed.

At nine, I lay Casper back. He is tired but not exhausted like after the St. Lawrence game.

"Where is your mother? Isn't she coming to bed?" he asks.

"Gido, Tita is in heaven," Lila answers in the soft voice of a whispering baby. All she knows of my mother is the baby picture of her as an infant being held by a shrinking lady with sad eyes.

"Wasn't she at the game?" he asks.

"Yes. I think she was," I answer, somewhat with confidence.

"Oh, no," he sighs as if he is out of breath. "She is in heaven. And I am still here. I am the only one left. Why?"

"You are supposed to be here with us. I just do not know why," I answer.

"You have to be here to play with me," Lila interrupts. I realize she is unaware that Casper's age and failing health have anything to do with death.

"'Come upstairs with me,' were the greatest words ever said. You saved me that day. I never bet a horse after that."

"I did not save you. You saved yourself. You did not need me to bring you upstairs. It was inside of you all the time."

"Dad, what was inside of Gido? Something bad?" Lila is confused by the conversation.

"Yes, something bad, honey," Casper says to Lila. He gently weeps.

"No, something good was inside of you, not something bad." I speak a little more loudly than the gentle voices around me.

"You brought yourself upstairs and quit betting, not me," I say.

"You said, 'Come upstairs with me,' and I followed you up the stairs to see Anna."

"It was inside of you already, Dad," I answer.

"Come upstairs with me," he responds.

I know he is tired, but I want to explain. "It was like that old church reading that Moses said to his people."

Casper and Lila both look at me and wait for me to tell a story. "Moses said to his people, 'If I told you the mysteries of life were in the stars in the sky, you would ask me how to fly to get the answers. If I told you the mysteries of life were across the oceans, you would ask me how we could travel across the water. If they were on the other side of the desert, you would ask how can we travel across the desert to find the mysteries of life?' Then Moses said to his people, 'The mysteries of life are within you, not across the oceans, or in the sky or across the desert.'"

Casper looks as though he understands Moses.

There is a long silence. Lila and Casper study each other's face, as if they both know they feel the same way, and they are content with the silence.

One mind about to start a journey and another ending a journey, I think.

"Bill?"

"Yes, Dad?"

"Did I ever tell you that I went to Syracuse University for one semester when I was seventeen?"

"Yes. You told me once. And you told me you had to leave to go back to Myers."

"Did I tell you why?"

"Yes, you told me why, Dad."

"Will we ever take a trip back to Myers?" Casper asks.

"Of course, Dad." I used to think that he would ask about traveling to Myers more often in the past few years, but now I'm certain his memory has been drifting back there. I sense that he realizes his childhood has long since lapsed from Myers and the time that has passed now lives in his heart.

"Is anyone still there?" Casper asks.

"Marion and Gus," I tell him.

"Oh, good," is all Casper says as he closes his eyes.

CHAPTER 26

Time in Myers stood still over the next months. Myers had left for war like all of America, but the war had its way of keeping what it wants and exchanging human love for endless despair. Takla Moses had made herself invisible. She locked herself inside her house, never even looking out a window. She stayed awake at night until exhaustion would put her to sleep for an hour or sometimes two. She did not eat or drink for days and sipped water out of instinct, usually in the middle of the night when she did not even realize she was awake. She would nibble on bites of Syrian bread when hunger raged.

Martha Saleem, like her sisters Mary and Scandera, and her father, lived without smiling. They worried about not just Nemo, but their brother, Sam, as well. Like every family not yet torn apart by war, they lived with the desperate fear that it soon would. Martha noticed how sullen and empty the tiny village of Myers now appeared. She tried to think of life when she was a little girl and her mother was alive and everything seemed so peaceful and happy. She remembered how much better she felt when Nemo had the chance to come home after basic training, and she climbed on the train, and they laughed when he left for good. The reality of the war had marched her off, as well. Martha, like Takla, had in some emotional ways blocked out the death of Puppy. If she did not think about it or let herself understand it, then she would not dwell deeply on Nemo and what could happen to him. Martha could feel herself withdraw from the world around her, only caring and praying about the fate of her brothers.

Martha limited her trips off Syrian Hill. Whenever she did walk down into Myers, she quickly crossed the bridge, never allowing herself to study the beauty of the creek. Martha kept her distance from Takla, which was simple as Takla, whose mind drifted farther and farther away from reality, never left her house. "This is what purgatory must be like," Martha would say to herself. The only place she found solace was the Syrian Orthodox Church on the hill. The green-shingled church had become her second home, with her hiding away inside while the rest of the world, and the war, moved on.

On October 8, 1944, Private First Class Michael "Nemo" Saleem and twelve other soldiers from the 45th Infantry Division of the 179th Infantry Regiment were on patrol in the Montagne Forest and Hill 484, West Grandvillers, France. The mission of his unit was to remove Germans from foxholes.

Foxholes? he pondered. *I wonder if they will burrow deep like rabbits and we will have to dig them out. Or will they be waiting for us to look in? I hope they left for good and kept going all the way back to Germany. I hope there is no counterattack.* He thought about a previous battle.

The twelve soldiers from his infantry division moved slowly down a dirt road next to a patch of trees. It led to a field one hundred twenty yards long. At the end of the field was a road which led to the next French village they needed to capture from the Germans.

The field was open and dangerous. It could be booby-trapped with explosives or aligned with hidden snipers. Nemo's job was to make sure nothing leading up to the field would keep them from moving all the division to the edge of the field. There, they could take cover and shell the entire field and the opposite side.

Foxholes? I do not know what this has to do with foxholes, he thought.

They moved slowly, creeping down the road step by step. They crawled to the edge of the field and lay hidden in the thick, bushy hedgerow.

To the left was a small hill with spotty tree coverage that looked down onto the field. To the right, there was nothing but barren fields.

"They will either be to the left or ahead if they are anywhere at all," a sergeant figured aloud. "We have got to find out where the Germans are so the whole division can move forward from this spot." They waited for thirty minutes, surveying the silence and emptiness of a mild fall afternoon. "Let's move to the left up the hill, along the tree line. Maybe we can see something move from up there."

They crawled slowly, gaining a few precious feet at a time. Within an hour, they were three-quarters of the way up the hill. They looked down and across the field and saw no movement on the other side.

Nemo felt overcome by eeriness. Something was not right. He was seventh in line in the formation as it crawled up the hill. He looked down to the five men beneath him. Then, something behind them to their left in the bushes caught his eye. Before he had time to react, machine gun fire erupted.

The 111th Panzer Grenadiers of the 11th German Panzer Division had begun a counterattack.

The five men directly beneath Nemo were shot instantly. Blood spouted in all directions. Within an instant, the fire also came down from above and the first three men on the line were killed.

Three loud explosions ripped the air.

Nemo felt the spray of bullets hit the dirt around him. In an instant, his instincts told him to move, but another explosion stopped him before he could react. His eyes went black, and he instinctively pressed the palms of his hands against his ears to muffle the deafening blasts. Nemo Saleem could not see or hear, but he could feel the warmth of blood from his head soaking his hands.

BA-BOOM!

Another explosion ripped the ground near where he lay. Instantly, he felt a sharp, jabbing pain in his lower abdomen on the left side of his body and head. As he rolled on his stomach, he could feel the blood pooling in his pants and in his shirt around his navel. Nemo continued to roll until he came to rest sitting up against a fallen tree. Two of the soldiers that were still alive in the formation returned fire upward. A barrage of German machine gun fire now ripped in from both directions. Nemo drew his pistol with his right hand but as soon as he did, his arms went numb and he could no longer hold his weapon. It sat useless on his open palm. He could feel the blood pouring from his head as if he were standing in a shower. Then, silence set in, and so did the fear. His breathing shallowed and his eyeglasses dropped from his head and into a pool of blood. Expecting the enemy to approach, Nemo again tried to grip his pistol, but his arm was numb as blood continued to pour from his head and limbs.

Three German soldiers pulled back the brush and stared down at the dying American. One bent down and picked up Nemo's pistol, completely soaking in his blood, and another took his rifle, which lay a few feet away. Then, one of the Germans reached into Nemo's shirt pocket and removed a small photograph. The German stood and the others looked at the picture.

"Daughter?" he asked in English with a heavy German accent. "Daughter?" he said again, looking down at Nemo. War has an evil way of making the dying and the dead appear so much older than they are.

Nemo started to choke. He tried desperately to cough and clear his throat as his eyes swelled and as his mouth gasped for air he could not inhale.

The German bent down on one knee and held the black and white picture to Nemo's face.

Nemo cracked his left eye open, as if to respond to the Germans, and through his bloody vision he was able to see the photo of Dawn Worsell, standing on ice skates beneath the bridge in Myers at the age of eleven. She was wearing white leggings and a white dress with a white bow in the middle of her chest. Her smile in the photograph was frozen like the ice and snow around her.

A telegram that listed Michael Saleem's platoon as missing sent the family into panicked screams of hysteria. The hysteria only grew when no other word came for two weeks. Martha's older sister, Mary, had learned that the platoon leader of the small band of soldiers was from Syracuse, just sixty miles away. Mary tracked his parents down and traveled to Syracuse on an afternoon while they were at home. They knew nothing more.

Every day for almost two weeks in the late fall, Martha walked down the path and stood on the bridge. She waited each day for the salt plant shift to end and for her father to walk up from the road beneath Syrian Hill, and they would drag themselves up the path with shattered nerves. It had been a full two weeks since the telegram had arrived and, today, she did not pause on the bridge but walked toward the Moses house.

In the autumn sunshine, Martha could feel the first cool wind of late October turn the trees of Myers into songs as their leaves rustled. It had been a warm autumn and many of the trees were still full.

On the porch of the Moses house, Martha noticed a small bowl of milk that looked out of place, but she had too many worries to pay much attention. Martha knocked twice, softly, and when only silence stirred through the lace curtains of the door, she knocked a third time with much more force. With no answer, she turned the doorknob and walked in. Takla Moses sat still at her kitchen table, her face hollow. In front of her was a cup of tea with lemon and a small piece of bread. She looked straight into Martha's eyes and lowered her head as if she had not seen her at all.

"How are you?" Martha asked kindly.

Takla sipped her tea and took a small crumb from the bread. She broke off two other crumbs and dropped them in her tea. It was as if she knew, instinctively, that she needed to survive for her other children, but her heart had no desire to move on.

Martha watched Takla suffer for as long as she could then walked out and down past the Myers store and to the bridge. Her father, Abraham, was coming home from the salt plant and she met him at the end of the bridge, and they headed up the path to Syrian Hill together, his black metal lunch pail at his side and a Pall Mall cigarette in his mouth.

His gentle eyes always look so tired and sad, she thought. *What a gentle, loving person. But he is such a quiet, lonely man. He has his two boys in the war to worry about.*

Martha walked with her father past the Isaac house and straight across the hill through John George's yard to their house. They had arrived at their door when the black sedan with the flags appeared out of nowhere. The door of the car opened and, even before a word could be spoken, Abraham Saleem threw his heavy lunch pail in the air toward his house, screaming.

An instant later, the pail crashed through the kitchen window.

Abraham collapsed, kneeling at the foot of the messenger, weeping but not listening to the messenger's voice. All that could be heard besides his wailing was the name "Michael! Michael!" being screamed by Martha, as if she was trying to call him back from the dead. Her baby brother was gone, her companion, her best friend, her purpose in life after her mother's death. The wailing continued as Mary and her sister, Scandera, raced out after the crash of the pail through the window. The four of them huddled on the ground in a pile of tears, clutching each other.

Martha looked up a few minutes later, her eyes blurry with water and her stomach churning with pain, and she saw Dawn standing in front of her. The instant their eyes met, Dawn took a slow step backward, turned and sprinted through John George's garden to the yard between the Isaac house and the church and disappeared down the path and off Syrian Hill.

Later that day, while a freshman at Syracuse University, seventeen-year-old Casper George was told he had a phone call from his brother, Nick, in Myers.

"Hello," Casper said into the phone.

"Nemo's gone," was all Nick George said.

Casper returned to his dorm room, buried his face into his pillow and cried. After an hour, he nervously picked himself up off the bed and left for Myers, never to return to the university.

CHAPTER 27

It is easy for the coaches to drag themselves into the office the Sunday after our Merchant Marine win. The old cliché "business as usual," meaning working tirelessly and moving on to the next game, is more theory than practice. In truth, human nature escapes no one. We cruise through the Kings Point game film with joyous ease. Then we plow on to prepare for Hampden-Sydney. They crushed us last year and have most of their team back, a favorite to win their league and earn an NCAA playoff spot. In the coaches' offices, none of that matters. We have just beaten Merchant Marine for the first time in three years, most likely our best chance at doing so in the years ahead with declining male enrollment at the Academy. The excitement of the win has also buoyed our intensity. The reality is that we have eight games left but we feel like we have just won the national championship.

My early arrival at home pulls Lila out of bed and down the stairs.

"Bill?" Casper asks through the dimly lit living room.

"Hi, Gido." Lila answers for me.

"Oh, honey, I missed you," Casper says to Lila in a tone that sounds as if he has not seen her in ages.

"I just kissed you goodnight. Don't you remember?" she answers. "Here, I will kiss you again so you remember again." She climbs up and lays her head on his chest and Casper tilts his head and peers out of the corner of his eyes down to her and then looks back up at me.

"She has the most beautiful red hair." He pauses. "What is happening in Syria?"

"The Middle East is falling apart. Especially Syria," I say.

"I can't remember, but I think the news showed some horrible pictures about Syria. Especially the children," Casper says.

"I do not have an answer for you," I say desperately, not wanting to talk about destruction and death in front of Lila.

"Back to bed," Nancy says as she scoops her up. Lila grips her two hands onto Casper's white T-shirt, but they break free, leaving tiny finger marks where her hands have stretched the shirt.

Casper watches Lila's departure in silence. He looks up at her with a face of great despair. Nancy notices as she leaves the room.

"What if there is nothing after this?" he blurts.

"What do you mean after this?" I ask.

"After this. Everybody else is gone. I must have to go some time too," he said.

"You know you will go to heaven. You have always been a religious person." I can tell his sundown syndrome is floating in and out, but he has a deep awareness that has him thinking about the next world.

"Everybody is gone, and I am still here. Everybody's gone," he says sadly.

"Dad, you will go and be with them."

"What if this is it? What if it stops right here?" His face fills with panic and he starts to cry. "What if I have to leave that little girl and I do not see everyone else again?" his voice shakes softly.

"Dad, everything will be fine. You are not going anywhere."

Nancy, wracked from the guilt of Casper's sadness, walks back into the room with Lila asleep on her shoulder. Casper looks up and smiles.

"We are supposed to be like her," Casper says. "That is what Jesus said."

"What do you mean?" I ask.

"He is right," Nancy cuts in. "We are supposed to act like a little child. We are supposed to be humble, meek, innocent, loving, kind, gentle."

"Bill, I am glad you are helping all of the little children in the war in Syria," my father says from across the room. "I think about those little boys from Myers a lot."

The meds start to kick in as he fades and weeps. As I watch him slowly cry himself to sleep, I look up and see Lila peeking down.

Our victory celebration ends on Monday. The team meets at the Academy waterfront for what they think is a photo op for *The New London Day*. Having promised the team that spring that if we beat Kings Point, I would jump in the Thames River, I am hiding at the end of the dock behind the Coast Guard Sailing Center. I am dressed in a red Gumby survival suit, used only for rescue in icy, frozen waters such as Alaska.

While I wait, I can see the green trees on the other side of the Thames rise into the blue horizon. Everything seems bigger and clearer being this close to the water. I think of Anna and, somehow, she seems so far away. I feel guilty because I have not put pictures of her up around the house. I wonder if I am losing the memories of her or just selfishly moving on with life. Then it hits me; maybe I fear the pain the memories might bring.

I peek around the corner and see the team at the edge of the dock some two hundred yards away. Lila and Nancy are with them. As the team starts walking out on to the dock and down its length, I appear from behind the Sailing Center. As I flop step after step in the bulky suit, I can hear the laughter rising louder and louder as we near each other. The cheers and yelps crescendo when we meet halfway down the dock. When we join together, we scream with joy as we hold up the Secretaries' Cup one last time all together before it is put into storage until next year.

I turn and I jump in the Thames. After the initial shock of the plunge, I float on my back for a second, letting the suit do its job. I start a slow, backward paddle of my arms. I can see the cameras of the players for a second, but the only face I catch is Lila's, with Nancy holding her up in the middle of the team. She is expressionless. She may think it is funny, but somehow, I also think she does not know what is going on. I rest my sweating head backward, look up at the deep blue sky, close my eyes and try to think of my mother Anna's face when she was younger.

Late on Wednesday night, the bags in our living room are packed for everyone to head in every direction. The team will leave for Hampden-Sydney in Virginia on Thursday. Nancy and Lila will head up to Albany to see Nancy's mother, Eleanor McGraw, who is also being cared for at home. Dan will take Casper for four days, but we arrange the move so that Lila will not see him being driven away. I do not bring his suitcase out so that Lila will not think he is leaving. She is excited about seeing her relatives up north.

Casper is clearing his throat as if he is choking. Lila rushes over with a box of Kleenex, worried as if she needs to save his life.

"Here, Gido!" she shouts. Her tiny, white fingers press the Kleenex against the beaten and gnarled digits of his hand.

Casper catches his breath. "Oh, thank you, honey," he gasps.

Lila smiles at him with a soft face full of love. She stands quietly by, ready to help again if she is needed.

"She was sent from heaven," Casper sighs, as his breathing calms.

"Yes, she was," Nancy cuts in as she lays four pairs of Casper's newly washed pajamas next to his diapers.

"Aren't we all?" I ask.

There is silence as Lila fumbles with the Kleenex box and Casper stares into her face as if he does not hear me.

"What do you mean?" Nancy asks.

"Maybe we are all sent from heaven for our time here. For some it is quick and tragic and for others it is long and slow," I say.

"Maybe this is not our true place?"

"I just feel like the old cliché that we are all quickly running out of borrowed time," I say. "We walk around on this earth, some a lot longer than others. We all start off with a body, some good, some bad. If we are lucky, we get a lot of time to do good until something wears out like our heart or brain or any organ. I suppose some people get a very short life before time runs out or somebody steals our time."

"And that time is supposed to be used to do something more than beating the Merchant Marine Academy." Nancy teases, trying to get me to say more. "I know it is your job, but maybe you are finally thinking about the world and life outside of football."

"I don't know what I am thinking or saying," I keep talking. "Maybe we are all supposed to be some kind of angels sent from heaven for either a long time or a short time."

Nancy looks at me and then down to Casper, who is staring in a trance and straight ahead into Lila's eyes. "Give Gido a kiss good night," she says to Lila.

Casper does not notice Lila until she is right in front of his face. Instinctively, he reaches out to hold her as if Lila is coming to save him. He tilts his jaw forward and kisses her on the cheek. Then Lila turns her head slightly and she kisses Casper on the cheek.

"This is a kiss for you to save, Dad," I whisper to myself, "and take back to heaven and share with everyone."

Lila hears me and I wish I had said nothing. "How will Gido take my kiss to heaven?" she asks.

"He will take it in his heart," I say to her.

Nancy looks at me and smiles like the Mona Lisa, and I think of Adam Bryant as I watch Nancy take Lila up to bed.

In the darkness of the empty room, Casper asks me, "Can your heart go to heaven before the rest of you?"

"What are you talking about?" I ask, thinking his mind is drifting in confusion.

"Maybe some people are so hurt that part of them is in heaven already and part of them is still here," he says. "I think Myers was that way as I got older."

I ignore him and wait for my silence to help him rest. After ten minutes, I glance over and see that Casper is still awake but now he is ignoring me.

On the morning of the day before Thanksgiving in 1945, Martha Saleem stepped out of her house on Syrian Hill into the grayness of the November day. An immediate uncontrollable urge to cry overcame her. It happened often, triggered by a random thought about her life before 1941. Sometimes, it was the smell of food as she walked through the kitchen, or the sight of Nemo's clothes still in his room.

Martha looked across Syrian Hill at the Georges' home and garden. During the war, she knew exactly how John and Mary Anna felt with one son, Johnny Boy, in the South Pacific and another, Coach, in the Ardennes Forest in France. She could feel their pain through her own. Now, the war was over, and Johnny Boy was home and Coach had survived the Battle of the Bulge. Martha avoided them and the Isaac house; she could not bring herself to look at Gus or Decker, who too were now home from the war for good.

They are all back on Syrian Hill and Nemo and Puppy are gone forever, thought Martha. *Gus Isaac might have been the last person to see either Nemo or Puppy alive.* The thought gave her chills, as if Gus had something left to say or a message to carry. They were all back, but for some unknown reason it was Gus Isaac she feared seeing more than the others.

Martha had not taken the Syrian Hill path in a month, but today, instead of walking around the hill and down the road to avoid the Isaac boys, her mind drifted. She thought of Dawn, but they had not talked. She knew it was far too painful for either of them. They had one thing in common and it was death. *Dawn is very young,* Martha thought. *The pain may go away for her someday. She might meet someone who will help take the pain away, but I can never replace Nemo.*

"Martha, there is a package at Abraham's store," her father had told her that morning. Abraham Saleem then walked to the salt plant, torn between his own past and the future his daughters would have to endure. Martha knew he could not bear to pick up the package.

Instinctively, she cut through John and Mary Anna's garden next to her house and across the hill. Then she tiptoed, one soft step after another as if trying to make herself invisible, through the grass between the Isaac house and the church toward the top of the path.

She did not want to look back, but before she could turn around, the sight of Myers in late November caught her eye. It was the barren, brown sight of the leafless trees with long arms waiting for the drizzle that might come from the dull gray sky. She looked down the path and it was clear and barren, but so was the entire side of the hill and the shrubs which bordered the path. The short, dark days of November had eaten away the vegetation.

I am in a different world, she thought. *When did all the leaves fall? Did summer come and go without any warmth?* She wondered if she had been removed from the earth, put in hell and had just returned to Myers. *No, I am still in hell, and I will be there forever. We did not even plan a meal for Thanksgiving.*

Martha turned and looked up at the far bedroom window in the Isaac house. She thought she saw a curtain move and froze with fear. She did not want to see Gus Isaac.

In the room above, Gus Isaac lay on his bed crying. He could feel the tears roll down the outside corners of both his eyes and wet the pillow. He rubbed his head, trying to feel the German shrapnel still in his skull.

He would tell no one about what happened. *I can't believe I am back in Myers.* He was lost in every way. He knew he was lucky, but he also knew he was an ugly, walking monument. He thought back to Italy, standing right next to a boy who had never shaved. *That boy was vaporized,* he thought. *He just disappeared. Nothing left.* He remembered shaking in a fear so intense and horrible. Now, he knew he had to live with a fear he once conquered. In the war, it was a fear he had to survive with. Now, the fear was baked into him, not letting him forget the pain of war.

Gus could hear Decker in the next room. They had both made it back, but they were still ghosts walking around Myers. He lifted himself off the bed and peeked in at Decker.

"Did I get a Bronze Star at Anzio and a Purple Heart at the Battle of Colmar Pocket, or was it the other way around?" Gus asked his brother. "My mind won't let me forget about the war, no matter how hard I try."

Mike "Decker" Isaac was reading the letter they had written together dated June 2, 1944, in the middle of bloodshed. Decker looked up at Gus. "I'm trying hard enough to forget about my own medals. I don't want to talk about the war now or ever." Decker returned to the letter, and Gus returned to his bed.

Killing and death, Gus thought, staring at the ceiling. *Years of horror and now I am here living in the peace of Myers with war trapped inside my head.*

Gus leaned up and peeked out the window and saw, Martha who, upon being seen, turned and sprinted back to her house. By the time he was outside the front of his house, she was gone. He looked over at the church and knew he had to find her.

At the Saleem house, Mary answered the door and led Gus upstairs into the emptiness of one of the small bedrooms.

Martha lay beneath the bed, hidden in silence and covered by the long drapery of the white bed linen which stretched to the floor. She lay frozen on the hardwood floor, holding her breath when she saw Gus's brown beaten shoes walk into the room.

Gus started to turn away when he heard soft sobbing come from beneath the bed. Gus walked to the window and listened to her tears, as if it was his duty to feel her pain. He pulled the white lace curtain back and stared out the window onto the dark, blue waters of Cayuga Lake. He cried quietly, at first to himself and then in quiet unison with Martha. While he wept, he became mesmerized by the stillness of the vast, blue lake. And once his mind dulled, the vision of the water turned his fear into sorrow. Gus waited for several minutes, crying softly and hoping Martha would emerge. When she did not appear, he left without saying anything.

Martha lay paralyzed underneath the bed with a fright she could not understand. It was not the horror of the tragedies engulfing her, but the fear of the life that lay ahead. She slipped into an hour-long nap of exhaustion, dreaming of her father, Abraham. He was standing in front of her house holding his lunch pail, just as he was the day the news of Nemo's death came. The sky above him was bright and massive rays of sunshine covered all of Cayuga Lake and Syrian Hill. Abraham stood looking at the front porch, where the only darkness of the day, a thin black cloud, floated a few feet above him. In the depth of her unconscious, Martha heard the cloud say to Abraham, *That is all you get. Nineteen years is all you get with Michael.*

When she opened her eyes, Martha could see the daylight from the gray day on the wood floor. *Nemo,* she thought. *Where is Nemo?* As she slowly woke, all she could focus on was the white, lace curtains of the silent room. "Oh, my God," she panted, "the package."

Martha hurried to the path and, for the first time in over a month, walked between the Isaac house and the church and down the path. She entered Abraham's store and looked behind the cash register in the front. Among the dozen packages wrapped in brown paper, her eye caught the lettering *Department of the Army* on the return address of a package twice the size of a shoe box. When she lifted it from the pile, she could clearly see that it was addressed to Abraham Saleem.

When she turned to leave, she looked up and saw her uncle looking at her trying to smile. She tried to smile back but could not, and then left. Once outside the store with the package, she no longer felt hurried. She glanced down the tiny lane to the Moses house.

She did not want to go home. *Maybe it is a good time to see her,* she thought about Takla's misery instead of her own.

Daniel Moses walked toward her and noticed the package under her arm. "She will not leave the house," he said, referring to his wife. "It is hard. We can't touch anything or move anything." He pointed to the package under her arm, "She hides stuff around the house."

Martha tiptoed up the porch steps and stopped, noticing the small pie tin of milk on the Moses porch. She knocked twice, but there was no answer. She looked down at the tin of milk again and then turned and walked away with her head down. At the bottom of the porch steps, she startled when she noticed her eighteen-year-old cousin, Casper George, quietly staring at her. Casper had four large loaves of Syrian bread wrapped in a white linen cloth tucked underneath his arm. Their eyes connected for a moment and the creaking of the door, as it opened slowly, deflected their vison up to the six-inch crack in the door.

Takla peeked out. "Casper, come here."

Casper stood motionless, trapped between sorrow and shock.

"Casper, come here. My Puppy will be home from the war soon."

Taka looks a hundred years old, Martha thought in disbelief.

"Martha, my Puppy will be coming home from the war soon." She tried to smile at Martha, but her heart pulled her facial muscles tightly against her jaw and her face remained stoic.

She opened the door a little wider and handed Martha a package. "Puppy will be coming home from the war soon." Takla smiled softly. "He will be looking for you in Myers."

Martha looked down at the package that was addressed to Daniel and Takla Moses from the Department of the Army. The door closed before Martha could finish reading the address.

Martha took both packages and left. At the top of the path, she walked toward the church and paused. *I am not going in,* she thought. *I have lost something inside of me. I do not know what, but every time I sit in this church, all I have is fear.*

Martha walked around to the far side, away from the Isaac house. She sat on the November ground and looked over the salt plant to the lake and the far hills. The gray sky stretched forever.

"Maybe if I walk forever, I will find a spot where the sky is connected to the earth and I will find the past," she said aloud.

Martha sat, pulled her legs in, and rested her head on her knees. She looked down the green grass of the field as it stretched away from the church before it turned into the back side of Syrian Hill and sloped down to the salt plant and the lake. She watched a small animal she could not identify scurry off the field and down the slope. *Maybe a rabbit or a muskrat.*

It seemed like only days ago this field would be filled with ten-year-old Syrian boys playing football. Their names gushed forward. *Nemo, Puppy, Coach, Johnny Boy, Gus, Decker, Abrahams, Caliels, Solomons, the Georges.* Her depression turned to anger. *Little boys go to war. Even Jacko and the Solomon boys, before the flood, would be here.*

Then she remembered the puppy. It caught her off guard and she wondered why she had not thought of that little dog in years. She lay back on the ground and stretched her legs out from underneath her. The cold November earth easily crept up and into her bones as if she were a skeleton with no flesh to protect her. The chill chased her from the ground, and she sat back up. Instantly, she swallowed to wet the dryness in her throat. Her body never reacted to hunger, but thirst was different; thirst had no feelings or ties to the soul. The dryness in her throat made her think of Thanksgiving, and that made her think of Christmas for the first time in a year.

"Ugh," she grunted in horror, reaching to the package with the Saleem name on it and tore the brown paper.

Inside, she found a tightly wrapped ten-inch ball of cotton. Her fingers felt something inside as she held it for a moment. Then, her fingers gently sifted through until she felt a soft metal object and pulled it out.

"OHHH!" she screamed in horror as she looked at her brother's glasses, lifted from his dead body on the battlefield and still covered with his dried blood. She lovingly pressed them against the softness of her left cheek, cupping them softly, as if she were holding his face, and then cried inconsolably for minutes. When she stopped, she moved the glasses away from her face and looked down at them. She watched as one round tear lay on one spot of dried blood, turning it watery and bright red. She looked outward across the lake where the trees faded into the grayness of the horizon. *Maybe if I find that spot where the heavens meet the earth, I will find him, and he will be alive again.*

Martha looked down and saw the package addressed to the Moses family. She put the glasses in her sweater pocket and opened the package. It was larger and filled with wrapping paper. On top of the wrapping paper was a letter addressed to her.

When she opened it, a thin, gold chain fell out and into her lap. The chain had one gold piece, the shape of a dime. She held it close to her face and saw her name, MARTHA, inscribed. She put the chain in her palm and pressed her hand against her cheek.

> *Dear Martha,*
>
> *I wanted to give you this chain in person, but I could not. It is not to remind you of me, but for you to enjoy as you go through life.*
>
> *I wanted to tell you that life is not quite what we think it is. I cannot explain what I mean by that, other than it is so much more than we think it is while we travel through each day. I pray, more than any other thought in my mind or heart, that your days are full of all the love that life gives you. I know you as someone who will always give all their love back to life. To have known you, and more importantly to have fallen in love with you, even from a silent distance, was worth more than anything else I could have had in this short life. Sometimes, late on a clear night when I would stand on the bridge in Myers and see the sky full of stars, I would think that beyond the farthest star was a star that I could not see but it could see me. I will be a star that you cannot see but will see you.*

If Nemo is standing next you, please kiss him softly on the cheek for me. And if he is not there standing next to you but instead here, standing next to me, then I will kiss him on the cheek for you. I know he will be working to cure the leukemias and sicknesses of the world from here, just as if he had never left.

With all the love that I was never able to express,
Puppy Moses

Martha stared at the letter, frozen with lost emotions. After several minutes, she watched the November sky finally start to spit a few shivery drops of water on the letter.

Plip, plip, plip.

She watched the drops fall and leave their dotted marks as if they were desperately trying to become part of the words.

Martha gently folded the letter and placed it into her pocket next to the glasses. She could feel a chilly breeze brush across the bottom of her hairline. She listened as the breeze picked up and rustled the brown paper of the packages she had not finished opening. The drizzle and the wind weakened, fading away as quickly as they had arrived. She stood and gathered the packages and paper wrappings and cradled them in her arms and started back to the front of the church and to the dirt road in the middle of Syrian Hill. When she reached the front of the church, she heard a faint yelp as she caught sight of something out of the corner of her eye race past the front door and into the brush. *A little rabbit,* she thought. Martha blinked her eyes and it was gone. *I am like the rabbit,* she thought. *I scurry out into the day for a moment and then I rush back into the bushes to hide from the world.*

The rain was starting to fall harder as she turned her back to the church and walked past the Isaac house. The dirt road of Syrian Hill was now moist, and the rain turned the tan dust into dark brown dirt.

I am very tired and mixed up, she told herself.

She tucked the packages under her arm and turned back to look at the church. She kept her eyes open and tilted her head up at the grayness as the chilling water landed on her face. "I heard you. I heard what you said that day," she said out loud, as if she could talk to the letter that Puppy Moses had written her. "I heard what you said about the clouds when we were at the tennis court. I heard you say, 'Are they racing across the sky trying to catch tomorrow before they are left behind or racing after yesterday before it is gone forever?' I should have told you then that I heard you." Feeling numb and empty, she lowered her face to the ground, turned away from the church and walked toward the center of Syrian Hill and into the hopeless path of life that she had to travel.

CHAPTER 28

Seven days after Coast Guard looked so spectacular in victory against Kings Point, this Saturday's nonleague contest against Hampden-Sydney turns quickly into a disappointment. We trail miserably, 28-0, when the clock runs down to end the half. We look nothing like we had the week before.

I follow the team into the locker room. The Hampden-Sydney crowd respectfully waits until the team passes and then starts walking to the tailgate parties in the parking lot. The coaches are caught up in the traffic. I stop and look at the beautiful, white clouds rolling in across the rich Virginia sky. I feel as if the ghost I thought I had caught last week is slipping away from me and blending into the passing crowd. It was just as Casper had said after returning from his mini stroke and slowly gained his senses, "You look like my son Bill, but Bill is a much younger and much more handsome man."

Then I remember that once I was in San Antonio at a coaches' convention after my mother died, and as I walked by a church downtown I saw a homeless old lady standing on the side of the church in an alley. I looked into her large despondent eyes and she looked deep into my eyes as if they were trying to speak to me. I walked past her and moved on. A few minutes later I thought, "That lady looked just like Anna." I raced back but she was gone. I frantically searched for a few blocks, then ran into Coach LaForte and told him about the lady and that I was trying to find her.

"It wasn't your mother," Ray said, trying to get me to regain my senses.

"What do you mean?" I asked.

"You're running around San Antonio trying to find some lady who was not your mother. Even if you find the lady, it wasn't your mother."

Then it hit me. It wasn't my mother. Maybe deep down I knew it was not Anna, but something in the way her eyes pleaded with me made me want to believe it could have been Anna. "I could find her anyway," I said. "I'll flip her a few bucks."

"So," Ray spoke in a sly tone, "you walked by a homeless lady standing next to a church who reminded you of your mother and you did not flip her a few bucks?"

My heart sank. *Oh my God,* I thought. *What if it was some kind of test from God? What if it was my mother? What if I had a chance to see her again, even for a moment, and I just kept walking?* Then I thought, disgusted with myself, *No, it was not Anna, it was just some homeless old lady who was all alone and I just kept walking.* I looked around at all the people walking by Ray and me in downtown San Antonio. *Maybe it really was a test from God,* I thought.

We fumble the second-half opening kickoff and they take it in and score. The game ends at 56-0.

The bus ride home is long and dark and lonely. At four in the morning I sit alone in my living room. The emptiness of the house makes me think of the letter Nancy had written in 2001, thirteen years ago.

I really have led an empty life, I think. I have failed at football, although I am the winningest coach at Coast Guard, but I have also lost more games than anyone. *Lila is the only joy I have.* I think what life would be without Lila. I was the one who balked at adoption. I look over at Casper's empty bed. *I do not treat him kindly enough. I lose my patience and yell like an angry football coach.* I move an *old man a hundred miles an hour while he uses a walker. I loved my parents but not nearly as much as they loved and gave to me.* I know I have let my ego overshadow what is truly important in the world.

The empty gloom sets in and I have no one to turn to. I realize half my life has been paved with gold by my parents and the other half paved with silver by Nancy and Lila. If left to me, my life would be a lonely nightmare. "'Come upstairs with me,'" I can hear Casper say, "those were the greatest words ever spoken." I had said them to him but maybe I needed to come upstairs as well, I thought to myself.

Suddenly, my mother's aging face pops into my head. It was Sunday morning one week before Lila was born and three months before Anna fell and hit her head, which caused her death. I had gone for an early morning jog and when I returned, she was sitting in our living room in my childhood home, waiting for my father to take her to church. Anna smiled at me when I walked in the door.

"Is it cold?" she asked.

"No, not for February in upstate New York," I answered.

As I studied her, it came to me that since I had spent so much time worrying about the adoption, I had forgotten about worrying about my mother. Her face was gaunt, and her tiny frame was always thin, but now she seemed frail. Her white hair tried its best to cover her scalp. She was always very light-skinned for a woman of Middle Eastern descent, but now the skin on her face looked ghostly.

"I think I am being driven by a greater force," I said to her.

"You mean about adopting a newborn baby?" she asked.

"Yes. It is like I have not paid much attention to anything in life, and now this life-changing event has snuck up on me at the age of fifty-two," I answered.

"I know you will be a good father and you will love your child with all of your heart," she said.

"Mom, when I was a little boy, you used to say to me and Danny that Christ said, 'Many are called but few are chosen.'"

"Yes," she answered.

"Am I being chosen now?" I asked.

"No. That is not what our Lord meant by that," she replied. Her soft eyes stared at me. "I think everyone has that wrong."

"What do you mean?" I asked.

"We are all called," she said. "But it is us, not the Lord who chooses."

"I don't understand," I said.

"We are all called to follow the teachings of Jesus Christ, but only a few truly choose to do so. It is not our Lord who chooses, but us," she explained.

"And what are we supposed to choose?" I asked.

"We are supposed to live a life in which every moment is dedicated to kindness, whether it is toward a stranger we pass on the street or a human being suffering halfway around the world. Christ said, 'Love everyone, help everyone, forgive everyone.' And when he said forgive everyone, he also meant accept everyone and love them no matter who they are," she said.

I looked deep into the flesh of her eyes and I noticed that they were full of life, unlike the rest of her body. I wondered why the flesh of her eyes had not aged like the skin on her face or the bones of her body. Her eyes started to water as they looked back at me. I wanted to cry, but I kept my feelings locked within me. I wanted to say something, but I did not feel I could carry on the conversation, so I stayed silent. It dawned on me that she had always been so religious but just led us through love and had not pushed or pounded us about religion.

Anna started softly speaking again. "When the Lord pointed at strangers and said 'This is my brother, my mother, my sister,' I think he meant that you must love everybody, just like you love me, Billy. You have to walk every step with love and kindness to everyone like our Lord did. If you can do that, then you have been chosen. And then the world in front of you and the suffering world you cannot see will be better."

"The world I cannot see?" I asked.

"Yes. The world is bigger than what is in front of you," she said. She stood and readied herself to leave for church.

"Is it too late for me to choose?" I asked.

"No, it is never too late. Our Lord will always be waiting for you whenever you decide to help him."

"And if I decide to choose, what does that mean?"

"That means you will walk through life and help anyone suffering from anything," she said. "Most all of us do that already, just not to the degree we should."

I noticed a sadness as she glanced away from me. It was as if what was in her heart was trying to tell me something she did not want me to know.

"I will see you in church," I said. "I will get there as soon as I can."

"Come whenever you can. Just get there before it is over," she said. "And when you get there, you will kiss me and hold me tight and pay attention to me, but not to the church service." She smiled.

"Is that bad?" I asked.

"No," the smile widened until it turned into a small laugh. "How could that possibly be bad? That is the most wonderful thing that you could do."

As I sat there alone in the empty house, I remembered asking my father many years ago when we were visiting Myers why he had left.

"I love Myers, but Myers was not the same with Puppy and Nemo gone. I was eighteen and the war was over. It was as if they took some part of me when they left. I would stand on the bridge or walk up the path and around the Syrian Hill, but I felt empty. I was thinking maybe I would give Syracuse another try. George was starting a restaurant in Glens Falls. I went up to help him and never came back. That is where I met your mother. You would not be here if I had not left Myers."

The next few years passed slowly, and time carried Martha Saleem along as if she was walking through life in a coma. In the spring of 1948, she stood at the far end of Syrian Hill and looked down past the few houses on each side to the brown door of the green-shingled church. The afternoon breeze in the air chilled her, and she tightened her sweater around her white blouse, which was covered with red roses. The big cumulus clouds had gray edges as they shielded the earth from the sun, only letting a few rays of sunshine sneak past for a moment before evaporating in the bleak darkness of the day. Martha studied the stillness of Syrian Hill, ignoring which direction the cool day might take, sunlight and warmth or dark clouds and cool rain. She had not walked down the path at all and had only walked down through Myers a few times in the past year, using the road at the far end of Syrian Hill.

Martha had not been to church much in the last few years; she harbored no bitterness, but it stirred nothing inside of her anymore. The church was like the food she ate, dull, tasteless and never satisfying. Martha ate when her stomach subconsciously told her brain to eat, not when the spices tickled her appetite. Food became like church and church became like all her life, a bland task.

"Myers is tasteless and odorless," she sighed aloud to herself in despair. "I am walking around in the world alone. The people around me are moving but I am not. Time is moving, life is moving, but not me."

Martha turned her back to the houses on each side of her and the church at the end of Syrian Hill and walked across the big bridge. She stopped in front of the Ludlowville school on her left as she passed it. *If I walked into Miss Fisher's sixth-grade class, they would be there,* she thought. *Puppy and Nemo, they both had perfect attendance in the sixth grade. They would be in there.* She walked up the front lawn of the school and peeked into a classroom. Her mind made her see Puppy, with his round face and bushy hair, and handsome, young Nemo. She could see them smiling at each other as if something had made them both happy. As she stared at the vison of the boys, her sorrow swelled into a fear. *Where is Dawn?* she thought desperately. *Dawn was in the sixth grade with them.* In a panic, Martha ran from the school and onto Ludlowville Road and toward Dawn Worsell's house.

Inside the house, Martha calmed herself as she was led to the bed in the living room where Dawn lay barely breathing. The curtains were open, but the room seemed dark, as if the clouds had won the battle with the sunlight and the afternoon would stay chilly and drab.

Martha sat alone with Dawn, looking down at her, and thought, *She looks white like the bed sheet. Her beauty is gone. Her eyes look like an old lady's eyes.* Then Martha thought of her mother. *She did not have old eyes when she died. They were not young, but they were not old like Dawn's eyes.* Suddenly, panic from the vision of the boys returned and she wanted to run out of the house, but she did not. She took three deep breaths to calm herself, loud breaths. Dawn cracked her eyes open and blinked at Martha. They stayed open for a second longer and then closed.

Martha remembered a conversation she had with Dawn three years after they learned Nemo died.

"I cannot go on or even forward," Dawn told her. "You can at least move forward."

"I cannot do either," Martha answered. "My heart has stopped."

"Yes. Both our hearts have stopped but your body is moving. My body is stopping. It has been starting and stopping for years."

"And just where is my body, without a heart beating, supposed to take me?" Martha asked her.

"I don't know. I suppose only God knows," Dawn answered.

Martha looked down at Dawn. *I wonder why some people die young like this or younger. From sickness or anything when they are young and healthy?* Then she thought of her mother. *And why do some die in the middle of their life or some live old and long and die late?*

She thought of Nemo, and of Puppy. *And some die young in war. And we go on here in life and are supposed to carry on.*

Then Martha remembered what Nemo had told her years ago before he left for war, something Puppy once said to him, *"We die who we are and we die who we are not."*

"Do not die yet," she whispered to Dawn as she moved closer. "Nemo is going to cure leukemia. Hang on. Don't go to see him yet. Give him some more time, he will cure it." She put her ear to Dawn's lips and listened to the silence. After a few moments, she calmly rose and walked out of the house, not saying a word.

As Martha walked past the tennis courts, a lump in her throat swelled and drew heavy tears. She moved past the school and crossed Route 34B and headed down American Hill, descending into Myers, her mind blank and numb. She stopped outside Abraham's small store and, through the window, watched the grocer cut meat on the butcher's block. She looked for his wife, her Aunt Helanie, but there was only one other customer in the store with Abraham. She wrapped her sweater tighter as the wind picked up and turned the chilly day into a cold one. She shivered as her bony arms held the sweater tight around her thin, tight stomach. As the cold spring air cut through her body, she shivered again. She looked down the short dirt road to Puppy's house. She had not seen Takla in two years. *I wonder what they think about or talk about. I wonder if they can put anything behind them. I wonder if anyone can put this war behind them.*

Then she thought about Dawn. *I wonder if the war killed her, too, or if life would have taken her anyway? How can I move forward in this life?*

Down the street, she stopped in front of Abraham's house and leaned against one of the cement pillars, which were at the end of the path to the front door. *I hope she sees me.* She was thinking of her Aunt Helanie, who had been at their house many times in the past years, but Martha always avoided her. *I do not know why, but I* want to see her face right now. I want to look into her eyes and see my mother. They were sisters. I will see my mother in her face.*

The door opened and ten-year-old Marion George stepped out onto the porch. He held the door ajar and looked down the cement walkway to where Martha stood. "Ma!" he yelled back into the house through the open door. "Ma!" he yelled again, "Martha Saleem is here."

He looks a little bit like Puppy with his bushy hair, Martha thought. *That is odd. He calls his grandmother "Ma," like it is his mother. He treats Helanie like she is his mother, and I am trying to make her remind me of my mother.* Then Martha thought of the dream she had where God spoke to her father, *Nineteen years, that is all you get.*

Maybe, Martha thought, *God said to Marion and his mother when he was just a few moments old and she was bleeding to death, "One minute, that is all you get."*

Martha thought of Dawn and Nemo and of Puppy Moses and what he had said. *"We die who we are and we die who we are not."* Her lower lip trembled, and she bit into it to stop herself from crying. *I know Puppy better now, after he has gone, than when he was alive.*

Moments later, Helanie walked down the path carrying a paper bag. "Martha," she said with her deep Arabic accent.

Martha leaned forward and kissed her aunt on the cheek. When she leaned back, she stared deeply into Helanie's eyes, but she did not see her mother.

Her aunt reached out and held her. She cried into her aunt's thick, dark sweater and she could smell the fragrance of lilacs, which reminded her of her mother. Martha broke her embrace and, as she turned away, she could see Helanie making the sign of the cross with her fingers toward her.

"Wait," Helanie said. "Syrian bread, for your sister, Mary." Helanie handed her the paper bag. Martha took the bread and looked into Helanie's eyes again, rose to her tiptoes and kissed her softly again on the cheek. Kissing her aunt felt good to her again.

Martha took the bread and walked until she stopped on the

bridge and looked back at Marion and Helanie as they stood on the porch staring back. Martha looked down at the creek looking toward the railroad trestle. She closed her eyes and listened to the creek move for a moment and then walked to the path. Halfway up, she looked down on Myers and searched for Marion and Helanie, but they had disappeared. She turned and started to walk back up the rest of the path and suddenly she saw something quickly disappear above her up the path. *A possum,* she thought. At the top of the path, she walked past the Isaac house and noticed the door of the church cracked opened slightly. The church was always unlocked, but the door was usually closed. As she pushed it shut, Martha heard a whimper from inside. On the second whimper, she opened the door and in the middle of the church, as the fading light crept through the stained-glass windows, she saw a small animal. It was a tiny beagle puppy. The resemblance of the dog startled her. She bent down in front of the puppy and the tiny dog looked up at her with its large eyes glistening with life. When she touched it, she felt it trembling with cold. *It is soaking wet and freezing. Where did it get wet? It did not rain at all today.*

Martha placed it on her lap as she sat in one of the church chairs. She dried the dog the best she could with her clothes as it sat in her lap. The puppy trembled as if it had hypothermia and Martha sensed the dog's condition. She opened her sweater and unbuttoned her flowered blouse and placed the dog against the center of her thin, gaunt belly.

She felt the puppy sink deep into her body, settling against her body heat, and started to breathe normally. After a short while, Martha stood and held the dog with one hand tightly against her body and buttoned her blouse and sweater around the dog with her other hand. Before she turned to leave, she looked into the rays of daylight as they left the dark church. On the altar, she saw Jesus crucified on the cross. She looked down at the dog wrapped beneath her clothes and readied herself to move into the swift uncertainty of the future.

CHAPTER 29

Life at home became harder for Nancy and me three weeks later, at the midpoint of the football season. Hat, our primary caregiver, had increasing health problems and his time became very limited through the rest of the season. By the first of November, he was unable to help at all. Nancy carried most of the load, using all her vacation days and luckily being able to work from home on some days. We reverted to paying heavy prices for outside caregivers from professional agencies. Casper had withered but was still finding joy. The loss of his companion, Hat, left him lonely, with Lila out of the house during the day. The football season withered as well. Coast Guard struggled to barely defeat two of the weaker teams on our schedule. Halfway through the season, smiley Jordan Groff, who had scored the two late touchdowns against Kings Point, was blindsided with a violent intentional late hit, the kind that gives football a bad name. He was carried off the field with a shattered arm, never to return in a football uniform. The next time he set foot on the football field was at graduation as an ensign, which is why they are all really here. The season, which started so wonderfully, ended in defeat, as we finished 3-7.

After Christmas, in early January, the hospice administrators returned and this time, although Casper was weakening, they deemed him as thriving and he was removed from hospice care. The daily aides who cleaned him were gone, the nurses gone, the love they gave him gone. Nancy took time off, and Michelle LaForte, Ray's wife, helped us ease the load.

That February, less than one month after Casper had been

removed from hospice care, Michelle was caring for Casper while he was fighting a cold and slipped into a deep sleep. Michelle called me while I was teaching personal defense at the Academy.

"I thought he was dead. I called 9-1-1." She had no other choice.

I met her at the hospital. Casper was motionless. He looked much like he had for the last year, barely alive but his vitals had been stabilized. I explained the past year to the emergency room doctor. Within an hour, a drowsy Casper slowly emerged from his deep sleep.

I put the doctor on the phone with my brother, Dan, and waited as the two doctors talked for twenty minutes.

"He is a dying man, but he seems to be breathing normally for the moment," the doctor said. The doctor looked at me and whispered, "What do you want me to do?"

"What are my options?" I asked.

"I can hospitalize him for a few days," the doctor said.

That would give Nancy and me a few days of a break, I thought.

"Or, you can take him home. Your brother said it is your decision."

"Can you put him back on hospice?" I do not know why I asked that. I had thought a few days in the hospital would give us break.

"Yes, I can do that," the doctor said.

Two hours later, in the darkness of an early February night, the nurses wheeled Casper out of the hospital and we all carefully lifted him into the passenger side of the car and on his way home.

The next day, Casper was home and the head nurse came by and certified him again. It was easy for the certifying nurse, as he looked near death, with no emotion or happiness, and a faint heartbeat. He had new caregivers who still came with love, but Debbie was now reassigned. The nurses were new also, replacing Jessica and Amy, but they still came with love. And Lila would be here around him. It was the single best decision I had ever made considering the past year.

Casper was in and out for a few days, but then he drifted into deep sleep with little or no food. He would barely sip water or an energy drink; even then, we had to force it into his mouth.

Dan came over every night and on the second night he said, "He does not want to drink."

On Friday, a few days later, I awoke on the couch. I thought I heard the motor on his hospital bed running. It was a dull, repetitive grinding that would start and stop every few seconds. I listened, half asleep, but then thought, *What the hell is that noise?* I got up and flipped the light on and looked at Casper. It was him. He was wheezing loudly as he struggled for air. He was looking at me with terror, gasping for life, and begging with his eyes for mercy. I called hospice and they came at two that morning, and we started morphine.

"Get in bed with him," Nancy said to me softly. "Sleep with him."

I cradled his head as the two of us crammed into the upright hospital bed and slept. I was scared for him, but more scared for me. I was holding all my memories of life and they were being pulled from me by a force I could not defeat. I held him tight. Fear ran though me. Now I was the little boy scared of the night who crawled into his father's bed. Then, I thought about a sunny morning in my parents' living room in Glens Falls five years ago, a week before Anna fell and hit her head. All of life seemed to be traveling on its redundant course. Lila was two months old, sitting back on a portable car seat, her eyes wide open and looking around as if she understood everything that surrounded her. Nancy and Anna sat on one side of the room, and Casper and I sat on one side.

"Sometimes, a lot of times," Casper said as he leaned over to me, "I'm not sure if there is a God."

I was shocked. "You of all people, Dad? You go to church every day during Easter season. You say your prayers three times a day." I watched him as he stared down at Lila.

"I am going for a walk," was all Casper said as he got up and left the house.

An hour later, he walked back in and said to me, "I believe there is a God."

"What convinced you?" I asked.

"When I was a little boy in Myers, I could not ice skate. I was trying, I was scared. One time I was falling and going to hit my head right on the ice and I yelled out, 'God help me' and instantly my head and shoulders popped up at my waist and I was fine."

On a dark, January afternoon of 1935, seven-year-old Casper Abraham George sat crying on the frozen ice, halfway between the Myers bridge and the railroad trestle. The sky, a deep navy blue with hints of the darkest purple on its edges, captured winter's beauty above the world. The cold dusk was rolling in to swallow that last light of day. Flakes of ice chips covered Casper's red and black wool pants. He turned his ankles and rolled his skates against the frozen creek but did not attempt to lift himself. He buried his face in his wool mittens and tiny chips of ice touched his warm tears. He looked up to the bridge with tearing eyes to the Myers mothers who looked down on him. They were aligned across the bridge and when he spotted his mother, Helanie, standing between Atina and Takla he felt a sense of relief. Dawn Worsell, dressed all in white with a white hat and a white bow over her heart, skated by from his right, changing Casper's line of vison. He followed her until she stopped near the snow-covered gravel on the bank to his left.

"Take my picture," Dawn said to Abraham Saleem, Nemo's father, who stood in the middle of the snow-covered gravel bank. He took off his gloves and snapped a picture of Dawn, who was smiling and standing still as if she, and all of Myers, was frozen forever in a photograph.

After a moment, she slowly moved her feet and danced her way upstream and underneath the bridge and, as she did, all the faces on the bridge lowered in unison until she was out of their sight. Then the faces looked up and back to Casper. He looked to his right and saw Gus and his brothers Decker and Jacko sitting on the big rocks on the steep, banked side of the creek with their skates dangling inches above the ice.

Maybe Jacko will come and help me off, Casper thought in desperation. They did not move and neither did Casper's cousin, Martha, who stood on the ice next to the Isaac brothers, balancing against the rocks while she watched Casper.

Martha hopped off the rocks. Then gliding gently on the ice from underneath the bridge, Nemo and Puppy appeared, smiling softly like angels coming to the rescue. They each grabbed Casper beneath an arm, stood him up and pointed him downstream toward the railroad trestle and the wider part of the creek.

"No! No! I will fall!" Casper begged. "I can't skate. All I do is fall." He was starting to cry as they escorted him for a few glides on the ice.

Nemo and Puppy watched Casper's feet move with theirs as they held his arms until they reached the middle of the pool, just about the trestle, then Puppy winked at Nemo and Nemo winked back, and they both let go of Casper's arms. Casper glided for two steps and started to lose his balance backward, his hips locked, his eyes closed, and his shoulders swung his arms in wide circles to shift his weight forward. He was gaining speed as his arms generated more motion. Then Casper's weight shifted and now he was falling forward as he moved beneath the railroad trestle. Casper's skates started to slip from underneath him, as he screamed aloud. "God help me!"

Suddenly, he reversed his forward motion and his weight shifted upright, his feet wild with confidence, and he skated downstream beyond the trestle. Casper Abraham George opened his eyes as he moved and looked far downstream toward the deep blue waters of Cayuga Lake. He watched the whitecaps rise from the water and fall back into the lake, as if they were jumping and trying to escape into the air and join the purple dusk above the tree line on the far side.

Lila was visibly distant as Casper rapidly declined on Saturday. She would not go near him or acknowledge his presence. That night, cousin Regina came, and so did Dan and his kids, Jacqueline, Mary Kate, Michael, and Christopher. Jacqueline came up from her job in New York and Mary Kate came up from the middle of her first year at law school at the University of Virginia. The girls hovered over Casper's sleeping body, kissing him and talking to him. Lila watched them and followed their actions. She made him a star out of popsicle sticks, drew him pictures and kissed him like she had done every day. Hat hobbled, barely able to walk, to sit at the foot of the hospital bed and wept uncontrollably. He left without saying a word.

I contacted the local Orthodox diocese, and we were able to get a priest to arrive at the house late in the afternoon for last rites. They were in town that morning for the funeral of a young priest who had died in a car accident, leaving a widow and five children. Now the priests were here for a dying old man who had lived a very wonderful life. They had long beards and wore long robes. They chanted like they had one foot in the history of Constantinople and another foot two centuries ahead in America.

Later that day, Hat called me at around five. I was sitting next to Casper as he breathed once every four seconds. My face was only a foot away from his as I talked to Hat.

"I feel bad if I ever lost my patience with him," Hat said to me over the phone.

"You were always kind," I said. "I was the one who lost my patience all the time. I was the one who was too tough too many times." I was staring at the ground in the light of the late afternoon when I realized I didn't hear a breath.

I looked up to see Casper looking at me with his eyes open for the first time in days. There was no breathing, and as I screamed for Dan and Nancy, Mary Kate and Jacqueline wisely scooped up Lila and took her upstairs. Hospice came and pronounced Casper deceased.

Nancy went upstairs and brought Lila down. "Lila," she said.

"Remember when I told you that everybody just has a body that is like a shell? And we all live inside this shell. And the shells are all different colors and sizes and shapes, and some are boy shells and some are girl shells. But inside is where we really live?"

Lila looked down at Casper. She was sad but not overly stressed.

"Gido's shell has worn out and he cannot use it anymore. That happens to people, and so his spirit is going to heaven to keep living. And that is his shell. But he is not in there. He is in heaven with Anna and his mother and father and all his friends and relatives from Myers."

Nancy leaned Lila closer to Casper's face and she kissed him on the cheek. Then the girls took her back upstairs until Casper had been taken away.

I followed and watched cartoons with Lila.

When we came back downstairs, Lila saw the empty bed. "Where is my Gido's shell!" she screamed. In the next few minutes, her fright escalated, and she went ballistic. She screamed and cried with terror like nothing I have ever seen.

Even Dan, the normally calm doctor, started to get worried. "This is not good. We are going to have to get her calmed down or to the hospital."

We were only minutes from taking her to the emergency room when she tired herself out, falling asleep in Nancy's lap.

The next morning, when she came downstairs, she went in the dining room and sat underneath the dining room table, and we could not get her out. She just sat there in silence. Nancy crawled underneath and Lila ate her breakfast on the floor, hidden from the world.

Later that day, I had to make a stop at the Academy and when Lila and I and Nancy drove through the main gate, Lila started to sob again.

"Her whole life has been with him and a lot of it has been here at the Academy with him," Nancy said.

I stopped the car at the entrance to the football field and Lila stopped crying when she walked out onto the green, empty turf. The field was covered with the early spring sunshine of March. Lila walked over to the blue pad, just past the south goal post and sat quietly. We stayed for thirty minutes, until we felt we could move on with the day.

At the funeral, five-year-old Lila and I held hands, and together we followed the casket out of church with Nancy and Dan behind us. The whole church stared at the gentle, little red-headed girl with the black French bonnet and white leggings and black coat. It was as if she understood everything, and she wanted everyone to know she understood.

I remember looking around and, among the mourners who came from Glens Falls and Myers, I saw all my first cousins, who were the progeny of my immigrant grandparents. On my mother's side, there were the Toney boys, Mike, David, Jeff, Johnny and the Jacobs brothers, Jimmy and Bobby. The cousins on my father's side were Marion, Gary, Regina, Sheila and Jeff. We were all products of people who left one world to go to another and gave us a better life.

Eleanor McGraw, Nancy's mother, sat a row behind us with all of Nancy's siblings. There were the Brammers, including brother-in-law Dolan, who spent a year in Baghdad as a machine-gunner on a Black Hawk, and Kevin and Mary Lisa Lyons, who housed Casper on our trips up north before his health declined. Also, there were the Galarneaus, with brother-in-law Michael, who had helped Nancy with all of Lila's adoption paperwork. Others included the D'Angelicos, the Pytells, and Nancy's brothers Barry and Joe.

After Casper's funeral, time moved on in its peculiar way of disappearing quickly. When spring ended, we had one last summer before kindergarten and, sadly, Nancy and I realized it would have been nearly impossible to have taken care of him much longer. I sometimes thought Anna realized this, also, and that any longer would have taken time away from Lila, so maybe she called for him. In the next year, we slowly adjusted to being a smaller, simpler family—not just caregivers. Somehow, all the burdens were forgotten. Lila did not forget; her questions were typical, but I was prepared for her statements.

"I miss Gido," Lila sprung upon me and Nancy in the most unusual of times. We knew her thoughts were filled with him. I was stunned at how much of his presence she retained.

"I do too, but he is with Tita," I would often say. And to myself I would think, "And he is with Puppy and Nemo and all of Myers with all of its love."

One year later, on a Saturday in late July of 2016, Nancy was staying with her mother in Troy for a few days as her family cared for Eleanor McGraw at home.

At fifty-eight years old, I put Lila, now six and having graduated from kindergarten, in the car and headed for Myers. I stayed with Nemo and Martha's nephew, my cousin Gibran Baida, and his wife Mary. My grandmother, Helanie, and Gibran's grandmother, Atina, were sisters. I was godfather to Mary and Gibran's two grown children, Samira and Gabe, who were Nemo's great-niece and nephew.

Gibran now lived in the Isaac house next to the church. Lila slept in the same room that Jacko and Gus had slept in. "It is such a tiny room. It is like a being in little house," she marveled with her eyes twinkling. She sat on the white linen bed and gently touched the thin, white curtains. Her eyes softly gazed out onto Cayuga Lake. She was quiet at first, as if she sensed she had to process everything herself.

Then we walked the path and down onto the bridge in Myers with Mary and Gibran.

We stood on the bridge in Myers and watched the shallow waters of summer gently swim past us. Lila would look down at the water and then up at us and smile. We went down along the side of the creek and Gibran tried to teach Lila how to skip stones across the top of the water. Lila was more interested in watching a crab hiding in a rock on the edge of the water. We walked along the side of the pool upstream from the railroad trestle. When we reached the bank below the railroad trestle, we climbed up and walked over the creek one railroad tie at a time. Lila walked carefully, stepping on each old tie, trying to miss the spots of black tar on each one. At night, we sat in Gibran's yard on the hill, right next to the church, and watched the lights of Ithaca shine down the lake toward Myers.

The next day, we entered the church for Orthodox Mass. Gibran and his wife, Mary, had refurnished the inside of the church and painted the green shingles white. For the first time in fifty years, there was a weekly Eastern Orthodox Mass.

"It is such a tiny church," Lila said with amazement. "I have never been in a church so small. Is this real or make believe?"

There were eight people in the church. *All leftovers from a Myers that had long since left for heaven*, I thought. There was my cousin Marion, and the Abraham girls, all in their nineties, who were the only older Syrians remaining. Sitting next to them was Riad Shalaby and his mother, Margie.

Across the aisle was the biggest smile I had seen in years. It was ninety-two-year-old Gus Isaac, with his daughter and granddaughter. Gus always loved my father and my father always loved Gus, and he smiled ear-to-ear when he made eye contact with me. I felt a lump in my throat. Gus and my father were always the best people to listen to when I was young when they told stories of their childhood. They always remembered details.

I was around five years old the first time I met Gus. It was sometime in the early 1960s. I was standing with Casper on the bridge in Myers on a sunny April morning. Gus walked up to us and Casper said, "You see this guy? He's got metal from a German bomb still in his head. They couldn't take the piece of metal out, so they sewed his head back up with the German bomb still in his head." I vividly remember Gus bending his ever-smiling face down to me and turning his head to the side so I could reach up and put my fingers on the spot where the shrapnel was still lodged. Gus spent his whole life walking around not only with the horrors of war stuck in his head but the weapons of war, as well.

There was a small coffee hour after church, and I stood next to Gus and admired how healthy he looked for his age. I had talked to him many times over the years about the war. Then I asked Gus about Puppy.

"Why don't you ask Marty Moses?" He pointed to one of the few other people who had been in the church that morning, a lady about my age who stood quietly by herself in the corner of the basement. "That is his niece. Her father was George Moses, Puppy's brother."

I walked over to her. "Excuse me, was Puppy Moses your uncle?" I asked.

Marty Moses looked at me with a blank face, but I could tell she was searching for a childhood memory of a story she had once been told. "No. I don't know who Puppy Moses is."

"Puppy Moses, he was killed in World War II," I said.

"My father, George, served in World War II, and so did his brother, my Uncle Joe. They both came home alive," she said. "But they are both gone now."

I waited a moment but said nothing.

Then she added, "I had an uncle, Michael Moses, who was killed in the war. Long before I was born."

"That was Puppy, his nickname was Puppy."

"I have never heard the name Puppy Moses," Marty said.

"My father and everyone in Myers knew him as Puppy Moses. My father talked about him through the years. Twenty years ago, I asked your Uncle Joe about him."

"What did he say?" Marty's voice grew excited.

I recalled the conversation that occurred sometime around the mid-to-late 1990s.

One muggy July afternoon, I walked into a laundromat in Ithaca near the Cornell campus. The heat outside was unbearable, and the heat inside the laundromat was worse. I walked toward the back of the thin room with the dryers on one side and the washers on the other, spinning and churning. At the desk in the back, a short, tired old man, who was folding shirts with his crooked hands, looked up at me with his white beard. His face was square with a lantern jaw and hard features like a Greek sculpture. I remember thinking in amazement that Joe Moses actually had a face that looked like every drawing or likeness of the Biblical Moses I had ever seen. I could tell he was short when he looked up at me with his sad eyes. His face and body were not like the round, soft images I had seen of Puppy Moses, or Casper's vivid descriptions of him. His eyes looked at me like those of Puppy Moses.

"Joe Moses?" I asked a question I already knew. "Are you Joe Moses?"

"Yes," he said softly. He looked up at me, waiting for me to say something else.

I introduced myself.

"Yes, I know," he said quietly.

"How do you know who I am?" I asked.

"Your cousin Marion told me you wanted to talk to me," he said sadly. "And I knew your father, Casper."

"Did Marion tell you why I wanted to see you?" I asked hesitantly.

"Yes," his voice was cracking. "Go ahead, I might not be able to talk long."

I knew he had all afternoon to sit alone but maybe not more than a few moments to talk about painful memories before they dragged him backward into the horrors of the past. "How did your brother get the nickname Puppy?"

"He found a puppy and it followed him everywhere," Joe said of his brother.

"My father told me stories about your brother. I know your brother was killed in World War II," I said.

"Yes," he answered. "In Normandy, during the D-Day invasion."

He stared at me with empty eyes, as if the years had vanished all at once and, now, he realized time was gone forever.

"Where were you when you found out?" I asked.

"I was in the Army. I was in Europe. I was cooking eggs. They walked in and tapped me on the shoulder and said, 'Your brother Michael was killed.'"

"What did you do?" I dared to ask.

"I just kept cooking eggs," was all he said.

I looked at him and now his eyes were not empty. Now they were filled with the sorrow of lost years. I could actually see his throat swell. I stared into the mask of pain on his face and his eyes told me to stop. I never saw Joe Moses again.

After I finished telling Marty Moses the story, I told her I needed to see her again before Lila and I left Myers to return home.

I spent three hours the next morning with Gus Isaac. I had talked to him a lot over the years, but now I taped the conversation and went into greater detail.

In the afternoon, I met with my cousin, Tamam Baida, Nemo's niece. Tamam brought me letters and pictures of Nemo's past that she had shared with me years ago, but now they seemed to come to life before my eyes.

That evening I met with Marty Moses. We talked and looked at pictures for a good two hours. In the pictures, Joe Moses was square and slight and solid. Puppy, however, was different; his face was round, almost too gentle looking to believe he was real. I told the Puppy Moses stories that Casper had told me when I was a child and he brought me to Myers. He repeated many of those same stories when a failing old man.

"This is his funeral record," Marty Moses said, putting a stack of papers in front of me.

"Funeral record?" I said, stunned.

"Yes. They brought his body back in 1948. He was buried in the North Lansing Cemetery."

I looked at the paperwork. Gus Isaac was one of the pallbearers. So was my uncle John's son, Casper "Coach" George, who was in the Battle of the Bulge. I saw my grandparents' names, Abraham and Helanie George, on the registry. What I did not realize was that President Eisenhower brought back one hundred and fifty thousand soldiers to have them buried on American soil after the war.

On the way out of town the next day, Tuesday, Lila and I pulled into the North Lansing Cemetery. I stepped out into the beautiful sunshine of July 26.

"Is Gido buried here?" Lila asked. She was smiling and eating a bagel.

"No, someone else, one of Gido's friends." I was worried that too much of her time was around aging and death. I was shielding her as much I could, but she seemed okay.

"Marty?" I asked on the phone. "I have found your father's headstone but not Puppy's."

"It is back about ten rows and on the other side."

I hung the phone up and backed the car up and opened the door so I could see Lila.

I looked down at the stone. "Born July 26, 1923." I was stunned. "Today is July 26. I had never known his birthday before." I shook my head in amazement.

"Dad," Lila called.

I turned and stuck my head into the open door of the backseat. "What, my love?"

"Are you okay?"

"Yes, why?"

She studied my face with her eyes, as if I were different. "Because you are crying. I have never seen you cry, not even after Gido went to heaven."

I could feel the tears rolling onto my lips as I said, "I love you more than anyone ever loved anyone."

"Gido used to say that." She smiled, barely moving her lips but enough to show her deep love. Her eyes looked at me as if her whole being was to give me and all the world love and make us well. Lila then took her right index finger and put it on my cheek and watched a tear roll onto it. Lila brought her moist finger to her face, her blue eyes studied it for a moment as if she was waiting for the teardrop to tell her something. Lila leaned her head a few inches forward, her red curls fell off her shoulders, and she kissed the tear drop as if it were alive and she could keep it forever.

ACKNOWLEDGMENTS

Vickie Fulkerson spent nearly a decade assisting me with researching and editing and made this book possible. Through all the work, arguments, shared memories, and most of all love, she did what few human beings can do and turned a dream into a miracle.

Vice Admiral Sandra Stosz, USCG (Ret.), came to my rescue, giving life to the story and leading me into the published world. She is a living symbol of kindness and leadership who turned the miracle into a book.

A portion of the proceeds of this book will benefit Lauren's First and Goal Foundation. Lauren's First and Goal is a charitable, volunteer-driven, nonprofit organization founded in 2004 to provide financial support for brain tumor research and cancer services and to offer financial and emotional support to families living with pediatric cancer. Please visit www.lfgf.org to learn how you can do more to help children and families living with a pediatric cancer diagnosis.

In memory of Scott Odell, whose father, CAPT John Odell USCG (Ret.) was the first to read the unpublished manuscript and convince me to believe in it.

Visit www.homefieldsbook.com for pictures.

www.ingramcontent.com/pod-product-compliance
Lightning Source LLC
LaVergne TN
LVHW091631070526
838199LV00044B/1019